Edmond Holmes and Progressive Education

Although considered a figure of great importance and influence by his contemporaries, Edmond Holmes has been consigned to relative obscurity in the progressive educational tradition. This book reinstates Holmes as a key figure in the history of progressive education, both as a school inspector and educational thinker, who was instrumental in forming a set of ideas and principles which continue to resonate in education today. Combining biographical detail and key critical analysis, *Edmond Holmes and Progressive Education* brings together the central ideas and aspects of Holmes' life and establishes his writings as amongst the most insightful ever produced by an educationalist.

Throughout his inspectorial career, Holmes scorned mechanical obedience in the classroom and was appalled by the inability of teachers to allow pupils to express themselves freely and imaginatively. His seminal publications positioned him at the vanguard of educational reforms. His work, however, was not exclusively educational, and throughout his life Holmes published on religion, philosophy, poetry and literature, subsuming his educational viewpoint into a much wider 'philosophy of life'. His spiritual leanings and call for an improved education system, which would draw out the potential for development from *within* the child, inspired successive generations of progressive educators.

In studying Edmond Holmes in detail, this book makes an important contribution to current debates surrounding creativity and the curriculum, in particular the need for alternative educational voices within the state system of regulation. This book will be key reading for postgraduate students and researchers who are interested in progressive education, the history of education and educational policy and politics.

John Howlett is Lecturer in Education Studies in the School of Social Science and Public Policy at the University of Keele, UK.

Edmond Holmes and Progressive Education

John Howlett

LONDON AND NEW YORK

First published 2017
by Routledge
2 Park Square, Milton Park, Abingdon, Oxon OX14 4RN

and by Routledge
711 Third Avenue, New York, NY 10017

Routledge is an imprint of the Taylor & Francis Group, an informa business

© 2017 John Howlett

The right of John Howlett to be identified as author of this work has been asserted by him in accordance with sections 77 and 78 of the Copyright, Designs and Patents Act 1988.

All rights reserved. No part of this book may be reprinted or reproduced or utilised in any form or by any electronic, mechanical, or other means, now known or hereafter invented, including photocopying and recording, or in any information storage or retrieval system, without permission in writing from the publishers.

Trademark notice: Product or corporate names may be trademarks or registered trademarks, and are used only for identification and explanation without intent to infringe.

British Library Cataloguing in Publication Data
A catalogue record for this book is available from the British Library

Library of Congress Cataloging in Publication Data
Names: Howlett, John, author.
Title: Edmond Holmes and progressive education / John Howlett.
Description: New York, NY : Routledge, 2017.
Identifiers: LCCN 2016009969| ISBN 9781138777866 (hardcover) | ISBN 9781315772370 (electronic)
Subjects: LCSH: Holmes, Edmond, 1850-1936. | Progressive education. | Educators--Ireland--Biography.
Classification: LCC LA2375.I732 H684 2017 | DDC 370.92--dc23
LC record available at https://lccn.loc.gov/2016009969

ISBN: 978-1-138-77786-6 (hbk)
ISBN: 978-1-315-77237-0 (ebk)

Typeset in Bembo
by GreenGate Publishing Services, Tonbridge, Kent

Contents

Introduction 1

1 Beginnings and influences 19

2 The years of Inspection 36

3 Edmond Holmes as poet and religious writer 65

4 *What is* and the key educational works 92

5 Holmes, society and the later writings 123

6 Final years and legacy 152

Appendix 168
Bibliography 172
Index 182

Introduction

Edmond Holmes in historical context

W.H. Auden's characteristically laconic remark about some books being undeservedly forgotten whilst none are undeservedly remembered (Auden, 1962, 10) may have been squarely aimed at his own profession yet in many ways the sentiment expressed in the aphorism resonates in the field of education where historical reputations of both individuals and their texts have waxed and waned according (at least in part) to prevailing ideology, dogma and political need. Within the field of *progressive* education for example, works as far back in time as Jean Jacques Rousseau's *Emile* (1979, originally published in 1762) and Friedrich Froebel's *Education of Man* (1898, originally published in 1826) have retained their popularity and status as 'classics' and continue to be the focus of intellectual and scholarly endeavour, often appropriated in the process into a more general child-centred and often, by extension, anti-establishment lineage. Such arrogation belies of course the inhering difficulties in translating across time ideas whose gestation, conception and form emanated in contextual conditions quite alien to those in which they have subsequently sought to be used and deployed.

By contrast, certain texts nearer to our own time carrying, one would imagine, far more relevance for contemporary practice have been correspondingly forgotten and neglected by both the academic and practitioner communities and their authors respectively marginalized. This abandonment has often emanated from a desire to ostracize either those individuals whose lives have become tarnished by controversy, those whose views appear unfashionable and anachronistic today or else by a need to dismiss unthinkingly those whose very *raison d'être* has been to court controversy and make problematic the seemingly 'straightforward' nature of educational practice. Such was the fate for example that befell the American educator Homer Lane amid the allegations of sexual impropriety surrounding his exit from the Little Commonwealth community in Dorset in 1918. It is only as recently as 2005 and Judith Stinton's fine biography that the name of Lane has re-entered the popular consciousness after a pronounced lull. Similarly the quixotic, contrarian and anti-establishment tones of A.S. Neill have likewise relegated their author to the margins of mainstream educational discourse which has remained both unprepared and disinclined to engage actively with his thorny critiques of conventional education systems and pedagogic methods. Whilst his works, particularly the various editions of *Summerhill*, continue to sell well and provoke discussion there is often great reluctance to embrace his far-reaching philosophy *in toto* with key phrases selected and particular tenets adopted in order to pay loose lip-service to the dogmas of his unique brand of schooling. This process of cherry-picking thereby fails perhaps to fully grasp the wider intentions behind many of Neill's extensive writings which, at a more fundamental level, saw the ills of education and especially a lack of play as being a root cause of many of the problems of contemporary civilization.

Nor has it always been the most abstrusely radical and controversial who have suffered; who today for example would know the name Henry Caldwell Cook? A cursory search of the recent literature indicates no major piece of scholarship addressing him yet, as David Hornbrook has shown, Cook's *The Play Way* of 1917 written in the trenches of the First World War 'became the first [text] to describe a comprehensive programme for what we now might recognize as drama-in-education' (Hornbrook, 1998, 8). Cook achieved this by placing free and dramatic play at the forefront of the curriculum and whilst he was a schoolmaster at the prestigious and somewhat conventional Perse School in Cambridge. Equally, at a more official level, texts which have not conformed to prevailing ideological norms such as the recent findings of the *Cambridge Primary Review* (Alexander, 2010) – whose advocacy of a strong child-centredness proved unpalatable for the New Labour and subsequent administrations – have been subject to acts of political violence with their rhetoric shunned and findings ignored or discounted. Whilst this particular disparagement could of course be attributed to recent parliamentary moves toward a central consensus and its attendant 'conventional' pedagogic understanding, as far back in time as the Hadow Reports (variously published between 1923 and 1933) governments of all political hues have long appeared at best tentative and at worst downright reluctant in endorsing ideas which challenge received orthodoxy and opinion on educational practice despite simultaneously tipping their hat to the need for evidence-based policy making. Even the state-sanctioned Plowden Report of 1967, although monumental in its scope, was never a project for genuine and long-term intellectual investment. This was shown by the later investigations of both Neville Bennett (1976) and Maurice Galton *et al.* (1980) who uncovered a marked hesitancy on the parts of supposedly supportive practitioners to engage with its more progressive tenets.

Nevertheless it is not always sufficient to explain such historical neglect by citing shifts in ideological and social opinion or else as a consequence of being contested subjects in the political arena. There have, as well, been those rarer cases in which neither author nor text have been the subject of *active* intellectual disregard but which have instead simply not been addressed in any meaningful way and thereby subsequently forgotten by the academic community to the extent that they have long since unwittingly and unintendedly resided in Trotsky's 'dustbin of history'. Nowhere is this collective amnesia better manifest than in considering the life and works of the subject of this current volume – Edmond Gore Alexander Holmes (1850–1936). Despite in his own time being, as this book will attempt to show, a figure of considerable importance as both a popular, innovative and best-selling writer as well as a key player within many educational developments that served to define the modern scholastic landscape, there is very little existing scholarship on Holmes. Indeed, the only published academic pieces which have him as their central focus are minimal to the extent that they can be briefly discussed here.

Foremost among these are a 1983 bibliographic article in the *History of Education* journal by Peter Gordon – the author of Holmes' expectedly short *Dictionary of National Biography* entry – and a brief 58 page pamphlet (1998) by Chris Shute entitled *Edmond Holmes and the Tragedy of Education* published by the Educational Heretics Press. The first of these offers a brief biography of the key events in Holmes' life and discusses the contents of his extensive corpus of work many of which were helpfully collated and gathered by the author. All subsequent work on Holmes and educational idealism undoubtedly owes much to the pioneering endeavours of Gordon and this excellent contribution. By contrast, the second source is a more superficial book whose sole purpose (and no less noble for it) was to provide and illicit discussion of one half of Holmes' key text *What is and What Might Be*.

In addition to these there are also two brief pieces which take Holmes as their subject. The first of these by David McKenzie (1984) was published in the Australian journal *Education Research and Perspectives* and was speculatively entitled, 'The Legacy of Progressivism; Some Reflections on Edmond Holmes'. In an insightful publication, McKenzie builds on the earlier piece by Gordon and touches upon some of the key features and themes of Holmes' extensive body of writings. The second of these entries comprises two short related articles (2010 and 2011) by Colin Richards in the journal *FORUM: for promoting 3–19 comprehensive education* in which the author offered timely considerations on the relevance Holmes holds for today's children and educational system. Whilst useful for the practitioner and noteworthy for explicitly addressing the contemporary utility of Holmes neither of Richards' pieces sought to significantly locate their subject within the historical contexts in which he either lived or worked.

Residing in the archives of the University Library at Cambridge there is also an unpublished doctoral thesis by Paul McDonald (2008) concerning Edmond Holmes yet even this, by the author's own admission, was not designed to explicitly provide any new critical insights into his subject or 'tell his story' with a view to popularizing his canon. Instead, McDonald sought to use a select group of Holmes' works to advance a particularly innovative methodological model crafted around the particular linguistic insights of the historian of ideas Quentin Skinner. Whilst this model can be said, within its designated parameters, to have been highly successful in the sense of facilitating a new way of approaching historical educational texts (and latterly developed in subsequent publications including Howlett and McDonald 2011), it is explicitly focussed at the micro level of ideas and intentions inherent within individual utterances rather than seeking to generate a more widespread appraisal of Holmes' biography and his longitudinal influence.

This is not to suggest though that Holmes remains invisible within the academic literature. A cursory browse on Google Scholar displays (at the time of writing) 55 educational entries containing the search term 'Edmond Holmes' and in many of these he is indiscreetly cited for the impact he had on the development of a wide range of pedagogic fields. John White (2007) for example invokes him as a precursor to the now more accepted belief that education should enhance well-being, Margaret Mathieson (1991) mentions him in the context of the teaching of English, E.W. Jenkins (1980) saw fit to cite Holmes in his discussion of the development of science education whilst Gordon Cox (1996) touches upon his influence in the field of music and the development of British folk song. Yoko Yamasaki (2010 and 2013) further hints at an *international* stature in outlining how Holmes' key texts were widely translated into Japanese and contributed to what she identifies as the strong influence such progressive ideas briefly held in that country. Paradoxically however, whilst all of these pieces carry a level of implicit assumption about his work, none place Holmes at the forefront of the developments they describe and he is often tellingly mentioned only *en passant*. Indeed, the limitations of the literature surrounding Holmes were made apparent in Catherine Burke's (2005) wonderfully detailed and erudite discussion of E.F. O'Neill's school in Prestolee in which Peter Gordon's earlier brief article was invoked as the best source of insight into Holmes' life.

Aside from these more specialist entries, Holmes also appears either very cursorily or as non-existent within many of the older and standard works on English progressivism such as those by R.J.W. Selleck (1972), Robert Skidelsky (1969) and W.A.C. Stewart (1968 and 1972). Selleck's contribution aside however, even in these cornerstone works, Holmes is not central to the story. In Stewart for example he merits four skirting references and he is not mentioned at all in Skidelsky's account of pioneering progressive schools despite many of these institutions having displayed practices that echoed some of Holmes' earlier naturalistic ideas. Whilst therefore recognizing that he had a role to play in the development of the progressive educational narrative in the United Kingdom, authors such as these have never sought in any meaningful way to explore either the innovation inherent within Holmes' own corpus of work, the ideas and principles that lay behind it or the direct influence and contribution this was to make upon later educators and theorists such as A.S. Neill, Beatrice Ensor, Cecil Reddie, Susan Isaacs and others who were to play such a significant part in re-shaping pedagogic understanding across the century. This scholarly neglect can then be seen as a microcosm of that which has pertained to Holmes amongst the wider academic and pedagogic communities.

Perhaps the best of these longitudinal historical accounts in relation to Holmes is that of Peter Gordon and John White (1979) whose ground-breaking discussion on the intersection of philosophy and educational policy contained the most expansive and direct discussion to date (albeit only four pages!) of his role in influencing the currents of educational thought and legislation. Nonetheless, even though Holmes is bracketed there alongside the mighty John Dewey, it is only in the context of their close relationship to philosophical idealism and not perhaps as being indicative of any comparable level of influence between the two. It is furthermore a limited discussion as it suggests Holmes' importance was chiefly due to his immersion in, and promulgation of, a particular strand of idealism (specifically 'self-realization') which was to impact on later progressive thought rather than in seeing Holmes' contribution as distinctive in its own right and this particular concept as but one aspect in his much larger canvas of thought. It is a subtle distinction and was evidently not the intention of the authors to denigrate Holmes but it is implicit nonetheless. The constraints imposed by the nature of that book left no room either for any consideration of the multifarious contributions made by Holmes to other cognate fields such as poetry, philosophy and theological thinking in which many of these educational ideas found both their origin and subsequent development. Furthermore in common with many of the other aforementioned secondary works this account is over thirty years old and (save for a welcome recent Routledge re-publishing) difficult to obtain thereby adding still further to the general level of inscrutability and mystery surrounding Holmes.

Aside even from his connection to the development of the so-called progressive narrative there has been little sustained mention either of Holmes' role at the Board of Education or in the infamous 'Holmes-Morant Circular' of 1911 – an event significant to his life as the leaking of this confidential document served to instigate a minor political furore and provoked contemporary outrage amongst the teaching profession alarmed at his high-handed attitude. Whilst, as M.J. Wilkinson (1980) long ago made clear, it is quite possible to argue that the importance of the event was more symbolic than real it nevertheless raised important questions about educational governance and the nature and composition of the government Inspectorate. It does seem however that it has been both Holmes' correspondent and administrative colleague at the Board Robert Morant and, as well, Walter Runciman (then President of the Board of Education) who have borne much of the brunt for its contents. Given that the affair cost Morant – no stranger to controversy as his earlier dismissal from the court of Siam indicated[1] – his educational career and heaped upon the Liberal Government much contemporary opprobrium they clearly had the most to lose from its leaking yet it seems that Holmes has remained by contrast relatively immune to the subsequent fall out. History has here (for once!) favoured the progressive educator over the civil servant and politician.[2]

Of course the common-sense explanation for the paucity of scholarship on Holmes would be that he is not worth writing about in the first place and that the filters of history have somehow 'got it right'. Such a view represents the traditional and, in this author's opinion, ultimately mistaken assumption of seeing Holmes as an 'adjunct' or 'prop' whose educational ideas served only to feed into and buttress those of the more well known and later figures of the mid-twentieth century. Whilst these other significant names of the period in which Holmes was operating – Neill, Maria Montessori, Susan Isaacs to name but three – have been well documented and explored by historians and biographers, it seems Holmes, and he is hardly alone in this, has been relegated to the second rank of educational thinkers and perhaps even behind those. There is for example no official biography of Holmes; although his friend and colleague E. Sharwood Smith did produce a contemporaneous account it remains unpublished and its current whereabouts unknown.[3] Similarly, there is only one extant image of Holmes[4] in which, wearing formal collar and tie and with the prim neat moustache characteristic of the Edwardian period gentleman, he embodies both donnish respectability and anonymity and appears anything but the intellectual firebrand he was to become. In that respect, Peter Gordon typically puts it best:

> It is widely acknowledged that the writings of Edmond Holmes have influenced the educational philosophy of generations of students, teachers and administrators. Few textbooks on the history of English education omit at least a mention of him. Yet Holmes remains a curiously shadowy figure; there is no full-length biography of the man and there are few modern editions of his books.
> (Gordon, 1983, 15)

This situation thus ultimately makes little sense particularly given the recent trend within history of education writing which has rightly begun to recognize the unique contributions made by educators operating in a range of different contexts and levels and which has afforded prominence to even those figures who have not necessarily garnered *national* and widespread acclaim but who have nevertheless added in some way to our understanding of the development of pedagogy.[5] It is though the contention here – and hopefully one borne out by this present work – that this is a case in which the judgments of history have proved incorrect, its practitioners surprisingly neglectful and that Holmes fully deserves to be bracketed alongside his more famous contemporaries and forebears.

The achievement of Holmes

My own interest in Holmes arose out of personal investigations into the history and accomplishment of the New Education Fellowship, a discussion of which formed part of a previous book detailing the development of the progressive education movement. Despite the scope of that particular project being necessarily broad it nonetheless became rapidly apparent that Holmes' influence on those thinkers associated with the Fellowship was positively out of all proportion to the minimal scholarly recognition and space he had been afforded. Furthermore, it was noticeable how frequently he was often name checked by his younger contemporaries as one of the organization's founding fathers and leading ideological lights. His key text *What is and What Might Be* for instance was cited by (amongst other luminaries) A.S. Neill, Caldwell Cook and Norman MacMunn as propounding an important critique of existing schooling provision whilst, more indirectly, J.H. Simpson, E. Sharwood Smith and Edward O'Neill all credited it as having a defining influence on their later reforming practices. There was also a very direct link to be traced with Beatrice Ensor who, having read the book, later founded the Theosophical Fraternity which was itself a forerunner of the New Education Fellowship and initially redolent of the quasi-mysticism found within the pages of Holmes.

Through the indefatigable work done by Derek Gillard in maintaining his excellent website – www.educationengland.org.uk – I too was permitted an easy opportunity to read this important work in its entirety online whilst the University Library of Cambridge held copies of nearly all of Holmes' other published works. Although ultimately only garnering a small sub-section in the finished text, this initial foray nonetheless stoked my interest in Holmes who increasingly emerged as a figure of fascination and deserving of a book in his own right, particularly, as has already been mentioned, given that what little extant scholarship there is on Holmes remained tucked away in ageing and hard-to-access academic journals.

His later influence on educational thinking aside, the principal reason why Holmes became seen as a character of such interest was heavily attributable to the *breadth* of his intellectual achievements and endeavours. As has been alluded to, he initially made his name as a School Inspector and oversaw the emerging state educational system through his various postings, rising ultimately to the rank of Chief Inspector of Elementary Schools by 1905. This in its own right would have certainly marked him out as a figure of distinction although not necessarily of great significance particularly when one considers that the vast majority of his important texts were written after the age of 50 and because there had been many previous Chief Inspectors whose names have been long since forgotten to history. However, these facts aside, this should not be to denigrate the prominence of his earlier career particularly given the critical nature of his two published Inspection Reports which offered – within the limitations afforded by such formal publications intended for official audiences – implied trenchant criticisms of the 'payment by results' system which had been previously introduced in 1863. Although initially designed as a way of making teachers and schools accountable for their practice, in a theme that was to emerge throughout much of his subsequent writing, Holmes took to task the rigid and narrow strictures in schools that sought to simply impart factual information in a way that was both novel and savage. He saw little practical, moral or indeed philosophical value in a system which favoured traditional didactics and rote learning and bravely argued against the very policy he, as an Inspector, had been expected for many years to implement.

More tangentially, many of the later official publications of the period such as the *Handbook of Suggestions for the Consideration of Teachers* (1905) as well as its later manifestations which contributed in liberating teachers from those earlier shackles were marked by Holmes' fingerprints (if not his explicit authorship) and betray evidence of his centrality to the key educational developments of the period and his role in shaping governmental policy and general outlook. As shall be illustrated more directly in the concluding chapter, his critiques of an education system rigorously driven by examinations and the needs of a fixed curriculum are but one example where his remarks can be seen to prefigure many of the concerns of the modern age. This is particularly prescient in light of recent Coalition and Conservative Government moves to impose both a retrograde agenda demanding simple recall – reminiscent of Holmes' concept of 'mechanical obedience' – at the expense of skills, imagination and critical thinking, the rise in the number of formal examinations for children as well as the increasing constraints imposed upon the teaching profession which has served to stifle innovation, originality, creativity and more rounded growth amongst young children. In that regard, and signalling his continuing relevance, Colin Richards is right therefore to say that many of Holmes' most important pronouncements should make for 'cautionary reading' (Richards, 2010, 345) for contemporary policy-makers whilst for,

> those schools and teachers feeling isolated and disheartened at current trends Holmes reminds them that they are not alone, that pioneering teachers (female as well as male!) are 'abroad in the land' and that change for the better (however defined) is still possible.
>
> (Ibid., 346)

Whilst these concerns are important, and undoubtedly make him a figure for the modern age, Holmes' life was not solely defined by his Inspectorial career which was inevitably heavily administrative and it is his subsequent literary outpouring which, for this author, raises him to the highest plane of educational thinkers and away from those whose successes were a result merely of bureaucratic and political manoeuvring and policy development. Appropriately, in the year following his enforced retirement, in 1911 Holmes published his *magnum opus What is and What Might Be* which, notwithstanding the influence it was to bestow upon later thinkers, stands, still, as one of the key texts when attempting to understand twentieth century progressivism particularly through its invocation of mystical and spiritual dimensions to learning. As R.J.W. Selleck informs us, 'If a time has to be set for the beginning of progressivism in England, May 1911 when the ex-chief inspector published his attack on the conventional school is probably the best date' (Selleck, 1972, 26). Such is its enduring reputation this work remains perhaps the one thing those with only a passing interest in Holmes and progressivism are acquainted with and it is almost exclusively the sole focus of many of the aforementioned secondary accounts concerning its author.

Like so many of his other educational works which have themselves been traditionally neglected and under-read, this book was heavily informed and influenced by his earlier Inspections – in this case a school in Sompting, West Sussex run by Harriet Finlay-Johnson – yet characteristically it uses these observations to delineate a very particular educational philosophy informed by elements of theology, spirituality and otherworldliness. Whilst his educational writings and pronouncements occasionally betray the speculative quality associated with such fields they were never less than informed by his own empirical and observational evidence gathered throughout his long earlier career and it is this which grounds much of his rhetoric in reality and makes him even more of a figure for our own age in which evidence-based policy making has become a key watchword.

Further to *What is* and his other educational writings, including a brilliant yet today largely unread follow-up *In Defence of What Might Be* (1914), throughout the course of his long life Holmes published variously on religion, philosophy, poetry (a life-long passion) as well an autobiography. Peter Gordon's (1983) cataloguing of Holmes' writings in fact divides the published work up under those headings and includes not merely twenty full-length books but also pamphlets, reviews, official publications and specialist and general interest journal articles which Holmes often used as a way of working out ideas which later became expanded into book form. His was a work ethic of seemingly Stakhanovite proportions, emblematic of another age and it undoubtedly ensured Holmes in his time reached the widest possible readership from theologians to teachers, policy-makers to poets. In ranging so widely it also meant that his educational viewpoint became subsumed within a much wider 'philosophy of life' in a way that was almost wholly unique through its incorporation of intellectual, mystical and ethereal dimensions. It was this combination of contrasting cultures and systems of belief which both integrated and (to borrow Bernard Leech's wonderful phrase) went beyond East and West to forge in the process something clearly distinctive within the progressive canon. R.J.W. Selleck further suggests something of that rounded hinterland by proposing that, 'Those who knew Holmes thought of him as much a poet as an inspector and probably he was as much philosopher as poet' (Selleck, 1972, 25).

Although fond of claiming that he was merely an amateur within these other areas – he described for example his philosophical endeavours as 'informal, unscientific, unprofessional, untechnical' (Holmes, 1905a, 83) – this was false modesty on Holmes' part and does disservice to his vast scholarly powers and command of a range of cognate fields. Further, it detracts hugely from his most considerable achievement which was to bring together ideas from various strands of intellectual thought (education, theology, philosophy and so on) into a unique and evolving inter-connectedness which sought to provide an explanation for the condition of Man and, in the process, to delineate a particular framework of moral action. Ironically, such grand ambition has had its negative side. It is precisely because of this great variety of writings, often held within specialist libraries and with different publishers (some now defunct), that has meant an overall appraisal and conspectus of Holmes has proven hitherto intellectually and logistically difficult for the interested scholar and has perhaps contributed to the aforementioned lack of general scholarship.

However with the modern benefits of digitized readings and more comprehensive cataloguing facilitating general access, it is now quite possible in fact, after that fashion, for one to carve up Holmes' writing career into particular phases. Whilst compartmentalization of this type is to some extent an artificial exercise, imposed retrospectively and does not ever fully represent the lived experience of a writer, it is useful here in order to give both trajectory and direction to Holmes' thought processes and career. As a young man, very much still under the formative influence of his Oxford experiences, Holmes' first published efforts were two volumes of poems (1876 and 1879b) and – with four later collections, a critical study of the discipline and a selection of Walt Whitman still to be written – it is clear that this was a medium which he felt comfortable returning to in expressing many of his central ideas often those concerning love, spiritual wholeness and his particular brand of Wordsworthian pantheism. Concomitant to this, and then up until 1924, were all of Holmes' *educational* writings although even within this group most came after his retirement from the Inspectorate in 1910 when being freed from the burdens of official position allowed him time to fully devote himself to the endeavours of scholarship. In these works one can further identify Holmes moving from those which are grounded very much in the lived day-to-day experiences of school observation such as his two Reports to the Councils on Education, three addresses and papers to various educational groups and his accounts of the Montessori system sourced from his own visit to Rome, to those broader educational writings (after *What is*) which started to locate education within a much broader intellectual and philosophical context and the ways in which the rigid structures of schools were seen as routed in the dominance of a particular form of religious morality.

It is therefore within these latter pieces that we see both the clearest evidence of the wide scope of Holmes' cerebral interests and his active engagement with many of the nascent philosophical debates, contemporary events like the Great War and academic communities of practice of the time. Ever the polemicist, Holmes frequently took to task those with whom he disagreed and nowhere was this more apparent than in the aforementioned *In Defence of What Might Be* in which a number of combative chapters saw Holmes setting himself against his critical contemporaries including the neo-Herbartians[6] (a particular bug-bear) whom he saw as innately conservative and wedded to a view of child development predicated upon an education imposed externally and conceived as a form of social utility. Such a view, which Holmes saw as dangerously instrumental, stood in opposition to his preferred neo-Romantic notion of growth as stemming from the child's innate impulses and *instincts* – a position more in accordance with his own adherence to the principles of Friedrich Froebel and the essential goodness, capacity and wisdom of the child. Whilst the whole of that particular book can be read, as indicated by the title, as a justification against those who sought to criticise Holmes' particular strictures it is indicative very much of the man as a whole whose writing was continually permeated by powerful rhetoric and persuasive argument railing as it did against the deepest restrictions on Man's freedom and the problems which that had created for the modern civilized world.

From 1924 until 1934 (which one can consider as the third 'phase' of his writing career) there are then significantly no educational works or volumes of poetry but, instead, the majority of Holmes' *philosophical* writings and various of his religious tracts. In many ways this represented a natural development and evolution of Holmes' thinking as, even when earlier commenting on education, it was clear that he believed organizations of schooling could only be reformed by corresponding improvements to the political, social and most importantly moral and philosophical outlooks of the society in which they were located. In his last reflective educational writings for example which had emerged in the aftermath of the Great War – *Give me the Young* (1921d) and *Can Education Give us Peace?* (1924a) – Holmes had indicated this new direction through talking of the need to encourage and foster community and cooperative spirit amongst young children with a view to preventing the sorts of bloodshed which had only very recently scarred the globe. This was not to be achieved however simply by classes in citizenship, patriotism or specific communal events like assemblies but instead through changing and reconstituting the very fabric and culture of education in which collective spirit and not egoism was the driving force behind children's actions. Indeed, such grandiose concerns were typical of Holmes who was never parochial; his visit to Montessori's schools in Italy, his long interest with all things German (the intellectual home of idealism and according to Holmes the most 'slavishly docile' of races) and his loose connection to the pan-national New Education Fellowship meant his outlook was both international and universal with schooling seen as having a lavish role to play in the spiritual advancement of a global humanity.

Within then that last decade or so of his life, whilst still connected to education through his association with the New Ideals in Education conferences, Holmes' preoccupations were much more with *religion* and his invocation of Eastern mysticism and Buddhism – including being involved with the now obsolete Quest Society[7] – was offered as a unique solution to what he saw as the national and indeed international moral malaise in the years following the Great War. In particular, Holmes desired individuals to cultivate the elevation of their souls to a higher plane which allowed them to grow and develop on the path toward expressing their infinite and limitless potential. This conception of 'soul-growth' was one which Holmes had earlier written about as being one of the central purposes of education and was facilitated by allowing children's innate creativity and self-expression to flourish with none of the limits imposed upon their development which was an unfortunate feature of contemporary systems of schooling. This form of growth was also intended to elevate their spiritual understanding to a level which fostered both integration and unity. In reflecting upon the philosophy of his last two decades Holmes was quite explicit in acknowledging this point: 'If I had to give a name to the philosophy in which my soul has found refuge…I would call it the philosophy of *wholeness*' (Holmes, 1920a, 1, original italics). It was Holmes' contention, as we shall see, that the impulses toward this state of being had been intentionally stunted and twisted by civilization and its composite institutions which predicated themselves upon a belief in the child's Original Sin and their subsequent necessary obedience through prescribed moral action. The originality of Holmes in comparison to other educational thinkers was then to lie in his incorporation of a range of disparate fields – religion, philosophy, morality and education – to construct a distinct view of life drawing upon and reflecting a markedly different (Eastern) tradition.

Holmes' relationship to his contemporaries

Although the ability to extemporize in a wide range of cognate fields was not of course peculiar to him or his time – when the genuine 'Man of Letters' was an established part of the academic landscape – and other public intellectuals such as Bertrand Russell were to later turn their attention to education[8], Holmes was unique in the way in which his starting point was the very discipline itself drawn from long experience of having observed pedagogic practice at close quarters. Nor was his radicalism of the sort envisaged by other contemporary progressive thinkers who conceived of education as having a role to play in overturning existing social structures and with a pedagogy enmeshed in the revealing of class inequality – a theme latterly explored in the accounts of both Brian Simon (1972) and Harold Silver (1975).

Whilst like them Holmes saw traditionalist approaches to education and the seeming need for 'accountability' 'regulation' 'testing' and 'standards' as imposing curbing patterns of conformity and a stifling of children's growth he was nevertheless as distrustful of emergent socialist ideas as he was of those on the right. At the heart of Holmes' philosophy lay the tenet of *spiritual* emancipation and the desire to awaken conscience and perception of reality through free activity and association and he therefore found within the creeds of the left dogmas and doctrines which contributed ultimately to having similarly detrimental effects on the child as those emanating from the more Gradgrindian mould. This was particularly apparent in the attendant arms of socialism – trades unions, cooperatives and the like – who sought to enforce unquestioning patterns of behaviour, thought and belief on their members; ultimately the power of the collective was as evil as that of the individualist.

Correspondingly Holmes 'had no faith whatever that people could [first] be improved through legislative reform' (McKenzie, 1984, 8) and he chided the socialist movement for its ultimately unrealistic expectations and as having, 'not lifted [its] little finger to change this de-socializing, de-humanizing trend of education' (Holmes, 1914, 259). For him, any attempts at improvements in social justice and welfare were antecedent to changing the ways that humans perceived reality, social systems and others around them. Even under such a socialist system, which argued hopefully for people working together collectively, if humans had not achieved the prior desired state of spiritual achievement and been placed on the path to 'self-realization', Holmes still feared that their old prevailing faults would remain:

> Competition for "the good things in life" would probably go on as fiercely as ever; but it would be a scramble among nations rather than individuals, and it might conceivably take the form of open warfare waged on a titanic scale.
> (Holmes, 1911, 289)

Such statements hinted therefore at a man whose social instincts, although derived from the promotion of communality, were innately *conservative*. These sentiments were further reinforced elsewhere; when addressing for example the issue of 'obedience' in schools – and this was a much recurring theme in his writings – Holmes was at pains to stress that whilst he opposed any education which sought to stunt the child's spiritual growth and which was based on the foisting of unthinking compliance, he was not opposed to discipline as a bulwark against potential lawlessness and anarchy which many critics had seen as the end-product of his ideas concerning freedom. For Holmes, such socially desirable characteristics would instead come quite instinctively to the child who had been allowed to develop naturally and his writings are peppered with glowing references to Montessori Schools in which cooperation, trust and genteel good manners were demonstrably evident. Whilst appearing therefore to some as an educational agitator and dangerous progressive meddler there were in Holmes' copious utterances much which seemed to carry a message that whilst its philosophy was radical it was not intent on overturning any form of existing social order. At a time when questions over national fitness and health (physical and moral) were paramount and remedies were sought from all quarters for the decline of Britain's global power, Holmes was seemingly quite happy to offer his own schema as a possibility. Although therefore naturally at home on the left (freely admitting his sympathy to the Fabian cause) his politics remained complex via a youthful attachment to the Empire and Tory Party and he embodied his solid gentrified background through relative social conservatism and years of service to successive Governments of varying political stripes.

This apparent contradiction at the heart of Holmes between the educational radical and more stolid learned intellectual is one replicated and paralleled within his more well-known contemporary Matthew Arnold (1822–1888) who, through his own inspectorial career and wide-ranging literary endeavours, stands initially and most obviously as a legitimate point of comparison to the current subject. Such association is given further prominence when one considers the formative influence the writings of Arnold particularly *Literature and Dogma* (1873) was to have on the young Oxford undergraduate particularly in the way in which its author sought to enlighten school children through exposure to the very best aspects of intellectual thought and sentiment. Both Holmes and Arnold ended up ultimately therefore sharing a common ambition which was to address the 'state of the nation' question and each individually adumbrated a series of responses to what they saw as the deficiencies of the existing education system of which they had, through their respective travails, intimate knowledge. Whilst Arnold sought solace in the liberalizing effects of high culture which he saw as necessarily emanating from the 'vanguard' middle class who would combat and resist the advances of barbarism, Holmes' rejoinder drew both on contemporary educational theory – notably Montessori – and elements of the spiritual as a way to achieving a broad level of emancipation.

One must however be wary of carrying such comparisons too far as their intellectual trajectories were ultimately to significantly diverge as were their posthumous reputations. Arnold for instance is today less remembered for any explicitly educational writings as he is for his poetry and literary and social criticism of which, in both cases, he was one of the finest exponents of the age. By contrast, Holmes' poetry – perhaps because of its adherence to traditional verse forms albeit couching radical ideas – has been treated less kindly by posterity and in any case he was far more intrinsically interested in the *processes* of education than was Arnold. More subtly however, both men can be seen to represent very particular and divergent responses to what many critics have identified as the apparent crisis in Victorian faith subsequent to the publication in 1859 of Charles Darwin's *On the Origin of the Species*. Despite the fact that Arnold, through his headmaster-father Thomas, had become acquainted with the poet William Wordsworth and whose influence was initially apparent in both his early poetry and louche Oxford lifestyle, like his close friend Arthur Hugh Clough he soon embodied the turn toward agnosticism with doubts raised over the accepted and established place of both God and religion. Certain of his key works, notably the brilliant poem *Dover Beach*, therefore encapsulated this perceived crisis in modern faith and, in seeking to address this loss of certainty, Arnold's diagnosis and solution to the ills of society were to reside in an education system in which the noble example set by the middle class was to be emulated by their working class counterparts. Although not nearly as disdainful of elementary education as many of his fellow Inspectors and undoubtedly a man of good moral conscience, Arnold's general attitude, if not demeanour, was well satirized by his fellow Inspector Sir Joshua Fitch who memorably referred to him as 'going through the world as one who held a moral smelling-bottle to his nose' (Fitch, 1897, 226).

In contrast to this more austere of solutions, Holmes sought instead to tap into the dormant spirit of Romanticism which, since the late eighteenth century, had been prevalent within British intellectual discourse and which was not as readily immersed in, or associated with, Arnold's grand rhetoric of social improvement and paternal benevolence. For him, the deficiencies in education would not be remedied by the following of socially superior example but by allowing each child, within an environment of freedom, to follow their own natural, free and creative impulses (or 'instincts') which would ultimately lead to a holistic out-growth of the soul. Nor were such impulses confined to one class; *all* children were seen as being born innocent and with limitless latent potential and earlier Romantic writing, stretching back to Rousseau's seminal *Emile* (1762), had emphasized the innocence of the child prior to worldly corruption. It therefore followed that Holmes was to place greater emphasis upon the individual and growing child and *their* experiences and environments rather than the wider attendant social structures which he saw as inherently damaging and dangerous to development. Characteristically, in much of Holmes' work there are therefore direct pleas to the benefits of an education conducted in a naturalistic setting and, in describing the pupils of his model institution Utopia, he was moved to write approvingly how, 'I have never been in a school in which the love of what is beautiful in Nature is so strong or so sincere as this' (Holmes, 1911, 160).

As has already been alluded to this was a strand of Romanticism which had been partially rejected by Arnold. In his own analysis of nature for example, whilst finding it tranquil, he could not fully accept its moral ascendancy concluding it both 'a tyrant as well an enlightened despot' (Silver, 1994, 11). Such a view thus negated the potential ethical benefits it could confer upon the young and it was this cleavage between the Romantic and the Rational which represented the key difference between these two seminal thinkers. Recognizing the more sentimental and paternalistic element of Arnold's pseudo-Victorianism which stood in contrast to his own more pantheistic beliefs, Holmes himself was quick to acknowledge their conflicting perspectives:

> Matthew Arnold defined religion as morality touched with emotion. This definition is, I think, wholly inadequate. Would it not be nearer to truth to say that religion is morality transformed and even transfigured by "the intuition of totality" and the consequent sense of obligation to the whole.
>
> (Holmes, 1920a, 134)

This is an important utterance as it indicated the very singular path Holmes was prepared to take in developing a connection between religious doctrines and education and overlaying both with a heavier Eastern philosophical emphasis. In that light, these become important considerations particularly when evaluating the *distinct* contribution made by Holmes and the way in which his work paved the way for later pronouncements by thinkers within the New Education Fellowship and beyond.

Although himself socially very separate from those about whom he observed and wrote – one cannot overlook his public school and Oxford education which gave him an easy social cachet – in departing from Arnold and his age, Holmes acted therefore as a key bridging figure between two distinct educational worlds. These can be characterized as the Victorian with at its heart an embryonic state education system and concern with moral improvement and, subsequent to that, the post-First World War era in which the emphasis was placed more firmly upon reconstruction and the emergence of new ideas drawn from budding pseudo-scientific disciplines. In bringing 'educational debate out of the drawing rooms' (McKenzie, 1984, 11) Holmes therefore opened up a range of new possibilities which were to be further explored by his successors and which evolved into the significant branch of thinking we now think of as twentieth-century progressivism. Indeed, it would not be stretching a point to suggest that nearly all progressive literature, policy and practice – at least in Britain – contains within it elements, concepts and critiques which had previously been adumbrated by Holmes. Under that aspect, he can thus be argued to be one of the pioneers of a particular strand of educational thinking which, to paraphrase the later Plowden Report, sought to place the child very much at the heart of the educational process and which can be traced through to the teaching practitioners of today.

Holmes the man

In any general appraisal of an individual it does not of course do us good to be blind to their faults and this is no less true of Holmes as it would be of Arnold, Neill or any other well-researched educational figure. After all this was a man who referred, infamously, in private to elementary teachers as being 'uncultured and imperfectly educated' (Holmes quoted in Gordon, 1983, 38) and Local Inspectors – who unlike him were not for the most part Oxbridge men – as being 'unequal to the discharge of their responsible duties' (Ibid.). Contentious at the time, if leaked today, the political ramifications of such a statement from the head of the Government Inspectorate hardly bear thinking about! Under a certain light, this indicates perhaps residual evidence of Holmes' attachment to his own background which, for want of a better word was, as has been alluded to, *privileged* and undoubtedly bred a particular cast of mind peculiar to those with both a keen austere intelligence coupled with perceived insights into the flawed nature of Humanity.

Nowhere was this more vividly illustrated than in his occasional condemnation of the 'average man', a term used by Holmes to serve as a catch-all embodiment for the prevailing system of thought which had served he believed to contribute to the debasement of both society and a morality which was driven by an excess of hedonism and sensuality. This denigration had been allowed to occur due to the willingness of the apparently simple multitudes to adhere blindly and without challenge to the strictures and dogma of organized monotheistic faiths and their attendant dualism which divorced Man from the Spirit. Although it would on balance be unfair to think of Holmes as being either illiberal or intolerant – he was after all equally fulsome in his praise of the average children housed in Finlay-Johnson's school – there is nevertheless something priggish about his attack on the 'whippet racing, pigeon fancying, attending football matches, betting and drinking' (Holmes, 1923f, 266) of the working classes who he argued had failed to fully develop spiritually as he would have desired.

This deficit model of working class culture was apparent too in Holmes' otherwise insightful discussion of the Spitalfield Weavers (from which the above quotation is taken) and whose example served he argued to demonstrate the importance of education in raising the lower classes to the level of the higher, implying therefore that the one culture should aspire to that which was intrinsically superior. As if aware of the acute tension between condemning individual licentiousness on the one hand and the desire to espouse a liberal humanism on the other, Holmes was to admit honestly that such a view stemmed from his long-held belief 'that the "lower orders" are by birth and breeding our inferiors in mentality and character' (Holmes, 1917a, 69), a view that was only to change upon greater exposure to the children in the school he had christened Utopia. Along similar lines, his racial views were equally rooted in their historical context as he referred to 'the existence of races, such as the Negro, which seem to be far below the normal level of human development' (Holmes, 1911, 302).

Whilst not seeking to act as an apologist for such views – and today such statements and terminology undoubtedly appear as both jarring and unpalatable – it must be remembered that such attitudes were not uncommon amongst the intelligentsia of the time and Holmes is hardly the first from that stratum to excite debate over their social attitudes many of which may have been bound by prevailing scientific limitations. Indeed in his case it was tempered with a high degree of self-reflection; in his autobiography for instance Holmes readily admitted that the quest to live out his philosophy and find ultimate self-realization through attaining a selfless love of Man was not instant and took over thirty years of contemplation and struggle including passing youthful attachments to the Tory Party and the doctrine of Imperialism. Such an admission thus belied the fact that his philosophy and social outlook was one that was not easily understood and enacted and contained within it elements of complexity and evolution. This was compounded perhaps by the ontological tautology involved in attempting to realize an ideal thereby, in the process, de-idealizing it and stripping it of its aspirant quality.

The failings, if we can call them that, of Holmes were not of course all *personal*. His radical educational ideas were themselves not universally feted and, notwithstanding the difficulties and toils progressive beliefs have had in finding a place within mainstream educational discourse, in the case of Holmes and his time these became more exacerbated as the particular scholastic and social settings in which he was operating maintained a close attachment to very static forms of pedagogy. It is also relevant perhaps to note that many of those within Holmes' orbit who were to be at the vanguard of the New Education Fellowship and their schools – for example Cecil Reddie, Kurt Hahn and J.H. Badley – were themselves rebelling directly against the English public school tradition and their (often fee-paying) establishments also reflected this through equally idiosyncratic structures, language and customs. Even then amongst Holmes' bedfellows, there was not always common consensus around the need for 'self-realization' and the more mystical later elements of his philosophy remained, it would be fair to say, a minority interest and have been largely ignored by the educational establishment.

In many ways this is a telling point as it indicates that over the course of a long life and an even longer list of publications which covered such a vast and potentially daunting terrain what mattered for Holmes and those with any interest in the man were his *ideas*. Certainly, these were ideas underpinned by the need to be both practised and enacted (particularly within schools) but with their tones of abstraction and, second, a desire to link together the practical with ideas and concepts drawn from disparate and heavily theorized fields such as philosophy, Holmes' books are those to be both ruminated upon and, ultimately, debated intellectually. This is not of course to suggest, in any pseudo-Derridian way, that Holmes' life did not matter and there is nothing of any value outside of those texts. This is far from the case and there were occasions, as we shall see, when the link between the two was both explicit and clear. However, much of that life was one spent either in the capacity of a working civil servant (within a department then of comparatively little prestige) or else the circumstance of quiet retirement neither of which, when taken in conjunction with Holmes' own introverted temperament, are preconditions for a substantively rich biography. This is exemplified for example by the lack of any official archive or cache of letters – what material has been found has been within the papers of others or else as part of the official Governmental collections held within the National Archive. Nor is this a problem common to Holmes; given its emphasis upon practice as well as the traditionally low social status of its protagonists (teachers) much educational, and for that matter, social history has been beset with the problem of reconciling theory and practice and has relied heavily upon interlocution and memory.

However, in Holmes' case, and given how little attention many of them have merited, to some extent the works are the archive and, that being so, we can identify a very rich and fulsome collection indeed. In that light, the following book will attempt to somehow make sense of this not merely by synthesizing the key ideas and aspects of his life which may have been seen to influence them but also by attempting to implicitly draw these strands together so as to give greater substance to a philosophy we could christen Holmesian. As one so committed to the principles of wholeness, integration and unity it would surely have upset Holmes to see his work treated in any other way! Indeed, it is in reality impossible to do otherwise as Holmes' views on religion were to have implications for his understanding of education which were to thus impact upon his views of democracy which was to shape his views on spiritualism and so on. It is then these broad areas that are the focus of the individual chapters which follow – first, Holmes' early life and long Inspectoral career (Chapters 1 and 2), second his religious and literary thinking (Chapter 3), third his major educational writing (Chapter 4) whilst the work concludes with an examination of his role in responding to the First World War and efforts within wider society (Chapter 5) and finally reflections on his late life (Chapter 6). Not for nothing can it therefore be said that the deeply unified canon of Holmes' writing is amongst the richest, most profound and deeply complex ever produced by an educationalist and it is hoped that what follows provides a testament to that assertion.

Notes

1 See B.M. Allen (1934, 43–88) for the fullest account of Morant's extraordinary time in Siam (which saw him rise from tutor to the Crown Prince to being an advisor on government policy) and his dismissal from the Court on account of political intrigue and complications over foreign affairs.
2 This is perhaps unfair to Morant who had previously worked at Toynbee Hall and was to show himself to be active in seeking to reform the education system through expanding provision.
3 Peter Gordon's (1983) access to this memoir was facilitated by his connection to E. Sharwood Smith's son who 'kept it in a locked drawer.' As far as this author is aware it has not been seen since.
4 The image is located as a frontispiece to *Freedom and Growth: and other essays* (1923).
5 For examples of where this has occurred see the following variety of publications: Jane Read (2003) 'Froebelian Women: Networking to Promote Professional Status and Education Change in the Nineteenth Century' in *History of Education*, 32(1); Jane Martin (2010) *Making Socialists: Mary Bridges Adams and the Fight for Knowledge and Power, 1855–1939* (Manchester University Press) and Philip Gardner (2004), 'There and Not Seen: E.B. Sargant and Educational Reform, 1884–1905' in *History of Education*, Volume 33, Issue 6.
6 The term used to describe those intellectuals who claimed allegiance to the educational thought of the German philosopher Johann Friedrich Herbart (1776–1841).
7 The Quest Society was founded in 1909 by the English critic G.R.S. Mead and was originally comprised of defectors from the Theosophical Society. It held regular talks in London and published a journal *The Quest: A Quarterly Review* which ran from 1909–1931. Holmes became President of the Society in 1921.
8 Bertrand Russell, with his then wife Dora, founded the Beacon Hill school in 1927. Dora's philosophy was later adumbrated within the pages of *In Defence of Children* (1932).

Chapter 1

Beginnings and influences

Early life and school

In one of the finest of his late poems Edmond Holmes was to refer lyrically to the 'speck-like seed' of the 'mighty banyan-tree...In which it hides its life's totality' (Holmes, 1918, 'The True Self'). Although he was here speaking metaphorically to describe what he saw as a timelessness to the nature of existence, such a reference seems to carry an additional importance as it indicated a knowing awareness on the part of its author that his own life, work and ideas had to that point been inexorably bound together. Whilst therefore on the surface Holmes' intention within that poem may indeed have been purely philosophical and an attempt to acknowledge his increasing indebtedness to an Eastern way of thinking which saw the inherent Oneness of the individual with the Universe, one cannot help wondering if he had as well somewhere in his mind reflections upon his own infancy and the idea of the child as 'father of the man'. At the age of 68 this would certainly not have been out of keeping with the need to contemplate on a life lived fully and its varied achievements and it certainly reflects the trend for poets and writers as they get older to become more meditative and worldly. More significantly however it betrays Holmes' close attachment to that most Romantic of conceits which placed great importance on the spiritual interconnectivity of both infant and adult. Although such speculation derived mainly, as we shall later see, from an emergent religious viewpoint which sought to develop a theory of spiritual and temporal unity, it also gives an indication of the close attention paid to the notion of the Self and its more global position in relation to both time and place – contained in both present, past and future simultaneously.

Holmes' later philosophy and its emphasis upon inward contemplation and outgrowth of the soul in many ways serves to give added primacy to the earlier years as, under this framework, one was contiguous with the other – the life course was not one that was static to be discretely compartmentalized but part instead of an idealized whole to be conceived of *holistically*. This represented then the adoption of a comparatively radical stance and, although personally a contemplative, gentle and benign individual, old age for Holmes certainly did not lead to a corresponding softening or mellowing of his views. By contrast, the passing years did nothing to blunt the anger of the earlier young man but were rather a time in which he became ever more set against the mainstream and prone to greater unorthodoxy of thought. With his later beliefs in the rebirth and infinite continuity of the soul and its regeneration his was a very loud raging against the dying of many established lights. The link therefore between the youthful Holmes and his later life and works should not, and indeed cannot, be ignored if only as a means of doing justice to his own intellectual prescription. Although such forms of 'psycho history' are notoriously problematic and speculative and should be treated with caution, given the philosophical importance Holmes himself attached to his early life it certainly befalls the historian to explore in greater depth the events within it and the later influences they were to have on his own writing. Such biographical explorations have equally long been fertile ground for historians of education (particularly given its close association to oral history) and nowhere is this more pertinent than in the case of Holmes, whose many and varied later ideas can be traced to aspects of his own life.

With the best of intentions however details of these early years are characteristically vague and not assisted by Holmes' own autobiography which is reticent and has little to say on the matter. Born in 1850 at Moycashel, County Westmeath, Holmes' father Robert (1803–1870) was an Irish landlord whilst his mother Jane, also Irish, originated from Dublin. Her father had been William Henn, a master in chancery, a position responsible for assisting the legal process through the gathering of evidence and which then carried with it the reputation of today's barristers. Holmes himself was the fourth son and, as one of seven, was to have four brothers (including T.R.E Holmes the noted historian and classical scholar[1]) and two sisters. His ancestors we are told came over with William of Orange and thus formed part of what today is referred to as the 'Protestant Ascendency'. This movement was characterized, as Claydon and McBride (1999) best tell us, by the establishment of a hegemony and dominance of the Protestant faith over that of the Catholics and other minorities which became enacted via a succession of early punitive measures designed to strip Catholic landowners of their former power and, in some cases, land and territory. Such supremacy was exemplified within Holmes' own family through his maternal grandfather who had inherited his position at the tender age of 24 in the main through his household connections.

At the time however of Holmes' birth (1850) such dominance had ceased to be so obviously political and instead was more focussed around the *cultural* restoration that was later to be closely associated with those intellectuals grouped around Lady Augusta Gregory[2] including W.B. Yeats, John Millington Synge and the renewal of the Abbey Theatre. We know that this milieu represented much of the world Holmes inhabited; one of his early family friends (and a cousin through marriage) for example was the composer Charles Villiers Stanford who, according to his official biographer, saw much of Holmes during school vacations and was later to be the subject of his friend's kindness as Holmes acted as a go-between for Stanford during his troubled courtship. Stanford's other early friends included the Graves brothers – Alfred Percival (born 1846) and Charles Larcom (born 1856) – both of whom were also to enjoy literary careers in their own right whilst the former is today equally well known as being the father of the poet Robert and a school inspector of some note.

It was this latter role, as we shall see in the following chapter, which was to bring Graves for a brief time into a close working relationship with Holmes at the Board of Education. Were they here, nearly forty years later, renewing old acquaintances? It seems unlikely that they did not know each other – Graves himself in his autobiography lists his families' friends, many of whom like Sir Thomas Larcom and Lord Dunraven were at the time key players in the political landscape of Dublin, as well as families such as 'the Joys, Wallaces, Blackburns, Gales, Lloyds and Stanfords' (Graves, 1930, 22). Landowners such as those within the various branches of the Holmes family would therefore, perhaps through politics or business, have intersected with these and formed part of a burgeoning and connected municipal middle class with close personal and professional ties. Regardless, Edmond was clearly raised in the cultured and connected environment characteristic of those within families of the Holmes' standing – upper-middle class almost minor gentry although with none of the lavishness or louche manner of those directly above. As he appositely puts it, 'for many generations my forbears on both sides had enjoyed possessions and privileges which were denied to the bulk of their fellow men. And they and we took all that for granted' (Holmes, 1920a, 8).

There is evidence too that Holmes visited much of the rest of Ireland during both his boyhood and as a returning young man and its landscapes were to imprint themselves clearly and powerfully upon his memory and conscience. This influence is most apparent when reading the poetry within his first two published collections (of 1876 and 1879b) much of which addressed, in very direct terms, real places on the West Coast of Ireland particularly those coastal spots within the Counties of Clare and Mayo. Such indeed was the strength of these associations that the landscapes within the poems (which ultimately were to be numbered amongst his best) became imbued with a *genius loci* which could not have come one feels from anything other than a close and nuanced attachment that went beyond mere superficial appreciation. Holmes himself spoke fondly of his earliest impressions as being of 'heather and cotton grass and bog ditches and the scent of "turf" smoke' (Ibid., 7–8). Poetic as such language is it is clear that, beyond such memories, the spirit of these rugged exteriors was to act as the basis for his later pantheist associations that equated God with a Nature in which, like Wordsworth whom he long admired, he was to find not merely aesthetic beauty but also a sense of guiding morality. Forged therefore in Ireland, his was to be an *active* and *lived* love of the outdoors; in later life, Holmes was to continually be attracted to rural locales and demonstrate prowess as a fisherman, rambler and mountaineer all of which brought him closer to the lands and landscapes he revered. This is an important point to note as this engagement with Nature was to represent the first phase of Holmes' mature philosophy and was ultimately to act as a stepping stone on the way to his more global theory of spiritual unity and love.

Enlightening as this world of literature, discourse and travel surely was, it was nonetheless offset by the increasing impact that more established and orthodox *religion* was having in the young boy's life. Initially this was to spring from his mother, a strict disciplinarian, who took it upon herself early on to take care of her children's religious upbringing which she seems to have done with quite characteristic verve and vigour: 'I was brought up with extreme and consistent severity...My mother, who was deeply and sincerely religious, had thought it her duty to drill religion into each of her children, and had done so by the forcible methods which were then in vogue' (Ibid., 9–11).

This boyhood obeisance was to be further reinforced following the Holmes' family move to London and Edmond's attendance, from 1863, at Merchant Taylors' School then housed in the heart of the City. Much of this stricture was to come via the teaching and sermonizing of the then headmaster James Augustus Hessey whose faith, as we shall see, was notably redoubtable and whose pronouncements accorded with much of the ethos and values of the Victorian public school system. It is indeed indicative in the first instance that Holmes was sent 'across the water' for his education and that the family moved with him; whilst the trappings and benefits of a traditional public school education were then as now self-evident, it still says much for his families' *Anglo-Irish* descent that he was not home-schooled or sent to a religious institution within the land of his birth. Those from the Holmes' social stratum inevitably looked to England and the Union for guidance and governance, part of which involved deference to the continued authority of the Church of England whose principles underlay the development of the Empire and the wider preservation of social order. Similarly, they themselves tended to follow English modes of thinking, culture and occupations with the law, the armed forces and politics being particularly common career destinations. Holmes' Irishness must therefore be couched in its very specific niche which led inevitably to a particular paternalistic and conservative way of thinking which was also to carry through into the early part of his adult life with, for example, his belief in the congenital superiority of particular groups (typically his own class) over others.

In many ways, this educational trajectory embodied perfectly that of a late Victorian gentleman and nowhere was this more evident in his parents' choice of school. Set up in the City of London in 1561, Merchant Taylors' was conceived originally as a place for scholars from both rich and poor backgrounds and under, initially, the dynamic guidance of Richard Mulcaster – one of the greatest early public school headmasters – it strove to promote a well-rounded curriculum focussing upon the many different branches of learning. This spirit continued into the succeeding centuries particularly through the endeavours of another equally dynamic figure James Townley who sought to bring both mathematics and drama into the curriculum, both of which were subjects that were then deeply unfashionable and perceived as superficial and lightweight. Today Merchant Taylors' no longer carries the reputation and lustre of the other schools who formed part of the 'Clarendon Nine'[3] (Eton, Harrow, Westminster, Winchester and so on) yet in its own time it was easily considered their equal and counted Edmund Spenser, John Webster, Lancelot Andrewes and Robert Herrick amongst its alumni. As David Turner has made clear, at this time Merchant Taylors' and its near neighbour St. Paul's 'continued to educate few landowners' sons, filling their rolls instead from the capital's highly varied middle class, including the sons of business men' (Turner, 2015, 114). Although not originally a native of either London or England, this was much more Holmes' demographic; being neither part of the socially well-connected ancient aristocracy or heavily landed new money of Eton nor having descended from the intellectual lineages of the Wykehamists, his parents' choice of school (middle class and haute bourgeois) was still highly indicative both of their background and the later career aspiration of their professional son.

The more ancient literary connections within the school may not though one feels have been lost on the young Holmes who during these years began writing the poetry that would, in the end, form such a major part of his literary output. Although dismissed within his autobiography as the kind of quickly dispensed with juvenilia rhymed out by many an adolescent public school boy on the cusp of manhood it at least indicates the intellectual world surrounding the young Holmes and the inspiration which the school and its distinguished old pupils seemed to generate. Although pertinent questions were then being asked about the composition of the curriculum within the public schools through the Clarendon Commission (1864) – the lack of and in some cases open hostility toward science and practical instruction was a prevailing concern – their emphasis upon Classics, Literature and more traditional branches of learning were to clearly give Holmes an intellectual grounding that he was to put more fully to good use later on in his own writings which covered such a wide hinterland.

Indeed, when considering the narrowness of what was taught in these schools, one can safely say that Merchant Taylors' was hardly amongst the worst offenders in that regard; under the stewardship of Hessey for example the school had worked hard to improve its staff to student ratio, introduced meals at lunchtime and begun to take more seriously the teaching of both mathematics and science. Whilst in part these moves were instigated by the major criticisms within the aforementioned Clarendon Commission, there was clearly too an *internal* impetus for change and this trend was allowed to continue as the school expanded via the creation of new premises for the teaching of modern languages, commerce, games and mathematics. Whilst these changes reached their full fruition mostly in the period just after Holmes left, he was nonetheless within an institution which was more clearly attenuated to the emergent needs of a transforming modern industrial society than some of its bedfellows who remained by comparison stuck within insular and archaic frameworks. Again, whilst impossible to attribute with any degree of accuracy, it is certainly conceivable that Holmes' interest in science and its advances which he was to use later to support his belief in the evolution of the soul found itself stoked by the classes taken whilst at school.

Despite these more positive moves and a commensurate widening of the intellectual horizons, there remained still however the shackles of a strong religious ethic and one cannot overlook either this aspect of Holmes' schooling particularly as it was to impinge upon much of his later educational thinking in a far more direct way. A cartoon of Hessey by 'Ape' in *Vanity Fair* in 1874 (by which time he was Archdeacon of Middlesex) portrays a somnambulant, heavily bewhiskered, *pince-nez* wearing priest dozing in a pulpit. As with so many of Pellegrini's[4] distinctive caricatures, this perfectly captures the essence of the man who was well known for his strict pronouncements on sin and who was to be both Holmes' Divinity teacher and beacon of sermonizing authority as his headmaster. Public school headmasters then, as to some extent now, had ample opportunity should they so wish to mould schools in their own image (one only has to think of Thomas Arnold's muscular Christianity) and one of Hessey's earlier and more successful publications had been *A Scripture Argument against Permitting Marriage with a Wife's Sister* (1850) the very title of which indicates both his general religious orthodoxy, moral rectitude and wide appeals to tradition. This was a point not lost on Holmes whose autobiography spoke – in hindsight perhaps a little harshly – of this influence permeating down to the classroom: 'There [at Merchant Taylors'] I was taught by Classics and mathematics, or rather I had to learn these subjects as best I could from dreary textbooks, with but little help or guidance and with no inspiration from our overburdened masters' (Holmes, 1920a, 10).

As will become evident in later chapters, Holmes' fully developed educational philosophy was one standing in marked contrast to the experiences of his childhood, thereby serving to indicate the importance of these early years, even if they acted only as a sacrificial 'straw man' by which he could outline his more radical vision of freedom. In particular, the ways in which he was variously force-fed religion both at home and at school in the hope of producing a Christian gentleman obeisant to the Scriptures came to indicate the futility of 'teaching' an ideal through simple ritualism and recitation. This was a fault he later observed both within schools in England in which Bible study was a cornerstone of many a curriculum and, from a different context, in Germany where the ideal was more militaristic. In both cases however, Holmes saw only attendant failure with the upshot being the creation of climates of disinterested atheism or else blind unthinking obedience.

Nevertheless, whilst he may have laboured under a self-perceived climate of fear, by Holmes' own admission these were years of academic success, particularly as he rose through the school. Driven by an avowed need to distinguish himself – perhaps through the need to compete with his equally cerebral older siblings – his 'periodic bursts of almost abnormal industry' (Ibid.) were to pay rich dividends and official probation books (lists of all pupils showing their academic performance in school examinations) indicate Holmes performed exceptionally well in his annual class examinations. Merchant Taylors' records further show Holmes to be a frequent prize winner and, in the year of his leaving, he is recorded as winning two prestigious awards including the prize for History. It was these endeavours that were to be a contributory factor in his obtaining a Thomas White Scholarship to study at Oxford.

Oxford and beyond

Holmes matriculated at St John's College Oxford on 28th June 1869. The course for which he was enrolled was *Literae Humaniores* (today called Classics) which then consisted of two parts and lasted four years. The first part of his degree programme (five terms) was known as Mods and was designed to provide a fluency in both Latin and Ancient Greek. The second part (seven terms) was colloquially called Greats and consisted, crudely, of demonstrating both knowledge of Greek History and Philosophy. In many ways this was an extension of much of the work he would have done in school although it would nonetheless be grossly unfair to dismiss this as an easy option for which he had been suitably prepared. It was after all a longer than average degree for which Holmes was ultimately awarded a First in both halves and whose examinations were fiendishly difficult including complex unseen passages and gobbets demanding elucidation as well as critical analysis. According to one contemporary, who was to later become a friend and educational colleague, Holmes easily wore the donnish costume of his surrounds and was 'even in youth so manifestly of the very choicest "cru" academically speaking' (Macan, 1937, 2). Although therefore still an intellectual high-flyer perhaps the difficulties and punishing reading demands of the course contributed later to Holmes' frank assessment:

> I loved Oxford and I had a happy time there. But my happiness was overclouded by my having to read for the two public examinations…I worked hard…not for the pleasure and profit of learning, but in order that I might get 'Firsts' in my examinations.
>
> (Holmes, 1920a, 14)

Given his later condemnation of school curricula driven by any form of 'teaching to the test' and instrumental learning this observation seems providential and ramifies with his earlier concerns over the religious instruction received at school which he felt had been similarly acquired by rote. Indeed, it was noticeable, and perhaps slightly unusual, that Holmes, as a Scholar and with a stellar academic track record, did not subsequently take up a College Fellowship. Whilst this was, by the time of his matriculation, no longer obligatory and may have been down simply to a lack of vacancy it also perhaps indicates that he had by now come to reject the more formal aspects of his academic training in pursuit of undertaking a more civic and public responsibility.

Equally important to his choice of degree was however his choice of College. From their founding the constituent colleges of both Oxford and Cambridge had their own particular traditions, characters and specialisms and, even into the nineteenth century, this trend had persisted. Today one of the wealthiest Oxford Colleges, it was during Holmes' time that the foundation for much of the St John's fortune was accrued mostly through the commercial expansion of the city which took place upon land in north Oxford owned by the College and for which it could now directly benefit as the proprietor. Aside from its increasing financial status, St John's was also a highly appropriate choice given that it had a long established academic link with Holmes' old school. The College's founder Sir Thomas White had been a cloth merchant (hence the Merchant Taylors' designation) and he was involved in setting up not only the school but also the College as a centre for the Counter-Reformation designed to produce Roman Catholic priests whose duty and responsibility was to preserve many of the traditions which had been swept away under the earlier religious reforms of Henry VIII and his Chief Minister Robert Cromwell. Although by the mid-nineteenth century strict adherence to Rome had long since disappeared and the University was loosening its strictures for Fellows to be celibate, to subscribe to the 39 Articles and so on, there still remained strong elements of this orthodoxy and conservatism.

The longstanding connection with Merchant Taylors' meant therefore that the College's demographic mirrored that of its feeder institution. This was not then a home for the sons of the aristocracy as say Christ Church or New College would have been or with a reputation for hearty sporting prowess as say Brasenose. Instead, St John's was very middle class, deeply conservative, resolutely clerical and comparatively unintellectual. In commenting on this peculiar atmosphere the College's official historian W.C. Costin was to say that, 'St. John's...[was] the "closest" of the colleges, and as such particularly suspect to the Liberal free traders, whose freedom of trade was part of a general doctrine of "la carrière ouverte aux talents"' (Costin, 1958, 255). Nor was this constancy to be merely confined to the more nebulous realms of ideology and tradition. Due to his successful procurement of a Scholarship, Holmes was one of four boys from Merchant Taylors' to go up to St John's in the same month (June) and furthermore was one of eleven old boys to be at the College upon his arrival. Whilst this must have made the transition for the young man easier through personal familiarity it also provided for the development of a burgeoning nexus of contacts and acquaintances which were then such a vital part of Oxbridge life. Exact contemporaries of Holmes for example included men such as Charles Gibson who was to become a Master at Merchant Taylors' as well as later producing editions of Shakespeare, Horace Elam who was Master for thirty years at St Paul's and also the noted religious and theological scholar Henry Ottley. The latter is in fact noted in the College battel books (records of accommodation and expenses) as picking up one of Holmes' bills. Although these names represent but a handful from his old school who one presumes Holmes may have known, it still gives an insight into the type of institution he had entered – devotional certainly but also, in the best sense of the word, arcane.

After that fashion, within St John's, change seemed anathema. Throughout the whole of the nineteenth century there were only three Presidents[5] indicating a marked hesitancy – verging on occasional hostility – to progress on the parts of the College's governing body and a clear desire to preserve the somewhat turgid *status quo* found within its walls. Holmes' period of residency overlapped with two of these figures; the first Philip Wynter was, somewhat aptly, a noted scholar of the devotional writer Joseph Hall[6] whilst, following his death in 1871, he was succeeded by another religious conservative, James Bellamy. The latter in particular exerted a wide reach through his founding of the Non-Placet Society the members of which, as William Whyte informs us, 'saw themselves as defenders of an unchanging university, the true Oxford, against an invasion of the Greekless, the Godless, and – worst of all – women' (Whyte, 2006, 91). Through Bellamy's tireless efforts St. John's became then the centre of that reactionary cause and so there was much within its intellectual fabric which mirrored that of Holmes' earlier life and undoubtedly provided for a continuation in the sorts of ideology and expectation amongst its members that had been earlier passed down via Hessey. Indeed, more so perhaps than any other College of the time, St John's had long resembled, to the outsider at least, a comparatively closed-shop with a designated number of Fellowships (typically between 37 to 43 out of 50) set aside for Scholars from Merchant Taylors'. The implications of this insularity, as well as the social and theological conservatism of his surrounds, would not one feels have gone unnoticed to such a keen, impressionable and observant mind as that possessed by Holmes.

At a more global level however, Oxford itself – the home after all of lost causes – was going through one of its periodic ructions as it sought to come to terms with the emergence of two distinct movements both of which continued to impact heavily upon the intellectual atmosphere and landscape of the university. On the one hand, it was still reminded of the earlier Tractarian Movement which had sought, through the work of its originators John Henry Newman and Edward Pusey, to re-introduce older and more traditional forms of worship and liturgy which they felt had been lost from the Church of England in the years following the Reformation. Very much enmeshed with the conservatism found within St. John's, this permanent legacy was embodied more grandiosely in the form of Keble College – founded during Holmes' second year in 1870 – and named after John Keble an even earlier progenitor of these traditionalist approaches to worship. Undoubtedly, the opening of a new College (the first since 1714) would have been important news for any undergraduate but, more than that, it would certainly have reminded Holmes yet further of the messages he had earlier acquired about the need for ritual and obedience within established religion. Even the distinctive architecture of Keble was designed by William Butterfield as a monument and homage to the Gothic revival and the need for more arcane forms of worship.

Indeed such was the attachment to these features and characteristics that Newman and latterly Henry Manning and others ultimately migrated to the Roman Catholic faith seeing within its precincts clearer evidence of the 'high' church approach to which they were devoted. As we have alluded to already, this air of religiosity permeated more widely too; it was after all only in 1854 that subscription to the 39 Articles was no longer a condition of matriculation at Oxford and certain religious tests were still required for some positions until 1870. It is worth therefore remembering, in that vein, that in condemning religious education in schools as little more than 'collective recitation and reading, gabbling and mumbling, collective answering [and] irregular answering' (Holmes, 1923e, 193) Holmes was not merely critiquing the lessons themselves but more widely those who stood for order and preservation of the Church and State duopoly – a key part of which was compulsory religious study for children. Adherence to this alliance and its dissemination was then widely found within contemporary Oxford. Furthermore the Catholic Church and its theology, whose presence lurked in the background during these debates, was later disparagingly singled out by Holmes as 'the central axis of Christian orthodoxy…the Church of Rome…[which] cannot afford to take part in or to countenance in any way the modern movements of speculative thought' (Holmes, 1924c, 49). He could almost, within this denunciation, have been talking not just about his College but also the tenor of much of his University experience.

These religious schisms and controversies inflecting Oxford were therefore not only important in their own right but were to be channelled later into Holmes' vociferous critique of Western religious belief which based itself, according to his premises, on fostering the sorts of obedience, ritualism and compulsion as was manifest within the educational institutions of his youth. Such ideas he believed were rooted in a faith that was both external and dependent in the main on the notion of a transcendent distant God which did not appeal to Holmes whose passions were now being stoked by Nature and whose dissatisfaction with the conventional we can trace to this time. A young man's rebellion is of course nothing new but how best, beyond simple atheistic disbelief, to articulate it? In this, the answer for Holmes was to lie within the second emergent intellectual school of thought within the University which, through its ideas and principles, was to provide him with a source of life-long intellectual ammunition by which he was able to successfully repel and repudiate many of the religious demands and claims which had to date been a significant part of his young life.

Known as 'British Idealism', and centred upon the academic hub of Balliol College where several of its key protagonists in particular Benjamin Jowett, T.H. Green and R.L. Nettleship held Fellowships, this important philosophical movement was to garner widespread support and interest from many inquisitive undergraduates. In particular it 'met the spiritual needs of young men brought up in some orthodox Christian faith who…could no longer accept without qualification both that faith and also the religious vocation which, for university students, so often went with it' (Gordon and White, 1979, 7). Such a description could almost have been penned with Holmes in mind and it was clear that he, along with others of his ilk including his later colleagues at the Board of Education Robert Morant and Michael Sadler, were attracted to the movement both through attendance at public lectures, courses and debates but also by the porous dissemination of ideas and formation of intellectual cliques so common within the major universities of the time. Holmes in particular fell under the spell of Green and was to find within his philosophical ideas an intellectual toolkit by which he could begin simultaneously to both understand and dismantle so much of the apparent truisms of orthodox Western religion.

In sum, the Idealists held true to a series of key essential principles. First, was belief in an Absolute which, although subject to the characteristic minutiae of philosophical wrangling, was broadly an attempt to 'dissolve all dualisms, for example, between "individual" and "other" (e.g. society), "nature" and "thought", and transcendence and immanence' (Sweet in Mander, 2014, 561). Second, was their belief in the essential unity between thought and object, in other words to reject the notion of matter as being in some sense separate from the lives of individuals. This was in part a denial of much of the hithertofore dominant native doctrine of empiricism which posited the existence of an objective independent reality that was solely apprehensible by the senses. As we shall later see, this material 'external' view of the world (and in particular its theological implications) was to be one roundly condemned by Holmes. Finally, the idealists believed that it was the faculty of Reason as opposed to superstition which was the main method by which the Structure of this Absolute was to be apprehended.

Becoming a disciple to such ideas inevitably changed the way men such as Holmes understood and perceived the world around them; it was no longer to be a concrete entity of the real and actual overseen by a supreme God but more to be appreciated instead as a unified whole whose existence was a reciprocal product of both thought and imagination. When considering Holmes' later writings many of which ascribed such centrality to concepts such as Unity, Wholeness and inseparability of Man and Spirit it is evident how such a belief found its genesis within this strand of idealistic thinking. The tension residing therefore within the young man between childhood Biblical literalism on the one hand and this new and emergent way of thinking on the other was clearly palpable as Holmes himself explained: 'strange as it may seem, I managed for some time to combine…rejection of much of the teaching of orthodox Christianity with belief that Christianity was divine in a sense which set it apart from rival religions' (Holmes, 1920a, 15). However, such pressures could not lie unresolved indefinitely and it was to be his reading (also whilst at Oxford) of Matthew Arnold's seminal work *Literature and Dogma* (1873) that served to push Holmes over the edge, not merely completing his intellectual apprenticeship but also severing for good all connection to more literal and material interpretations of Christianity. We have already discussed, rightly, in the Introduction the fallacy of attempting to bracket together Holmes and Arnold despite their shared public role as 'Inspector-Poets'. Nevertheless, in charting the origins of Holmes' later philosophy which sought to break away from orthodoxy and supernaturalism, it is clear that this discovery, in parallel with his proximity to the Oxford-based Idealists, was to prove equally revelatory and influential. His path may ultimately have led to the mystics of the East but the spectre of Arnold undoubtedly loomed large.

Literature and Dogma was in fact to be not only Arnold's last major original book but also his most popular quickly going through a number of editions and selling as many as 100,000 copies, a not inconsiderable number for a work of theological criticism. In part this was through its arrangement – a prose narrative rather than a series of essays – but also because its overall tone was both iconoclastic and sought to challenge many of the accepted tenets of the established Church. Capturing something of this tone, Arnold's most recent biographer tells us,

The argument in *Literature and Dogma* in essence was that Christianity could only survive if it jettisoned certain false dogmas – hostages to fortune that, if they were not got rid of, would start to furnish people with excuses for abandoning Christianity altogether.

(Murray, 1997, 267)

In particular, Arnold sought to dispute the anthropomorphism and what he saw as the other vulgar errors of popular religion including miracles which he considered as an example of *Aberglaube* ('extra belief'). Prevailing interpretations of the Bible had, after that fashion, been prone to this and so moved irrationally beyond what could be considered valid in an age that was becoming more sceptic and questioning in particular through the developments of science. It was the search for such an ultimate and unknown reality that had driven the greatest advancements in human achievement and so Arnold came to eventually posit a naturalistic approach to religion and one based less on cast-iron theological conviction and more upon faith, doubt, question and uncertainty. The overlaps between these ideas and those of the Idealists should be straightaway apparent particularly through the way in which science (or Reason) was being used here not as a way to crudely deny and demolish the idea of God but as a way instead of interrogating and questioning its actual form in an age in which new discoveries – the theory of evolution, atomic structures and so on – were offering a potentially new paradigmatic way of thinking.

It is worth noting here that, like Arnold and despite his later promotion of Eastern ways of thinking, Holmes retained a life-long attachment to the Christian faith. Although his was to be an interpretation filtered through a very novel lens which incorporated those aspects of science and wider spiritual growth, as late as 1927 he felt moved to write, 'It was as a suffering God that Jesus Christ first won our hearts. It is as a suffering God that he still commands our devotion, our service, and our love' (Holmes, 1927b, 504). Holmes' early devotion to the tenets of Idealism did not then mean any corresponding attempt to destroy the idea of religion or negate the primacy of the spirit. Rather, they served instead to mould his spiritual understanding into a shape more akin to that as recognized and understood by those such as Green who found within his own philosophical project a perspective that could hold fast to religious attitudes and values but without the dogma and with perhaps new metaphysical truths to replace devotion to the old gods. Overlaying the idea of an Absolute with his youthful Romantic tendencies created therefore for Holmes an intellectually buttressed understanding of God to be equated with something altogether more pantheist. As he was to neatly summarize, 'When I had finished the book [*Literature and Dogma*] I had said good-bye to the Supernatural…Henceforth Nature was enough for me' (Holmes, 1920a, 16). Evidence for this newly transformed way of thinking comes too from his first religious work – published comparatively soon after in 1898 and written as a series of numbered tenets of belief – in which Nature in this context was envisaged as something greater than that merely apprehended by the senses or as an external being worthy of simple supplication: 'I mean by Nature that order of things in which I find myself, and which…is infinite in all directions and all dimensions' (Holmes, 1898b, 4).

Arnold was also important too in another way for his young contemporary and this was through his recognition of the need for spiritual transcendence from the exigencies of modern life. Encapsulated brilliantly in the well-known poem *The Scholar-Gypsy* in which the protagonist through his 'heaven-sent moments' is allowed temporary intellectual refuge from the mundane and poisonous aspects of a culture on which he has turned his back, it was also during these early years that Holmes too first began to recognize the Wholeness inherent within the material world and to reject any separation of Man and God which was seen as a cankerous feature of the contemporary world. Indeed, the landscapes inscribed within Arnold's poem carry an additional significance as they constitute descriptions of areas around Oxford which Holmes himself may well have frequented. Indeed, one of Holmes' own early poems was entitled *To the Isis* (the name given to the part of the River Thames that runs through Oxford) and his first two volumes of poetry published shortly after his graduation have, as their theme, a proto-pantheism which recognized the sublime (Absolute) qualities inherent within nature and the natural world. This was important for two reasons; first, it represented the earliest stage of Holmes' appreciation of the inherent unity between Man and Nature and the worlds of the inner and the outer – what he dubbed 'the supreme standard and measure of truth' (Holmes, 1898b, 13). Second in setting himself up in thrall to an external entity and spirit which, in Wordsworth's terms, rolled through all things it represented the beginning of Holmes' most longstanding perennial idea which was that of self-transcendence through *self-loss*. There were to be ultimately three key manifestations of this concept which were, successively, self-loss to Nature, self-loss in thrall to a beloved/love and finally self-loss in relation to the Universe or Cosmos. It was this last grand idea, as we shall see, which was to end up underpinning Holmes' moral and indeed educational system of beliefs which were centred on developing a more nuanced recognition of the relationship of the Self to its surroundings. Whilst this full elaboration was to be nearly four decades in the future, its origins were very much found within the fundamental tenets of Idealism and Arnold.

Such was to be the transformative impact of these beliefs upon Holmes that they served as the catalyst for his first major foray into the printed word, written in order to justify his newly acquired and, at the time, still intellectually controversial way of thinking. According to his autobiography, from his Oxford days and on, he had envisioned an *opus magnum* which was to consist of a large three volume work bearing the title *God and Man: An Appeal to Nature* and which was intended to make the case for the spirit rather than matter as being the key pole of existence. Although this ambitious project was never to see the light of day, its core thesis was nevertheless to be enshrined in this first philosophical work entitled *Sursum Corda: A Defence of Idealism* (1898b). As its title would indicate, this represented Holmes offering a strident justification for an idealistic way of thinking opposing the charges levelled against it by those adherents of materialism particularly in the way that it appeared as too abstract and not grounded in any 'actual' reality.

Holmes' defence – for which his indebtedness to those such as Green was all too apparent – rested ultimately on a number of key points but was driven, in the main, by the principle that the ideas of materialism were associated very much with the body 'with its narrow range of perceptive faculties...It is his [Mankind's] "lower self"' (Holmes, 1898b, 20). This contrast of the lower order and the body with the higher order of the spirit hints once more at Holmes' later preoccupations with the transcendent nature of the soul and the importance of spiritual growth within education and was perhaps being fuelled by his continuing school inspections in which he was surely observing many of the spiritual defects (selfishness, competition etc.) that were to form part of his damning indictment. This dismissal of the lower order pleasures alludes too to his later panegyrics of Christ and the Buddha, men 'whose life is entirely transfigured by the clear-burning flame of spiritual faith' (Ibid., 34). Simply put, adherents to the ascetic life of the spirit were always to be held in higher regard and identified as having been (in Thomas Carlyle's terms) the Great Men rather than those who lived of and through the narrow material confines of the body. In penning such a defence it was clear that Holmes was now beginning to move beyond mere theoretical and ontological concerns – that is what could be simply known and apprehended (which had often been the concern of those scholars at Oxford) – and into the realm of the quasi-theological by looking at the impact the doctrine of materialism had on human conduct and behaviours. Holmes may have been first and foremost a philosopher but he was always to be as much concerned with religion and morality and saw in the Idealist project a way of moving beyond simple earthly considerations and its fetishization and attachment, literally, to material objects.

Ultimately as we shall see Holmes was to migrate away from more Western-inspired principles and find increased solace in the teachings of the East; nevertheless, although these were to represent a new direction and extension of his initial thinking by seeing every aspect of life as part of an infinite continuum there was a clear overlap with the principles of Idealism and its talk of the unity of the Absolute. In thus rejecting materialism and giving primacy to the spirit Holmes was also providing a signpost for his own moral framework which was optimistic and associated with *hope*. What else after all could drive a system of thought that had at its core a search for the infinite and was not satiated simply by unsophisticated sense-bound realities and truths? Not of course that Holmes would ever lose touch entirely with the Christian teaching of his youth and in language that deliberately mirrored the most famous of parables he was to confer on his readership the benefits of an idealistic series of beliefs:

> The movement towards the ideal takes different names according to the different sides of our being which it affects. In the region of thought it takes the name of *faith*...In...emotion it takes the name of *hope*...In the region of practice...it takes the name of *love*.
>
> (Ibid., 109–110)

It was this outwardly simple premise that was to form the basis of much of Holmes' later social and political thought and so once more indicates the enormous debt he was to owe to this early conversion. Although later works may have sought to move into wider aspects of intellectual territory (education, religion and so on) it was all to be forever grounded in a spiritual standpoint with a drive toward both perfection (a goal never to be reached) as well as a faith in the limitless possibilities of the world.

Holmes received his BA in 1874 and his MA (after nine terms of holding his BA) in 1877. Almost exactly a year after passing out of Oxford he was rewarded, on 1st April 1875, with his first Inspectorial appointment in the West Riding of Yorkshire and was to be based temporarily in Huddersfield. Details of this are once more frustratingly sketchy yet it seems that, mirroring somehow the uncertainty and conflict within his intellectual life as he sought to reconcile religion and Idealism, this was a peripatetic and uncertain year in which Holmes briefly held three temporary posts. Two of these were within schools (the prestigious Repton School and Wellington College) whilst he also served latterly as tutor to the family of the 11th Earl of Winchelsea who was to ultimately assist him in his promotion to the Board of Education and thus provided him, through the tried and trusted method of patronage, with a 'foot in the door' for a life-long career as a serving Inspector.

As an example of the lack of permanence from this period, it seems his first posting at Wellington College was during the summer term only of 1874 (April–June) and came as a result of the need for the then headmaster Edward Charles Wickham to conduct a full review of the workings of the school, a function he could not carry out alongside his ordinary teaching duties. His formal Report to the Governors spoke of the post of his temporary replacement as appealing to 'a really good scholar, who would undertake the place at a moderate salary, as offering a little school experience and considerable leisure' (Wickham, Headmaster's Reports 1874, 2). It seems, from a little further on in his statement, that he already had in mind Holmes who went on to serve for the duration of the school year. How he acquired the post so promptly we do not know however working in such a setting was not unusual for a gentleman of the period (particularly given Holmes' background and academic record) and it may well have been the case that he had time here to work on refining and compiling his earliest verses – a handful were published two years later in the school magazine alongside a favourable review of his first volume of poetry.

In a similar vein, the termly lists of pupils and staff would seem to show that Holmes was also at Repton for a very short amount of time – he appears first on the Christmas 1874 list, but is gone by the Midsummer 1875 list (which would have been published at Easter) indicating he was once more only here for a term. Whilst there, he had been placed in charge of the lower sixth and, from brief mentions within the *Reptonian* magazine, it seems he was to make occasional contributions to school debates which betray, even here, both a developing concern with the role and purpose of education as well as a desire to openly espouse those earlier ideas of Arnold concerning the 'best' aspects of culture. For example, in a debate on the effectiveness of classical education he is recorded as arguing that, 'there was a far higher aim than mere practical knowledge, – that excellence or perfection which should be the aim of all' (*The Reptonian*, Volume 2, Number 14). On a later occasion, and in a subsequent debate concerning all things horse racing, Holmes betrayed his conservative streak by putting forward the view that, 'the pleasure it afforded was a poor equivalent to the waste of time and money it necessitated' (Ibid.). A contempt for such 'lower class' pursuits and enjoyments was one he was to carry with him well into later life as they became seen as an embodiment of the sensualism fostered by outward externalism.

Unusually, Holmes is not listed as leaving the school within the *Reptonian's* 'Occasional Notes' section which traditionally carried such information. His was certainly a fleeting presence and it seems that, from there, as Peter Gordon (1983) informs us, he became tutor to the family of the Earl of Winchelsea. How Gordon knew this is uncertain; there is nothing pertaining to this appointment in the Winchelsea Archive nor does Holmes mention it by name. Presumably, the family in question would have been that belonging to the 11th Earl of Winchelsea not merely on account of the correspondence of dates in relation to the Earl's children but also his active political involvement. Holmes writes very generally that his Inspectorship was due 'entirely to political interest' (Holmes, 1920a, 17) and one cannot help but think this is a reference to the Earl's political connections; he had, after all, been an MP for four years before acceding to the House of Lords in 1858. This influence would have become even greater following the return, in February of 1874, of the Disraeli Government. Holmes therefore cannot have been tutor for very long however with his claim for an Inspectorship made official in April he was to therefore put behind him this period of uncertainty and temporary employment to take up what became a lifetime's service to the nation and from which his greatest achievements would derive.

Notes

1 Thomas Rice Edward Holmes (1855–1933) was, like his brother, educated at Merchant Taylors' School and Oxford (Christchurch rather than St John's) and moved into education working most notably at St. Paul's School from 1886. In retirement he devoted much time to the scholarship of Classical History publishing widely on Julius Caesar and the Gallic Wars. There are two photographic images of him within the National Portrait Gallery.
2 Famously invoked by Yeats within 'Coole Park, 1929' and 'Coole Park and Ballylee, 1931' Lady Augusta Gregory (1852–1932) served as a central figure behind the Irish Literary Revival not merely through her own writings but by acting too as a patron and convener of the arts. Her home – Coole Park – served initially as the hub for these activities.
3 The Clarendon Commission was a Royal Commission established in 1861 and which sat until 1864 when its Report was published. Its findings concerned seven boarding schools (Eton, Charterhouse, Harrow, Rugby, Shrewsbury, Westminster and Winchester), and two day schools (St Paul's and Merchant Taylors').

4 Ape was the *nom de plume* of Carlo Pellegrini (1839–1889) who was a caricaturist for *Vanity Fair* from 1869–1889.
5 These were Michael Marlow 1795–1828, Philip Wynter 1828–1871 and James Bellamy 1871–1909.
6 Joseph Hall (1574–1656) was an English Bishop, moralist and devotional writer who repudiated many of the more orthodox approaches to Christianity.

Chapter 2

The years of Inspection

Introduction and context

Holmes' Inspectorial career began when he was only 24 and lasted for nearly 37 years. Although still comparatively youthful and having worked for less than a year in schools (and even these were private establishments), such limitations were not then factors considered as barriers to becoming an HMI (Her Majesty's Inspector). Reference has already been made to how Holmes' initial appointment owed much to the influence of the Earl of Winchelsea and, as Lawton and Gordon have pointed out,

> Many of the appointments [to the Inspectorate] were made on the basis of personal recommendation or through acquaintance with the Lord President... Of the ninety-two Inspectors appointed between 1839 and 1870, eighty had been to Oxford or Cambridge, five to other universities...None had taught in elementary schools.
>
> (Lawton and Gordon, 1987, 9–10)

Nepotistic as this system may have appeared such lack of experience was excused on the basis that the Inspectorate's role was, in essence, a functionary one in carrying out the annual examination of pupil standards and providing reportage on 'the state of the schools under their inspection and to [making] practical suggestions for their improvement' (Lowe, 1861, quoted in Ibid., 11). Furthermore, it served to ensure (as far as the Board was concerned) a level of objectivity in relation to their duties and that it was the 'right sort' of men who were elevated to their appropriate station.

As a consequence, Holmes' first posting was in 1875 to the West Riding of Yorkshire succeeded shortly after in 1879 by an appointment to Kent (Ashford district) where he remained for nearly twenty years until 1897. Following a six-year period happily spent in his old stamping ground of Oxford (and in charge now of some 400 schools) he returned briefly to the north of England to Northumberland in 1903 as Divisional Inspector, a position which granted him responsibility for between eight to ten districts comprising the four Northern Counties. Finally, in 1905, his long career was rewarded with a last promotion to the post of Chief Inspector for Elementary Schools where he was to remain for five diligent years until his peaceful retirement in 1910. Such a peripatetic career was not then unusual at the time amongst School Inspectors and Holmes' movements around the country are therefore in no way indicative of a career representing either great success or marked failure. Indeed, his ascendency to the top of the 'greasy pole' designates a high value placed as much on his administrative and personal competence and ability to manage his Inspectors as it does his educational understanding and vision.

This formative and clearly hugely important period of his life is, like his earlier years addressed within the previous chapter, frustrating for the historian as there is likewise little direct evidence or insights into his experiences, movements and personal situation. Of the 150 pages in his 1920 autobiography for example only nine are concerned explicitly with this long period of his life and, even there, they are dealt with somewhat cursorily. In many ways then he remains still at this time the ghostly figure of common understanding, his life pieced together by inference, assumption and limited correspondence. This is not perhaps surprising; as the introductory chapter made clear it was only after his retirement that the vast majority of his written output emerged and by the time of 1911 and the watershed moment of *What is and What Might Be*, Holmes' most significant works had been his poetry and religious writings many of which had anyway been published anonymously. Indeed, prior to that point, his only educational publications had been two *Inspection Reports* (in 1879a and 1883) and two papers delivered first to the teachers of the Oxford district (1898a) and then to an education club (1908a) respectively. Although naturally receptive to their speaker and, in the latter's case, indicative of the developing dissemination of progressive ideas amongst interested practitioners, these town-hall platform style orations were not obvious signs at this juncture of a potentially burgeoning career and reputation as an educational visionary. Similarly, such extrinsic ventures in verse and theological speculation did not greatly distinguish him from many other educated late Victorian amateur intellectuals whose schooling had equally well prepared them for wide scholarly rumination and academic contribution.

This paucity of publication can of course be put down primarily to the demands of the job and constraints of time inevitably imposed upon literary productivity particularly as increased administrative responsibility weighed upon his shoulders. This was not merely confined to Holmes' duties within the elementary sector but also his role in inspecting institutions responsible for teacher training. In an unpublished Board of Education memorandum, Holmes is listed alongside four other senior figures as having responsibility for the inspection of fourteen such establishments, nine residential colleges (typically for elementary teachers) and five day training departments (for secondary teachers) within the north of England.[1] As Lawton and Gordon have additionally indicated, such procedure and accountability were, from the outset, key watchwords amongst the Board: 'Inspectors were, from the beginning, also expected to account for their time and movements to "the Office". The main check was made by means of official diaries in which Inspectors recorded daily how they spent their time' (Lawton and Gordon, 1987, 13).

More significantly though it seems, as time wore on, that the maturing Holmes was to become increasingly disillusioned with the role he was being asked to fulfill and it was the stultifying nature of his routine which he felt had initially blinded him from fully apprehending the pervading malaise affecting the education system and any desire to seek to challenge it in print. As he succinctly put it: 'For nearly twenty years the grooves in which I had been drawn held me fast' (Holmes, 1920a, 67). This implicit pessimism is further reinforced from another later reflective and more revealing documentary passage which found him musing on his time as an Inspector:

> What was I doing during all those dreary years? Alas! I was a dutiful, industrious, and almost ultra-conscientious official, and the pity of it is that when an official is administering a pernicious system, the more dutiful, industrious and conscientious he is, the more mischief he is fated to do…I was well content to play my appointed part in that vast complex of machinery which had been elaborated by the wisdom and was controlled by the authority of Whitehall.
>
> (Holmes, 1922, 726–727)

Such a statement clearly indicates the over-riding and frustrating sense of conformity and constraint felt within his career and much Inspectorial work, beyond Holmes' immediate ideological opposition, was indeed drudgery of the geographic and intellectual kind involving widespread travel and often mundane school observation. This perhaps explains why he was so loathe to later dwell on this lengthy part of his life candidly admitting that he felt much of it wasted in deadening routine and toil. Nevertheless, if anything can be said to have been noteworthy about this work it is that its exigencies caused not only an ideological *volte-face* but also that they pushed Holmes into closer association with sets of radical and challenging ideas which were to form the basis of his later educational viewpoint and outlook. It was during his relatively lengthy tenure in Kent for example that Holmes developed his life-long interest in Theosophy through, as Peter Gordon (1983) notes, immersion in the works of Mabel Collins (1885), A.P. Sinnett (1883) and latterly and most significantly Rudolf Steiner (1908). Exposure to such Eastern-oriented literature undoubtedly planted the seed for a very particular intellectual framework and was clearly to provide a foundation for the ultimate development of an alternative and novel philosophy which drew upon those more esoteric and spiritual ideas.

Equally catalytic however to Holmes' shift in stance were the large-scale *political* and *policy* changes taking place contemporaneously and which he himself recognized as being of still greater significance in the course of his life. Indeed, after that fashion, the swing from over-worked Inspector to pioneering progressive was attributed in his writing to the abolition of the system of 'payment by results' in the 1890s and thus the alteration of his role from that of *examiner* designed merely to implement and oversee a grant-dependent test to school *inspector* whose role was far less rigid and proprietorial. This earlier system – which had been previously introduced in 1862 through the Revised Code – had been driven by the twin imperatives of efficiency and Benthamite utility with each school child for whom the government grant was claimed being examined every year on six standards mostly comprised of what were referred to colloquially as the traditional '3Rs' – reading, writing and arithmetic. As one of the architects of this system Robert Lowe[2] made clear in a revealing metaphor: 'Hitherto we have been living under a system of bounties and protection; now we propose to have a little free trade' (Lowe quoted in Hansard, clxiv, 1861, col. 736). This 'free trade' was to be built on the principle of schools having to earn, via academic attainment, the right to be funded by the government. As in any such system, competition and rivalry were key with some schools succeeding at the expense of others and performance therefore being determined by the individual efforts of the teachers who were to thus be held accountable for the results obtained.

Schools were therefore inspected annually in order to ascertain, through testing and examination, what children knew, the results of which determined much of the level of the grant paid by the government – in effect a rudimentary system of payment by pupil performance. Although there were occasional deviations in terms of the contents and formulation of the examination, the role of the Inspector remained essentially proprietorial and to test how successfully children had managed to learn the prescribed and narrow syllabus which in reality was often 'crammed' into them by anxious teachers immediately prior to the designated inspection date. The Committee of Council on Education gave official reinforcement to this the prevailing ideology by stressing that inspectors were to test, 'according to a certain standard [which] must always be, to a considerable extent, *mechanical*' (Annual Reports, 1862–1863, xviii, italics added). Even down to such details as insisting that children remain in their places throughout, the exact form of rubric to use when addressing them as well as recommending verbal dictation for certain parts of the examination, the Board it seemed were determined to retain a very particular form of control over all aspects of the bureaucratic framework.

Holmes' career is therefore significant for it very nearly perfectly bisects both this system and that which succeeded it in which simple 'block grants' were paid to schools on the basis both of their size and geographical location. This was envisaged as a welcome change and in characteristically grandiose language Holmes talked later of a seismic shift in the educational landscape as it moved from the Land of Bondage to, instead, being 'invited to enter the Promised Land – the Land of Freedom' (Holmes, 1920a, 67). This move was further significant in that it allowed for those with the cast of mind of Holmes to actually *inspect* schools (with all that term's particular connotations) rather than having to simply discern what those inside could repeat to order which often involved limited levels of interaction. Confirming this, Holmes was to write, 'Inspectors ceased to be mere examiners, mere appraisers and tabulators of cut-and-dried results, and became…*inspectors*'

(Holmes, 1922 727, italics added). Being asked therefore to better understand the *totality* of the child's educational experience via occasional visits rather than such factors being subsidiary to straightforward academic performance and attendance led, he believed, to a greater appreciation as to the truth of the numbing conditions in which the nation's young were then being schooled. In stressing that the role of the Inspectorate was as much about being 'observers of ways and works, students of method, critics of the atmosphere, the moral and the spirit of the school' (Ibid.) Holmes was evidencing a much wider range of success criteria in education than was then (or indeed now!) conventionally adopted.

Often, the earlier defects found by Holmes and his colleagues had been physical as well as intellectual; the *Newcastle Report* of 1861 for example had pointed out that,

> Of the 1,549,312 children whose names are on the books of public elementary day schools belonging to the religious denominations, only 19.3 per cent were in their 12th year or upwards, and only that proportion, therefore, can be regarded as educated up to the standard suited to their stations. As many as 786,202 [children] attend for less than 100 days in the year and can therefore hardly receive a serviceable amount of education.
> (The Royal Commission on the State of Popular Education in England, Parliamentary Papers, 1861, XXI.293–328; reprinted in Young and Hancock, 1956, 892–893)

The *Report* was also critical of much of the 'inefficient teaching' (Ibid., 893) which was seen to bedevil many institutions, a high proportion of which continued to be heavily populated by unqualified or pupil teachers.[3] Such statistics clearly placed Britain behind Prussia and other potential economic competitors in terms of the numbers of children receiving an education – a fact which did not go unnoticed amongst certain policy-makers of the time. In many cases, schools – particularly those maintained by the various church denominations and which had much older foundations – continued to be used throughout the duration of Holmes' long career without renewal or regeneration which meant not only a deterioration in their condition but also, due to their primitive layout often harking back to the monitorial system, negated any opportunities for the use of any type of progressive or child-centred pedagogical approaches.

Even newly founded Board Schools (following the Education Act of 1870) were often poorly designed and maintained, serving, as Andy Green has alluded to, as places merely to develop basic skills necessary for the demands of industry and built on a system more honed toward 'stunning its pupils into sullen quiescence that for honing alert and intelligent minds' (Green, 1990, 24). Frequently their limited curriculum and physical configuration seemed unwittingly to reflect a particular interpretation of the ideas of F.H. Bradley[4] in as much as the schools' hidden function became to instill elementary school children with a set of values (obedience, deference and obeisance) designed to reflect their pre-destined social station in life – in this case as grant and later wage-earning entities. It was therefore simply not the case that with a new system of funding and methods of inspection went significant changes to the educational experiences or life chances of all children; the system remained at best a mixed picture, a point acknowledged by Holmes:

> The Children of Israel wandered for forty years in the Wilderness before they entered the Promised Land; and it was long before inspectors or teachers could avail themselves in any appreciable degree of the freedom which had suddenly – perhaps too suddenly – been bestowed upon them.
> (Holmes, 1920a, 67)

Although more concerned about the stunting of spiritual growth rather than thinking of social or economic entitlement, the fact remains that one of the continuing themes even into his later books was the desire to confront the surface assumptions residing within the established educational system and to seek to constantly attenuate his intellectual compass toward that Land of Freedom.

Whilst then these aforementioned changes in political organization served to act as a Damascene moment in Holmes' life and undoubtedly coloured how he was to later perceive its trajectory this nonetheless somewhat overlooked and obscured the inhering possibilities that existed to oppose the system from within and the initial bold interventions he himself was to make in relation to education. Some of this was likewise encouraged by those free spirits at the Board of Education – particularly within the last decade of the nineteenth century – many of whom were of Holmes' generation and background, and who had been equally inspired by new and emergent philosophical trends. This was a point recognized by R.W. Macan who spoke of a 'New Spirit at work in the Education Office of the Nineties, which I associate with the presence of two other Oxford friends… Arthur Acland…and Sir Michael Sadler' (Macan, 1937, 5). Following that, it therefore surely behoves us to look in more detail at those early publications of the period to see how, in fact, Holmes was able to resist some of the state-sanctioned shackles and the 'iron of Whitehall' which he morosely claimed had 'entered his soul' and created within him a 'fatalistic apathy' (Ibid., 66). In particular, his two *General Reports for the Committee of Council on Education* seem to belie Holmes' suggestions of apparent personal constraint and provide instead pertinent examples of their author offering critiques of existing education within his allocated districts. Holmes was not of course the only dissenting voice; famously Matthew Arnold contended that the seeming need to constantly examine children was usurping the promotion of a more genuine intellectual development whilst his colleague W.P. Turnbull likewise reflected angrily on 'the open manipulation of the *child as a grant-earning thing*, rather than his treatment as trust' (Turnbull, 1919, 139, original italics). Although these men undoubtedly shared a common opposition to the instrumental payment by results system – influenced very often by their knowledge of child-centred ideas from the Continent and the United States – it was clearly Holmes who not only most readily articulated these fears and put them into permanent form through his many writings but who was also to bring these into a more coherent overall philosophy which challenged the system's hidden messages and underlying assumptions.

Furthermore, although comparatively brief, these *Reports*, along with a handful of other educational publications, represent the transformation of Holmes' newly found ontological convictions (addressed in the previous chapter) and implicit within the outlet of his early poetry into more concrete epistemological beliefs which carried with them practical and very real educational and curricular implications. In essence Holmes was here seeking to apply his reading of the idealist principles of *being* to the problem of knowledge and understanding particularly as they applied and were taught in schools. By so doing he allows us now to more accurately pinpoint the development of his evolving intellectual thought and signposts the foundations for many of his later more radical ideas.

The Inspection Reports

Both of these *Reports* were produced for the Committee of Council on Education – a Committee of the Privy Council[5] – and each represented a summation of Holmes' findings over the course of a particular year and across his own district. The first of these concerned the year 1878 and covered the West Riding district of Yorkshire. The other, of 1882, discusses the education system in the Ashford district of Kent and comes from the time of Holmes' second appointment. Within these *Reports* three main general themes can be seen to pervade; first the poor quality of much of the existing educational provision, second the general trend towards didactic knowledge imposition in the classrooms and, finally, the lack of relevance of much of what was taught and studied.

At the time of writing, despite the new Board Schools created by the 1870 Education Act, there was still, as Phil Gardner (1984) indicates, a large and pervasive system of working class private schools christened by many, including here Holmes in relation to Kent, as 'dame schools' which were named colloquially and somewhat disparagingly after the old ladies who were often to be found running them. Charles Dickens, typically, offers the best known description of such an establishment in his novel *Great Expectations* in which the stories' protagonist Pip attends a dame school run by Mr. Wopsle's great aunt and which is housed in the same room as her shop. For him the experience was underwhelming: 'I struggled through the alphabet as if it had been a bramble-bush; getting considerably worried and scratched by every letter' (Dickens, 1992, 35). Although characteristic of Dickens' satirical streak – and this was not the only occasion in which he mocked what he saw as the limitations of Victorian education – it was undoubtedly true that the provision in these establishments was patchy and variable. As W.B. Stephens points out, 'the concept of what kind of education should be provided was a restricted one. One dame school assisted by a 'wealthy person' in the 1840s contained not a single child able perfectly to tell all its letters' (Stephens, 1987, 183). Such indeed was the lowly status of these establishments – and the common day schools with which they were classified – that they were labelled within the 1851 Educational Census as 'Inferior Schools', a snobbish epithet which nonetheless indicated their widely perceived value.

It was therefore perhaps unsurprising that Holmes would be particularly forthright in his denunciation of their merits: 'Of all the evils with which the cause of elementary education has to contend, the permitted existence of inefficient private adventure schools is to my mind the most serious' (Holmes, 1883, 354). Such problems stemmed not merely from the poor quality of many of their facilities – Holmes recounts having to put his head amongst low-lying beams, a pervading slaughterhouse stench and cramped conditions – but more significantly from the irregular and scanty attendance amongst its intake. As such, the general culture in these schools was anti-intellectual, peripatetic and hardly conducive to either successful learning or teaching. This was of still greater significance given that, 'At the passing of the Education Act of 1870, it does not seem fanciful to suppose that something like a quarter of all working-class children at elementary schools were attending private schools' (Gardner, 1984, 188). Indeed, many of these establishments, according to Holmes, acted solely as a home for child 'refugees' seeking to escape the more onerous provisions of the Board Schools and from which it was more difficult to be absent given the presence, from 1881, of a nationwide inspectorate designed to enforce attendance. Understandable as this was with children required to assist parents during seasonal work in order to add to the family income – and Holmes' geographical sketch of the Kent area alludes to the local farming and hop-growing – it was nonetheless seen as a contributory factor in the apathy and hostility surrounding education within the neighbourhoods under his scrutiny. One can therefore gain a sense that much of Holmes' critique here stemmed from a belief *a la* that of Arnold that education – which he at this stage equated somewhat narrowly with being 'cultured' – had a role to play in emancipation and enlightenment and that the current system was in that regard failing children.

Culpable in this were the *teachers* within those schools who were berated for having, 'no sense of responsibility, no motive to exercise assertion, nothing to hope for and nothing to fear' (Holmes, 1883, 356). This denunciation explains in part why Holmes felt moved to comment on the lack of *discipline* and *manners* within the schools particularly when the children were at play and outside of the arena of the classroom where they still remained relatively docile. Although he writes more extensively on this in relation to the Board Schools in the first *Report* on the West Riding and not the dame schools of Kent, it is nonetheless an implicit theme within the two *Reports* generally and is an early indication of Holmes' dissatisfaction with general classroom practice. Importantly, Holmes did not at this stage openly attribute poor discipline to defects within the inherited characters of the pupils themselves – a common enough precept of the time – but instead it appears as yoked to the limited curriculum and poor instruction they received in their daily education. Likewise, the deficiencies of the teaching profession were seen, somewhat sympathetically, as stemming from the absence of leisure – 'a luxury few can afford' (Holmes, 1883, 594) – indicating perhaps how Holmes was unconsciously following in the footsteps of those such as Robert Owen and the rational recreationists who saw the importance both of the environment and recreational activity in shaping character and virtue. As we shall see, most notably in his discussion of the example set by the Spitalfield Weavers (1923f), this was a theme that was to preoccupy Holmes more extensively later on as he despaired of the use to which many working class people put their free hours, their seeming lack of inner aspiration and a reliance on lower order pleasures.

However this was in the future; for now at this stage of his life Holmes was still prepared to be critical of what he had observed. In an eerie foreshadowing of his later leaked correspondence with Robert Morant, Holmes, although not apportioning individual blame, argued that,

> elementary teachers are, as a rule, somewhat wanting in "intelligence", [that they] are too suspicious of new ideas, too prone to move blindly and mechanically along beaten tracks, [and] too ready to rest content with methods which have received the sanction of custom rather than the stamp of success.
> (Holmes, 1879a, 594)

This is the first recorded use of the term 'mechanical' in Holmes' *oeuvre* and it is significant to note not merely given its centrality to his later works in which it came to be used as an omnibus term expressing a deeper moral malaise but also as it appears to belie his convictions that he was inactive and neutered during this time. His stated desire to vary from the methods of his colleagues by examining, where possible, both informally and orally rather than in a written form also indicates that Holmes was (at least tangentially) aware not only of the limitation of the examination as defined in educational terms but also that it was important to take account of the heterogeneity inherent within groups of children within a class. Although at the time of these *Reports*' publication Holmes was still a long way from articulating his later deep-seated child-centredness, his awareness of such prevailing difficulties nevertheless offered a watered-down version of that creed and embodied, more globally, the evolution from the then nascent Child Study and social survey movements to a more progressive form of education as manifest in the later New Education Fellowship.

Whilst the former groups couched themselves heavily in the more paternalist discourses of *reform* and were driven by a 'concern about the quality of the child population and interest in the details of natural human development' (Wooldridge, 1994, 11) particularly as emergent from their own quasi-scientific observation, the Fellowship were to draw more explicitly on the new harder science of psychology which itself offered a more nuanced and critical understanding of individual difference. By so doing they were offering implicit support to the view that testing as envisaged in schools was not only immoral and problematic but also ultimately an inaccurate indicator of an individual's level of intelligence. As the psychologist Philip Ballard was to put it, 'The discerning teacher knows that there is no such thing as a homogenous class – a group of children at the same intellectual stage, ready for the same intellectual food, capable of making the same intellectual growth' (Ballard, 1925, 184–185). Such statements were a clear refutation of that earlier ethos (underpinned by the diktats of the Board) which saw children as a lumpen entity to be taught, examined and instructed together and which had significant implications for those who were seen as deviating from expectation. In contrasting calls in these *Reports* for the measuring of 'general intelligence…by general questions on the matter of the reading lesson' (Holmes, 1879a, 59) with his subsequent beliefs over thirty years later that, 'the idea of testing [it] in any way… [is] chimerical' (Holmes, 1911, 61) one can identify Holmes as embodying the change, alluded to in the introductory chapter, from reform as linked to middle-class philanthropy and from *within* the system to later, more complex and radical understandings of welfare and social structure.

One manifestation of this transformation comes in Holmes' comments pertaining to discipline in schools which betray, at this early stage in his career, a seeming desire to promulgate the existing social order. Somewhat surprisingly, particularly in light of his later condemnation of such practices, he suggests both that 'I should…be sorry to see corporal punishment abolished (Holmes, 1879a, 596) and that 'In such a district as mine….the drill sergeant's influence is wholly for the good' (Ibid., 604). As McDonald has argued such apparently conservative statements represent Holmes perhaps responding to recent trade union disturbances and the Murphy Riots[6] of the 1860s and 1870s and in so doing conveying a 'warning to the Committee of Council against the potential restiveness of the working classes' (McDonald, 2008, 91). If this is the case – and it seems a reasonable supposition – it finds Holmes arguing not merely that discipline in the form of drill was the best way to alleviate such agitation but also thereby betrayed a residual attachment to a preservation of the *status quo* and his own governing class.

Nor is this wholly surprising; quite apart from his youthful support for the more conventionally minded Tories and notions of Empire and Free Trade given his relatively junior departmental position at the time of writing it would perhaps have been unwise at this stage for him to rock too many boats in Whitehall. This dependency was exacerbated through changes to his immediate family situation; he was married in 1880 to Florence Mary Syme[7] and was to quickly have three children – two daughters and one son. Whilst an Inspector's remuneration was, by the standards of the time, very reasonable it would certainly not have allowed Holmes to live an overtly lavish lifestyle. Once more, there is a frustrating lack of documentation surrounding his personal life. Although much of his poetry which he produced around this time appears addressed to a 'beloved' and Holmes, as we shall see later, was to have a turbulent correspondence with one of his female inspectors there is no suggestion within his autobiography that his marriage was in any way unhappy and that his verse was dealing with anything other than archetypes. Similarly his later admiration and idealization of the work and persona of Harriet Finlay-Johnson stemmed from her practical articulation of a form of education that Holmes had only to that point imagined and not through any romantic or sexual impulse. In many ways then, his personal life seemed very much to live up to the dictum he himself was to prescribe which was ascetically rooted, free of lower order sensualism and which sought to exist in that state of idealized unrequited longing which led ultimately to its true fulfilment. Nonetheless, for all of its rude health his marriage and burgeoning family life would seem to have been yet one more reason why his work became tied to a particular pattern and routine which contributed to his intellectual stultification.

However, despite appearing in this instance to wish to preserve particular existing school practices in accordance with prevailing social attitudes concerning discipline and obedience, in other areas these Inspection *Reports* clearly indicate a more general and underlying sense of dissatisfaction with the system of schooling it had been Holmes' duty to both observe and tacitly support. After that fashion, one of the implicit themes of his remarks concerns the position and place of the child in relation to the adult and the sorts of teaching methods to which they were subject. In an important and indicative utterance Holmes asserts, 'What is needed is to draw out the knowledge latent in the children, not to pump useless knowledge into them from without' (Holmes, 1879a, 597) and it is this spirit that pervades much of the texts. As we shall later see in relation to his more fully worked-out belief in innate 'instincts', the idea of latent knowledge (or more accurately a desire to acquire such knowledge) within the child was to form a significant part of his thinking as it was this which was seen as notably lacking in Western education which laboured under the empiricist assumption that children were notably incapable of original and active thought and imagination.

'Interest' was also key and Holmes was adamant that children would not benefit from the study of subjects that appeared overtly dry and academic. This was a particularly appropriate observation given how recent educational Codes, such as those in 1871 and 1875, had raised the status of Literature and Grammar in schools to be equivalent with the Humanities. For Holmes 'books that catalogue facts and books that explain and expound ought…to be kept out of the hands of children' (Holmes, 1883, 359). He was therefore keen to stress in the *Reports* that the starting point for learning should be that knowledge which it was possible to derive from the child's own immediate environment and natural interests rather than lessons concerning 'ostriches or elephants, [on] rhomboids or trapeziums, or orange-yellow or indigo blue' (Holmes, 1879a, 597). Geography was cited as a case in point in which, 'the aim of [the] teaching…[is] to interest the children in things that surround them, [rather] than to cram their minds with ill-digested and therefore useless information' (Holmes, 1883, 369).

In essence then Holmes was here offering a primitive and tentative vision of education with 'appeals to the heart' (Ibid.) as its cornerstone. This was particularly apposite in the subject of English and it seems that in Kent – given incentive perhaps by his despair at the poor standards seen earlier in the West Riding – he had managed in a small way to put into practice some of his own educational ideas. He noted that English was now the most popular subject in schools and that the percentages pass rate had risen significantly in that time from 39.9 per cent to 61.8 per cent. This was clearly Holmes' doing: 'My own faith in the educational value of poetry is so strong that I have always encouraged the teachers in my district to take English' (Holmes, 1883, 359). Given his own proclivities, his support of poetry was wholly unsurprising and he argued that it better comprised shorter rhyming verse than long epics and should ultimately, after the precepts of Matthew Arnold, 'have real beauty of expression and feeling' (Ibid.) in order to hold any true and lasting value for children. This appeal to the noblest and most sublime elements inherent within English literature was equally timely given the proliferation of the genre known as the 'penny Dreadful'[8] which was seen by those supporters of high culture as having 'debased and falsified consciences' (Wernham, 1881, 361, quoted in McDonald, 2008, 99) and once more indicates Holmes' longstanding awareness of both social context and concern. It was to be a continuing feature of much of Holmes' writing that he was never to divorce his theories of schooling and education from wider and more circumstantial events. In this case the transformative and civilizing power of literature (particularly poetry) was one Holmes was to carry with him all his life.

In explicitly referring to Matthew Arnold here Holmes was not merely betraying adherence to the former's view of culture as civilizing for the masses but also advocating for a position which based itself around the contention that the educator's task was to draw out and nourish the child's latent knowledge through encouraging its relationship to new knowledge as presented by the teacher. This inevitably meant that knowledge, rather than being seen as discrete as tended to happen when for example it became compartmentalized for the purposes of examination, should be conceived of as a unified whole; as Peter Gordon (1983) reminds us, this approach derived primarily from Holmes' earlier reading of Arnold's *Literature and Dogma* in which the master law of Nature was driven by a wholeness or self-integration. For Holmes, in perhaps the best example of the application of his ontology, when placed in the context of a school classroom such a belief meant that it became inappropriate to break subjects into smaller, discrete blocks. Instead the relationship *between* different elements of knowledge was to be encouraged and Holmes was to make this particular point in relation to reading which was then in many schools kept separate from English which tended in its study to focus exclusively upon grammar and poetry. For Holmes, this made little sense and he was keen that the two activities be integrated together; in that notion he was clearly indebted too to the earlier work and practice of Friedrich Froebel which had also hinted at a belief in unity albeit one driven by a quest for the divine law present in Nature. Although at this stage Holmes may not have been especially familiar with these ideas and was undoubtedly a long way from articulating his later notions of Wholeness he can nevertheless be seen to be working here very much within the established progressive canon of his forebears. Indeed, the breaking down of traditional subject barriers and boundaries was to be a concern of many subsequent thinkers keen to avoid the rigid compartmentalization of knowledge as commonly espoused in mainstream schools.

Nor was such integration merely to be between the various academic subjects; at the micro level of practice Holmes wanted children to first learn to read words in isolation rather than in the context of whole sentences. This was seen as essential if they were to actually *comprehend* what it was they were required to read – after all if they could not understand each individual word within a sentence then discerning the meaning of that sentence or indeed the story within which they were contained became an almost impossible task. In asserting that it was bad practice to 'accustom a child to read as nonsense what is supposed to be read as sense' (Holmes, 1883, 362) Holmes was once more taking a sideswipe against those advocates of learning by recitation and rote which served purely instrumental ends often in order to pass the oral component of the examination. Since its original inclusion in the 1862 Revised Codes, reading in particular had been seen as a necessary element of the curriculum, not perhaps as it served particularly beneficial ends but more as it embodied the aim of those like Robert Lowe who were driven by the utilitarian aim of 'value for money' as well as seeking to plug the gaps left by the struggling voluntary schools.

Learning was thus beginning to be seen by Holmes as a two-way interactive process which responded to the natural interests of the child – a novel precept in the context of late nineteenth century Britain which still relied heavily upon didactic teaching methods and which had dragged its feet in coming to terms with Continental progressive ideas. In making these points Holmes was offering as well an implicit criticism (on moral and practical grounds) of the 'payment by results' system which had led to a narrowing of the curriculum and limited time for reflection upon new material. Although this was not a critique exclusive to Holmes and others were, over the course of his years of inspection, to make similar claims it was unique here in that served to mirror a later conviction that humans, if seeking to achieve true spiritual fulfilment, had to move across time from pre-natal purity to a Oneness with God and that this was only achievable through a very particular sort of education which eschewed many of the traditional approaches he himself observed in schools – homogeneity, recitation, obedience and the like. There is evidence therefore in these early *Reports* not merely of engagement with, and dissension toward, established government policy but the emergence of a truly innovative educational philosophy which was to be more fully worked out elsewhere.

Towards the top: Holmes at the Board of Education

The difficulties in attempting to trace Holmes directly during this period have already been mentioned not least as there is – in comparison to other comparable figures – very little direct correspondence between himself and those of his wider acquaintance. Just over twenty years separate the publication of his second Inspection *Report* (1883) to his promotion to Chief Inspector in 1905 and it was during these years that he was intimately involved in the school inspection process in different districts of the country. However through what limited archival material exists it is still possible (and indeed significant) to identify his involvement in a number of different causes within the framework of the Board of Education indicating not only his increasing seniority but also the respect with which he was coming to be regarded by his colleagues. Many of Holmes' interventions came of course at a time when there were increasing upheavals within the British education system. Following the Cockerton Judgement[9] which 'sealed the fate of advanced, or secondary, teaching fostered by the more radical and enterprising School Boards' (Chitty, 2007, 19), Robert Morant – appointed later as Permanent Secretary to the Board – had helped draft the 1902 Education Act which led to the creation of Local Education Authorities as well as, in the process, offering some relief to the flagging Anglican schools. This represented the first serious consideration by the state toward any form of schooling beyond that of the basic elementary level. Alongside such structural re-ordering, contemporary concerns were also being voiced both around the composition and also the *suitability* of the curriculum within British schools particularly in light of warnings such as those given by Michael Sadler which indicated a pronounced anxiety over Britain's waning global economic prestige and competitiveness. As Neil Daglish in his magisterial study of the period has rightly pointed out,

> the reorganization of secondary education in the 1890s resulted from two factors. The first was the power of the new county and county borough councils to aid secondary and technical education and the second was the growing impact of international economic competition, especially in Germany.
> (Daglish, 1996, 12–13)

The work therefore that Holmes was doing at the Board at this time (albeit with a focus more upon elementary education) came at a point of turbulence and transition particularly given the parallel rise of the new ideas of child-centredness and the creeping state control of the sector. Having already demonstrated, through his successful promotion of English in Kentish schools, his willingness to be active and involve himself in practical school initiatives it was perhaps then unsurprising that he sought to use both his authority and experience to promote more widely such forward-thinking ideas and it was these which were to form the basis of many of his continuing initiatives. Stemming for example from his earlier address (1898a) to the teachers of the Oxford district Holmes became interested as to the most effective means by which these new pedagogies could be more widely disseminated. As therefore Peter Gordon emphasizes, 'How to fill the schools with progressive teachers able and willing to undertake experimental work was a constant source of concern' (Gordon, 1983, 19). In that vein, an unpublished *General Report* on the schools in Oxfordshire written by Holmes called attention to the problems of infant education in which:

> To put a girl who knows nothing whatsoever about teaching in a class-room with 15 or 20 infants and tell her to educate them is a proceeding scarcely less foolish than that of placing a "land-lubber" on board of a battleship and telling him to take command of her.
> (ED 24/75, General Report for Oxfordshire, 1901)

This situation was best exemplified within his own district as here only around one in five of teachers had been found to have been properly trained. Seeking redress, Holmes' solution to this neglect had been to establish, in conjunction with Oxfordshire County Council, a scheme of in-service training within local schools and run by committed teachers and practitioners keen to share experience, knowledge and good practice. Although initially this had only been of four weeks duration, Holmes clearly envisaged something far grander notably a 'complete system of Training Colleges' (Ibid.) and this principle seemed to fall on sympathetic political ears. An appended letter to the original document addressed to Sir John Gorst[10] (then Vice President of the Committee of Council on Education) indicates that Holmes had met Gorst at the House of Commons and that he had asked for a copy of the *Report*. In Holmes' mind he looked upon this scheme as the 'very thin end of a very large and important wedge' (ED, 24/75, Holmes to Sir John Gorst, 4th March 1902) thereby signifying his commitment to forms of pedagogy rooted in the new emergent understanding of the condition of childhood. This was to be similarly reflected in the contemporary interest shown by Holmes in relation to systems of education such as the Montessori Method in which the role of the teacher (or *Directoress*) was so seminal.

Further to that, another area in which Holmes was active at this time was through his contributions to the *Handbook of Suggestions for the Consideration of Teachers* first published in 1905. The recent ending of the 'payment by results' system meant, as has been indicated, that government and the arms of Whitehall were now acting less proprietarily and elementary teachers in particular were increasingly freer to devise their own methods of teaching alongside having commensurate levels of autonomy to pursue their own interests and schemes of work. In response the Board of Education, mindful perhaps of the comments made earlier by those such as Holmes who had criticized existing educational provision, therefore produced a series of pamphlets (which carried on until 1937) designed to advise and recommend on best practice in light of these wider changes. These were a clear development and move forward from the earlier *Instructions to Inspectors* which, together with its companion *Specimen Schemes of Instructions*, had promoted a more rigid and unyielding framework when it came to curricular interpretation. As John Leese has also pointed out these new publications, of which the 1905 *Handbook* was the first and most important, were also very welcome as, in the aftermath of the ending of the old system, 'local authorities and teachers were given little comprehensive lead as to how to make use of their new freedom' (Leese, 1950, 235). This *Handbook* then was to ultimately be seen as 'representing a new liberal attitude by the Board towards teachers, pupils and the curriculum' (Gordon, 1985, 41) and embodied much of the ethos pertaining to elementary and primary education which was to prevail across the first four decades of the century. It was, after all, this particular period that Roy Lowe (2007) has rightly characterized (albeit with reservation) as the 'golden age' in which teachers' freedom away from government was at its highest.

In keeping with this sentiment, the spirit of these new publications was widely praised within the pages of contemporary educational journals and by far the most powerful and fulsome of tributes stemmed from the influential *The School Manager* whose editorial waxed poetically that despite a widespread perception that the Board of Education consisted of 'shrivelled, wind-dried mummies, who had been sitting there from time immemorial' (*The School Manager*, August 1905) the *Handbook* served to indicate instead that 'the members of this ghostly council have at last mouldered into dust and their places are now occupied by human beings' (Ibid.). It is significant therefore that Holmes was to be a central figure at a time when the Board was being both reorganized administratively via the creation of Local Educational Authorities but also changing its character with more recognition being given by policy-makers, at the elementary level at least, to the position of the teacher *vis-à-vis* the child. In relation to this particular pamphlet which was to be presented before the House of Commons, we know from a letter to Robert Morant that Holmes himself was one of the few inspectors allowed to make suggestions to it before publication and also that he 'criticized the book in its fairly complete form' (ED 24/233, W.R. Davies to Robert Morant, 9th October 1905).

In that spirit, there is then evidence of his fingerprints all over the *Handbook* both in its direct recommendations as well as its more general liberalizing tone. In particular its prefatory suggestion that the only thing that should be seen as uniform was 'that each teacher shall think for himself, and work out for himself such methods of teaching as may use his powers to the best advantage' (*Suggestions for the Consideration of Teachers*, 1905, 6) echo that of Holmes who had earlier criticized the prescriptive nature of the teaching being advocated by the Board of Education. Indeed, when read in its entirety, it is a quite remarkable document, progressive both in its tenor and nature and carried much within its 150 pages that accorded wittingly and unwittingly with the ideas and beliefs of Holmes and the burgeoning progressive faction. Of particular note is its contention that, 'The child's education should be useful to himself, and in so far as it makes him a better citizen, to the community' (Ibid., 5). How far this recommendation was ever put fully into practice within mainstream schools is hard to say however it is clear that it was given wholehearted support by the central authority of the Board who desired to devolve power back to the practitioners and their localities; a confidential memo to the Inspectorate regarding possible changes to the *Handbook's* contents finds them later stating that, 'We shall, of course, have to guard ourselves carefully against any accusation of attempting to fetter unduly the discretion of Authorities or teachers' (ED 22/9, *Proposed Revision of the "Suggestions"*, 14th May 1909). Given Holmes' later writings on the need for an individualized education that was, paradoxically, rooted in a particular sense of community (which he was to christen the *cosmic commonwealth*) it is a significant synergy and provides evidence both of his centrality to educational developments of the time but also as these ideas became incorporated into his own thinking.

Nor were Holmes' activities of this period confined solely to the printed word; he also worked with another H.M.I., A.P. Graves – mentioned in the previous chapter from his youth in Ireland – in the latter's scheme for providing playing-fields to those schools within the inner city slums. To that point school playgrounds were not generally seen as having any educational value and were more akin to schoolyards and places to simply dissipate excess energy as well as being in their rudimentary design extensions of the classroom in which children were, typically, confined and monitored for brief periods throughout the day. Graves' plan, betraying the essentially humane aspect to his character, was therefore designed to provide for 'properly organized games for older children under competent supervision and instruction' (Leese, 1950, 180). Holmes' involvement in this, and perhaps the reason why beyond their initial acquaintance Graves contacted him in the first place, is perhaps unsurprising especially given the high value he placed on the role and importance of Nature which had been such a feature of his early poetry in which, after Wordsworth, the *spiritual* value of landscape had been well adumbrated. This belief was echoed too in Holmes' concomitant religious writings which were occupying him during this period. In *A Confession of Faith* (1895) for example Holmes made his particular brand of pantheism very clear from the outset: 'I believe that Nature is all in all, and that there is nothing above it and beyond it' (Holmes, 1895, 3). Similarly in the *Creed of Christ* (1905b) which dates more directly from this time Holmes had made clear his belief in the 'wholeness' of God found in all things rather than in any form of duality between the internal human spirit and the external world of Nature.

In therefore drafting with Graves what was to become Article 44 of the Elementary School Code of 1906 which allowed local authorities the opportunity to expand their existing play areas, Holmes was indirectly voicing his recognition of the importance of the outside world for children's education drawing as it did on the spirit of Romanticism and the general good moral value which Nature could impart. Although such exigencies under the new Code led, as Colm Kerrigan (2004) has shown, to the expansion of games such as football which would not perhaps have met with Holmes' approval, the London County Council (LCC) for one was keen to stress that such games were not to be there merely as a reward for good behaviour but as being beneficial in their own right. This use of external space was indeed to be one of the key features of Harriet Finlay-Johnson's school in Sompting which Holmes first visited around this time (1907) and of which he was to later speak so fondly: 'I have never been in a school in which the love of what is beautiful in Nature is so strong or so sincere as in this' (Holmes, 1911, 160).

Ideological and philosophical justifications aside – and clearly the staple activities of Sompting such as sketching and outdoor folk song were a world away from any form of education taking place in urban environments – this was nevertheless a timely intervention for it echoed the important work being done by others including the pioneering McMillan sisters Rachel and Margaret.[11] The energies of these extraordinary siblings had been focussed initially in the northern town of Bradford however, by 1906, their attentions had switched to Deptford where their efforts were now concentrated in a crusade to improve the physical lives and condition of those in the inner cities. This was being achieved both through legislation designed to pressure local authorities to provide basic sanitation and medical care (they were well acquainted with a number of key political players) but also, latterly, by night camps designed to take children away from the noxious side-effects of industrialization and into the countryside. These developments therefore tied into nascent discussions around the 'state of the nation' question and demonstrated the increasing importance of *health* and *fitness* in supporting the vitality of the country. These were debates tied inexorably to the future prosperity of the nation and its Empire; in her seminal *Education through the Imagination* (whose very title must surely have appealed to Holmes!) Margaret McMillan made clear that any stifling of the child's imagination was to have effects beyond the classroom:

> The learning of facts and of formal arts, the training of the verbal memory, the discipline of the class-room and school may be good things in their way. But when the youth of the country have left the school-room, when they are out in the open of industrial life, competing with educated workmen of other lands, mechanical training and formal attainments will not carry them far.
> (McMillan, 1904, xi)

McMillan then was conscious of the more global implications and anxieties such debates would tap into and the same was ultimately to be true of Holmes. In a revealing passage from a later work, he cites a pupil from the Utopia/Sompting School whose first job on leaving was to collect flints and put them in piles. Although a seemingly mundane task Holmes reports the boy as carrying it out with 'cheery goodwill, [as] he sang his Folk Songs with all the spontaneous happiness of a soaring lark' (Holmes, 1911, 193). Unlike others, for example the Marxists, whose consciences were more politically attuned and who may have desired root and branch economic change, Holmes' democracy was always that of the *spirit* and his work and reform, even when at the Board, must be seen in that light. Although the McMillans and their ilk were politically aligned to the left they were nonetheless, as Carolyn Steedman (1990) makes clear, important in shaping the ideology of the New Education Fellowship particularly in the way in which they drew close connections between the child's capacity for creativity and the need for social reform. These moves indicated not just the broad church of that movement but also the way in which their ideas over health and welfare coalesced with those of Holmes.

It is then clear that much of Holmes' energy was spent, when possible, in promulgating ideas and causes which sought both to enact his developing progressive philosophy but also which ramified with and actively shaped many of the contemporary changes and developments in outlook regarding education. Whilst much of his work therefore found a broad level of support, this period was not completely free of controversy and one incident in particular sheds some light on Holmes the *man* and relates to his time in Oxfordshire (1897–1903) and his relationship to one Katherine ('Kitty') Bathurst. Bathurst was a woman sub-inspector – only the third ever created – and had, by 1901, transferred to work in Holmes' district. Clearly, his reputation as a fair minded and forward-thinking administrator preceded him with one colleague enviously writing to her that, 'There is no place in all the world in which I would rather work. You will I believe have an excellent chief' (KB/11/10, Letter from W. Home, 10th January 1902). Nonetheless, from the extant letters between Holmes and Bathurst which are preserved within the London Institute and which cover a period of eleven months, it is clear that things did not proceed as smoothly as this recommendation may have foreseen. Despite the initial establishment of good relations with Bathurst via her offer to introduce him to her cousin by marriage Sir John Gorst and Holmes noting that one of her letters remained 'one of [my] most prized possessions' (KB/13/3, Letter from Holmes, 15th November 1902) the remaining exchanges indicate that future dealings between the two were less than straightforward. Symbolizing Bathurst's destructive presence Holmes was to write,

> Since you came here my life has been a lasting storm… In its early stages, before it develops into a gale, a sou'wester is one of the most delightful and refreshing of winds, and as such may fitly symbolize my intercourse with you in the first four or five months of the year.
>
> (Ibid.)

Quite what form this prior intercourse took we do not know however seven months later Holmes, in response to Bathurst's accusations of 'lying and treachery' against him (KB/13/18, Letter from Holmes, 19th June 1903), was being forced to cede, 'I will have no further dealings with you, except such as are strictly official and absolutely unavoidable. So far as I am concerned, you have ceased to exist, except as an official under the Board of Education' (Ibid.).

Perhaps this antipathy was to be expected given Bathurst's own formidable reputation; as Peter Gordon (1988) has shown, Gorst himself had voiced prior concerns over her hot-headedness, fearing she was causing damage to the future chances of female inspectors and her career was in fact to later peter out without his influential support in the Commons. Much of the disagreement with Holmes however stemmed more immediately from Bathurst's school inspection reports which were both inaccurate and inappropriate in tone and scope and which therefore needed alteration from her superior so as to make them suitable for presentation to the Board. Whilst some of these details appear somewhat trite (in one letter KB/13/6 Holmes draws her attention to a complaint made by the Vicar of Brackley to Whitehall over Bathurst's suggestion that students with eye complaints should visit a specialist eye hospital) it nonetheless indicates the punctiliousness of a man with high expectations and standards of administrative competence but also with an added awareness that he may be destined soon for better things. Despite his aforementioned attempts to keep their relationship strictly professional, Bathurst nevertheless was indeed to report Holmes' alterations ('interferences') not merely to Gorst but also to Robert Morant and, later, the President of the Board himself – the Marquess of Londonderry. Interestingly, despite their disagreements, Holmes was generous both in not attempting to dissuade Bathurst from reporting the full facts of her complaint to his own superiors but also in latterly recommending her for her own district. Given that this would have set a precedent for other female inspectors this indicates forward-thinking views concerning equality on Holmes' part, opinions which, as he reported in a letter to Bathurst, were not shared at the time by Morant although his reasons were apparently 'purely impersonal' (KB/13/16, Letter from Holmes, 10th January 1903).

Whether it was this minor furore which caused Holmes to be moved away in 1903 to the more remote location of Northumberland (albeit with a promotion to Divisional Inspector) we do not know, however, it had clearly not been forgotten by the time of the resignation two years later of the Chief Inspector of Elementary Schools Cyril Jackson who had been disconcerted by the sweeping changes made by Morant in relation to administrative reorganization. In contemplating therefore the choice for his successor between the equally experienced E.M. Kenney-Herbert and Holmes, Morant mused at length to Sir William Anson:[12]

> I recognize on the one hand that Kenney-Herbert would be a 'safe' appointment and that there would probably be no difficulties arising under his regime in the handling of men; and that in the case of Holmes there would be a certain amount of uncertainty as to how successful he would be in this matter of the handling of men. At the same time, I think it is hardly fair or accurate to assume that his sad mishandling of Kitty shows that he would be specially fallible in handling men, since the difference of sex makes an enormous distinction. Moreover, he must have learnt a very bitter lesson from that episode...
> (ED 24/590, Robert Morant to William Anson, 24th November 1905)

Although betraying perhaps prevailing social attitudes concerning the disposition of women (there is no explanation given as to why they would need to be handled differently), it is curious to note that Holmes was more widely perceived as 'mishandling' Bathurst presumably on account of him failing to restrict her complaints to the local level, unable as he was to keep her from approaching his superiors in Whitehall. Still for all of the residual antipathy surrounding the incident, it is clear that Morant still held Holmes in high regard not merely in his ability to manage and administer competently within a range of settings (he had called on testimony from others working under him) but also through his knowledge of 'new educational developments' (Ibid.), a quality which set him apart from the more plodding Kenney-Herbert. Whether Holmes' other wider literary ventures contributed to this assessment we do not know but it seems highly unlikely that Morant would not have known of his earlier publications and prevailing intellectual preoccupations particularly given the friendship and common ideological ground they seemed to share which went beyond that of mere work colleagues. Taking all these factors into consideration it was therefore Holmes who was chosen to succeed Jackson as Chief Inspector in late 1905.

The end of the ideal – Holmes as Chief Inspector and the Holmes-Morant Circular

One of the immediate benefits to be gained from Holmes' new appointment was that he was no longer confined to particular areas of the country and so it was on 26th November 1907, through his now more roving brief, that he first visited the school which was to act not only as the living embodiment of his own developing educational philosophy but which was to also radically alter his views on human-kind. Sompting School in Sussex, catering for 120 pupils and run since 1897 by Harriet Finlay-Johnson and her sister, neither of whom incidentally had received formal training, was based on the principle of encouraging pupil self-expression and practical activity at the expense of more rigid and staid methods of learning. Whilst in its early years the school was 'still fairly firmly within the framework of conventional teaching' (Hyndman, 1980, 353) Finlay-Johnson quickly came to manifest and enshrine her child-centredness in as wide a range of activities imaginable including the encouragement of formal debating, singing, drawing, dancing and gardening all the while never losing sight of the more foundational subjects such as History and Literature which were often taught by recourse to *drama*.

As we shall see shortly these ideas around free activity were to percolate Holmes' later educational writings and act as a cornerstone of his mature philosophy as he sought to use Finlay-Johnson's ideas as the basis for a much broader theory of schooling. Not for nothing did Holmes later refer to this visit as a 'revelation' and state that, 'As a thinker and writer about education I owe my soul to her' (Holmes, 1922, 179). For now however, he was still in the process of developing that more radical viewpoint, in part through attempting the not inconsiderable task of reconciling his extensive knowledge of education with his prior religious critiques of Christianity and intellectual indebtedness to philosophical idealism. As has been suggested earlier these were ideas too that were receiving a wider appreciation; school log books indicate that on his initial visit to Sompting Holmes was accompanied by the local H.M.I. Edward Burrows who had himself first visited in 1904 with his companion's predecessor as Chief Inspector – Cyril Jackson. Both men were later to receive fulsome praise from Finlay-Johnson for their continued support in relation to her radical practices.

Although Holmes' previous published work had therefore sought to establish for himself a philosophical way of understanding the world (with of course religious implications), the first major written evidence we have of any connection between *education* and these wider currents came in 1908 though publication of a remarkable pamphlet entitled *A Village School*. Although this was a short piece (39 pages) it was still very important as it was designed as a means of supporting his newly formulated contentions that 'The function of education is to foster growth' (Holmes, 1908a, 3) and that 'The process of growing must be done by the growing organism, by the child, let us say, and no one else' (Ibid., 4). Although seemingly self-evident truisms, this was a new direction for Holmes and, when taken in context, they stood very much in contrast to his earlier experiences which had seen education reduced to mere instrumentalism and the imposition of knowledge by various forms of external authority – teachers, inspectors and the like. Crucially, Sompting was seen as the antithesis to this way of thinking and was referred to effusively: 'There is no fraud about it, no hypocrisy, no cant. Miss Johnson's one idea is to help the children educate themselves. She gives them the three things which every teacher ought to give his pupils, – material, stimulus, guidance' (Ibid., 18).

Interestingly, like the rest of his previous writings (except his more non-partisan poetry), his name was not attached to the title-page indicating maybe a desire to preserve his anonymity to the wider world. After all would it have done, for example, to have a Chief Inspector of Elementary Schools (the supposed pillar and mouthpiece of Government ideology) talking in bitter terms of, 'a vicious circle from which there seems to be no way of escape….Machine-made teachers are producing machine-made children, and machine-made children are developing into machine-made teachers' (Ibid., 36)? Whilst such pragmatism in this context was clearly warranted it did not however stop Holmes from airing his views privately amongst his colleagues as indicated in a remarkably long and candid note sent to the then President of the Board of Education Walter Runciman:[13]

> As things are, the child is bored to yawning-point by the teacher's insane distrust of him, and is secretly longing to be allowed to make use of his own natural faculties. The path of self-education is such a pleasant one that the child who is allowed to enter it will find in it that stimulus to work which is at present withheld from him, and the absence of which is seriously detrimental to his character as well as his mind!
> (Runciman Papers, WR 28, Holmes to Runciman, 3rd February 1909)

This note is worth quoting at some length for it indicates two key emerging elements of Holmes' system of explicitly educational beliefs; on the one hand, there is the notion of the importance of the child being *self-directed* in his own learning and the particular virtues this may serve to promote. Second, Holmes touches here upon one of the reasons why this idea continued to remain absent from mainstream schools, notably the innate distrust the teacher often had of their children. As we shall see in the next chapter, whilst this concern was to become enmeshed with Holmes' already established religious views pertaining to Original Sin, for the time being it was to more immediately inform his work as Chief Inspector in which he sought to continue to liberate formal education from its previous shackles and allow for an elementary curriculum that was both varied and driven as far as possible by the expertise and creativity of both the pupils and better educated *teachers*. Existing and often confidential files of minutes sent by Holmes to his Inspectorate signpost this as they show his desire to involve himself in a range of different causes and agendas but also as he strove to establish a regime founded on the progressive principles to which he held dear. One memo for example finds him supporting the introduction of dancing (both traditional and classical types) into the curriculum as a way both of 'greatly improving the carriage of the children, of making them less clumsy and more supple…alertness, precision, and self-control required by combined movements are valuable qualities' (ED 22/9, *The Teaching of Dancing Steps and Exercises to Scholars in Public Elementary Schools*, 24th July 1909). Its tacit recognition of the importance of creative and performing arts aside, the links with this and his earlier concerns over the 'state of the nation' question in which children's physical health was central should be all too apparent.

Likewise, there is evidence that Holmes was also keen to ensure that the previous ideology of 'payment by results' remained forever dead and buried. In setting out his criteria for the system of inspection of individual schools for example Holmes forcibly wrote to his Inspectors that they must, 'be careful to ask no question and set no exercise which will tend to encourage "cramming" at the expense of intelligent teaching' (ED 22/9, *Methods of Inspecting and Reporting on Public Elementary Schools*, May 1910). What a contrast this too provides with his own negative experiences and in addition requesting that 'It will be left to the discretion of each Inspector to decide what does and what does not constitute a formal visit of inspection' (ED 22/9, *"Formal" Visits of Inspection*, 15th December 1909) as well as allowing Inspectors to both write and re-draft their Reports, Holmes was clearly here attempting to minimize and streamline the level of Whitehall bureaucracy inherent within the system. Although keen to establish more formal arrangements for things like the training of teachers, it was nonetheless evident that elsewhere Holmes was seeking actively to promote and develop the liberation of practitioners away from what modern scholars have referred to as cultures of managerialism and performativity. Even where Inspections were to take place Holmes set himself against any form of summative judgment preferring instead dialogue and cooperation so as to foster a culture of improvement.

Sadly though, and for all of his diligence, Utopia was all too brief as Holmes was to retire (aged 60) after fulfilling a term of five years as Chief Inspector, a period which, despite the often bureaucratic, procedural and internecine nature of Whitehall politics, he was to describe as, 'the happiest period of a very happy official life' (Marvin Papers d. 261, Holmes to W.S. Marvin 25th January 1911). Such feeling and pride in his work seemed justifiable and was echoed in a private exchange with Runciman in which Holmes cited the 'very favorable reports on the work done' by his (Runciman's) administration (Runciman Papers, WR 35, Holmes to Runciman 1st December 1910). It was after all in this period – aside from individual initiatives and schemes – that Holmes was allowed to stamp most productively his own philosophy upon elementary education and which was now being enshrined both within official rhetoric and, increasingly, the practices of teachers. Many of these changes were to be immortalized not just within his own later reflections which show this to have been a time of ideological transformation but also as they became more widely imitated within the beliefs and actions of his official successors. In showing for example how the 1927 *Handbook* was more progressive than the 1905 version R.J.W. Selleck (1972) provides solid evidence that 'Holmes was by no means an isolated voice in the Inspectorate at that time' (Lawton and Gordon, 1987, 20) and that others were equally inspired by his example in seeking to use the freedom afforded to them to challenge the system. Furthermore, as Roy Lowe points out, this period can be conceptualized as one in which 'the chorus of voices calling for reform of classroom practice grew, with several leading figures in teacher education being identified as 'progressives' and polemicizing for change' (Lowe, 2007, 13).

However, even with his public life seemingly at an end, and as he sojourned leisurely in Rome both to holiday and report for his former employers on its Montessori schools, events were unfolding which were to forever tarnish his name, sour his reputation as a progressive and forward-thinking administrator and go some way toward undoing many years of diligent service to the Board. Although not exactly beset with stiff competition there is little doubt that the hullabaloo surrounding what became known as the 'Holmes-Morant Circular' is amongst the greatest to ever embroil the Board (now Department) of Education not least as it showed how easily its internal proceedings and machinery could become used as a vehicle for party-politicking and points-scoring. The story of the events surrounding the leaking of E. Memorandum No. 1 (to give it its full title) has been well told already notably in the accounts of M.J. Wilkinson (1980) and Peter Gordon (1978) the latter of which helpfully printed for the first time the only extant full copy of the Memorandum which resides in the papers belonging to Walter Runciman at the University of Newcastle and which is reproduced here as an Appendix. Given these previous efforts, it is not therefore the purpose of this narrative to detail the background and intricate political machinations surrounding the controversy and the reader is urged to consult these earlier articles particularly as they provide a more thorough overview of the broader political context from which much of the antagonism originated. Nevertheless, given its centrality to Holmes' life and career it is still important to consider in brief the detail if only to highlight the way in which Holmes was widely misrepresented and misinterpreted and not perhaps worthy of the critical mauling he was to take from various of his contemporaries.

In essence, the trouble stemmed from the leaking and subsequent reading out in the Commons by Samuel Hoare M.P. for Chelsea of sections of a private memorandum authored by Holmes a year earlier in January 1910 and sent to his Inspectors which appeared to be heavily critical of the local authority inspectorate. Whilst these reproaches, as we shall see, were not without foundation it was one particular section (five) of the Memorandum which was to ultimately stoke the ire of the teaching profession and be the catalyst for recrimination. The first sentence set the tone:

> Apart from the fact that elementary teachers are, as a rule, uncultured and imperfectly educated, and that many – if not most – of them are creatures of tradition and routine, there are special reasons why the bulk of the Local Inspectors in this country should be unequal to the discharge of their responsible duties.
>
> (Holmes, 6th January 1910 quoted in Gordon, 1978, 38)

Taken in isolation, and in conjunction with the last section in which he implied that it was solely men 'of the Public School and University type' (Ibid., 39) who made the best and most suitable Inspectors, such a statement undoubtedly seemed to reflect a particular class prejudice on Holmes' part and it is easy to see why subsequent howls of protest amongst both the teaching unions and the Conservative Party centred upon this precise aspect and charge of elitism. Nor in fact can we wholly excuse Holmes on this point; we have already mentioned *en passant* his condemnation of particular working class leisure activities and he was to frequently take issue with those who failed to meet his own high intellectual standards in particular the 'average man' who had he believed a tendency to favour lower order pleasures and, as he had made clear in *Sursum Corda*, to find sanctuary in simple unproblematic materialism or, in this case, examination results and tests.

However, a couple of points of mitigation do here need to be considered. First, the antipathy of Holmes towards the local inspectorate arose less from its members' social backgrounds and more because of their tendency to seemingly obfuscate and negate the advances being made more widely by those at the Board who desired never to return to the older system of payment by results. As Holmes had previously made clear to Runciman, there was a clearly an issue for those more forward-thinking Board Inspectors who were doing their best, often 'in the teeth of opposition from local authorities and local inspectors, to bring about a better state of things' (WR 35, Holmes to Runciman, 3rd February 1909). It was Holmes' belief that 'many of the older local inspectors had been appointed solely on their ability to produce a high percentage in examination results' (Wilkinson, 1980, 30) and not because of their understanding of the complex discipline of education or awareness of new approaches to educational thinking. Given that as recently as 1901 a report issued by seven London School Board inspectors had accused the Board of Education and its policies of contributing to a rise in school inefficiency one can easily see why Holmes took umbrage at those who sought to block and disparage the work of the HMIs. Nor was this a view confined to those bureaucrats and mandarins within Whitehall; as Holmes was to later make clear following a talk to the Cambridge University Fabian Society, these were concerns too of the General Secretary of the N.U.T. Sir James Yoxall who had called on Holmes 'with a complaint about the local Inspectors in certain districts who, he said…were departing from the practice of the Board of Education' (Holmes reported in *The Schoolmaster*, 2nd March 1912). If this was the view of the head of the organization tasked with representing those Inspectors, is it any wonder that Holmes would have sought a similar redress?

Second, the Memorandum itself was, to some degree, merely an attempt by Holmes to amalgamate and summarize the views of those Inspectors who had been requested to respond on matters such as salaries, efficiency, type of education and the like of their local counterparts. Following his earlier informal talk with Yoxall and a subsequent meeting with Morant, this information had initially been sought by Holmes in 1908 and was, upon receipt, then summarized and sent, along with a further Memorandum (the Circular itself) to the Inspectors.

Whilst it so happened that many of them shared his views on the parochialism and rigidity of the local Inspectors one must not assume again that Holmes was here making any form of personal attack but more expressing the concerns of those whose opinions he had been seeking to find out. In that sense the leaking of the contents of the Memorandum went very much against the intended spirit of the enquiry:

> It is obvious that the aim which the Chief Inspector had at heart was to rescue children of the elementary schools from the tyranny of the antiquated methods which had long been discarded by the Board…It is also obvious that, had his remarks been intended for the eyes of any but his own colleagues, Mr. Holmes would not have allowed the disparaging words that he used about elementary teachers to remain in the text of his Memorandum.
> (Allen, 1934, 256)

It is therefore understandable why, after that fashion, Holmes was shocked by the leaking; in a letter to W.S. Marvin he was to write that, 'As a matter of fact the Board issued the Circular (which was really not a circular, but a minute from me to Selby-Bigge) on *their* instruction without consulting me!' (Marvin Papers, d. 261, Holmes to W.S. Marvin, 26th March 1911). Retirement of course meant that there were to be no career ramifications for Holmes as there were for Morant and Runciman (both of whom were moved elsewhere with varying degrees of pleasure and relief) and so he could perhaps afford to take 'the whole affair very calmly' (Ibid.). Morant in particular seemed to attract a personal vendetta and it is indeed very much to Holmes' credit that in a series of letters to the national press – including *The Telegraph* and *The Morning Post* – he tried to absolve him of all responsibility. Despite his best efforts and loudest protestations, these missives were though summarily ignored and Morant remained for many the 'Monarch of Memoranda', the 'too-Permanent Secretary' and was widely branded as a scheming Machiavelli and 'the most disliked [Secretary] that ever was' (ED 24/101, *The Schoolmaster*, 25th April 1911). At a time when the House of Lords crisis[14] was threatening to overturn the established constitution, protocol over preserving the anonymity of civil servants in Parliament and the Press was equally subject to disruption – 'in the fierce tumult of emotions which was now being let loose [as] established practices were thrown to the winds' (Allen, 1934, 261). Such political tension (which also included agitation over Ireland and votes for women) perhaps serves to explain why no one paid much attention to Holmes' declarations of innocence; in any case he too as the Circular's author was very much yoked to its contents and not likely either to be quickly forgiven.

Despite much contemporary material being destroyed, there are still files within the National Archives, and particularly the Runciman Papers, housing detailed press and teachers' union reaction to the events. Far from the controversy blowing over swiftly, the whole affair dragged on and much of this was down to the opportunism of the N.U.T. who used it as a reason to air many of its current as well as longstanding grievances which often had little to do with the issue at hand. Conciliation was far from anyone's mind and, in refusing to accept Runciman's assuaging offer to Sir James Yoxall to view the Circular in private, much of its speechifying was used as a vehicle to attack what it viewed as the wider failings of the Board in recent years. Extracts from a speech given by Yoxall – reported in the *Manchester Guardian* – indicate this as he spoke angrily of the Board's 'reaction and caste felling' (WR 46, *The Manchester Guardian*, 1st April 1911) in relation to particular policies notably higher elementary schools, the abolition of teacher-pupil centres and recruitment to the inspectorate. These were seen as 'inimical to a popular and democratic spirit in education' (Ibid.) and, once more, the austere Morant was cast as the chief villain. Given that it was Yoxall who first raised concerns to Holmes over the actions of the local inspectorate it is easy to see how political capital was rapidly being made out of this whole affair.

In a similar vein, speaking in Dudley on the theme of 'The Child and the Ladder' Yoxall (who seemed to be quite enjoying his moment in the sun) was to attack what he saw as the prevailing elitism within educational circles which precluded bright working class children becoming inspectors if they had not attended the right schools. Characterized as 'a symptom of disease in the body' (ED 24/101, *The Herald*, 7th October 1911) such snobbishness served as an 'artificial barrier' (Ibid.) to the prospects of many. Interestingly, this classification ramified with that from other works of the period; F.H. Hayward for example referred to 'The Holmes Prejudice' (Hayward, 1912, 326) which was his term for that body of opinion which sought to preserve the hegemony of those from within the 'right' schools and, as well, Oxbridge. Although Holmes himself later commented (and probably believed) that, for an Inspector, personal background was secondary to objective detachment and wider experience, given the relatively narrow social strata represented by many of his colleagues – Morant, Runciman and Sadler for example were all educated at public schools and Oxbridge – there was more than a little truth to these claims.

Such accusations of elitism then were to be the catalyst for much of the subsequent anger; by August of that year, 140 resolutions from local educational associations had been received, many of which demanded an exploration of the wider political ramifications and implications. There were also a number of flyers issued by the N.U.T. (copies of which are in the Runciman archive) calling for the petitioning of MPs and which used attention-grabbing headlines such as 'Schools and Serfs' and 'A Plot against Elementary Schoolchildren' and which characterized The Holmes-Morant Circular as the reason 'why your child can never rise high in the Civil Service' (WR 46, *The Protest Series No. 4*, The Secret Circular). Furthermore, another important and influential journal *The Schoolmaster* ran a number of features over the course of the year which singled out for attack both the incompetence and opacity of the Board which was widely seen as protecting its own and intentionally fostering class divisions. By this point Runciman's position had become untenable and he was moved by Prime Minister Asquith to the Board of Agriculture whilst Morant was also shifted sideways to begin drafting the Insurance Act and setting up the Department of Health, tasks well suited to his high level of administrative talent and eye for detail. This was perhaps the result that the militant N.U.T. had been angling for all along although, as M.J. Wikinson (1980) has shrewdly observed, this victory had something of the Pyrrhic about it for, with the benefit of hindsight, it is Morant (and by association Holmes) whose work at the Board can be re-assessed more positively: 'They [the N.U.T.] could not know of his unrelenting battle for resources to power educational advanced [sic] in staffing, building and curriculum and for political recognition of the important role of education in national affairs' (Wilkinson, 1980, 36).

Of course these events had no *direct* bearing on Holmes who no longer held official office; nonetheless they serve importantly to contextualize the climate of the time which was confrontational and set against denigrating those in educational authority. Such indeed was the level of anger and its forceful articulation that it risked forgetting all of the good work that he (and for that matter Morant) had done in his long and distinguished career of service. Whilst Holmes' choice of language in that one Memorandum was unfortunate it nevertheless was not intended for a wide audience nor was it designed to be any form of personal slight reflecting as it did instead Holmes' impatience with those less committed to educational reform as he. Although one could ascribe subsequent blame to Runciman who appeared as weak and vacillating in his reaction to events, Holmes was clearly not as portrayed and his outrage and surprise as expressed to friends afterwards seems genuine. The subsequent historical neglect pertaining to him can be put down to a whole host of factors – the diverse range of his publications, his reticence in self-promotion – however it is particularly telling that even his more radical ideas which he came to express so eloquently later on were tied invariably to his role in this one event. 'There must have been an incompatibility between the doer and the thinker' (ED 24/101, *The Schoolmaster*, 17th June 1911) wrote one anonymous contributor and it is this characterization that has sadly prevailed even amongst those who may otherwise have appeared as supportive, notably, those in the teaching profession.

Notes

1 See ED 22/4, Robert Morant, *Memorandum on the Inspection of Training Colleges*, 1904.
2 Robert Lowe (1811–1892) was Chancellor of the Exchequer and Home Secretary in the first Gladstone Ministry of 1868–1874. He had previously however in 1859 been appointed as Vice-President of the Committee of the Council on Education and was noted there for bringing in both the system of payment by results but also the Revised Codes of 1862.
3 In 1846 a national pupil–teacher scheme was launched for carefully selected elementary school pupils, aged 13 or more, who fulfilled particular intellectual and physical conditions. Whilst their numbers went into gradual decline, in the decade following the 1870 Education Act those numbers increased from 14,612 to 32,128. Over that period the number of Certificated teachers also rose from 12,467 to 31,422.

4. Francis Herbert (F.H.) Bradley (1846–1924) was a British Idealist philosopher. In a famous essay 'My Station and its Duties' – originally published in *Ethical Studies* (1876) – Bradley seemed to postulate a social conception of the self which grounded life fulfilment in terms of fulfilling one's duties. These were to be fulfilled regardless of wherever one happened to be on the social spectrum hence the need to find one's station.
5. The Committee of Council on Education, a committee of the Privy Council, and the central government agency concerned with the State's interest in public elementary education, was established in 1856 and was a direct ancestor of the Board of Education which superseded it in 1899.
6. The Murphy Riots was the collective name given to a series of disturbances that took place in the North-West of England during the late 1860s. Many of these were anti-Irish and inspired by the inflammatory rhetoric of William Murphy who gave anti-Catholic lectures. The most infamous took place at Ashton-under-Lyme in 1868.
7. Florence Mary Syme was the daughter of Captain P.M. Syme R.A. He is mentioned in *The East India Company's Arsenals and Manufactories* as being in charge of the Dum Dum Factory (near Calcutta) and holding the position of Deputy Commissary of Ordinance.
8. Penny Dreadful was a catch-all term used for a range of cheap, sensational, scandalous and highly illustrated booklets popular with the Victorian public.
9. The Cockerton Judgement was delivered on 20th December 1900 and was to have a detrimental effect on the development of technical and scientific education and training. Whilst the details of the case are complex, the judgement effectively decided that any expenditure outside the limits of the Code or instruction of adults was illegal.
10. Sir John Eldon Gorst (1835–1916) was a Tory politician who became Vice President of the Committee of Council on Education during the third Salisbury Ministry in 1895. He remained in this post until 1902.
11. The McMillan sisters, Rachel (1859–1917) and Margaret (1860–1931) were born in New York to Scottish parents. Upon returning to England they worked in deprived areas of the country – notably Bradford and Deptford – setting up school clinics and night camps. In addition they both campaigned stringently for reforms to improve the health of children.
12. Sir William Anson (1843–1914) was a Liberal Unionist politician who became a member of the consultative committee of the Board of Education in 1900. In 1902 he became the first Parliamentary Secretary to the Board of Education.
13. Sir Walter Runciman (1870–1949) was a Liberal politician who was President of the Board of Education from April 1908 to October 1911.
14. The House of Lords crisis resulted from the so-called People's Budget of 1909 which was – against precedent – vetoed by the House of Lords thereby leading to a subsequent undecided election and a potential standoff between the House of Lords and the House of Commons. Following the threat of intervention from George V, the Budget passed in 1910.

Chapter 3

Edmond Holmes as poet and religious writer

Holmes the poet

Although his long career as a School Inspector was to ultimately provide the inspiration, and pave the way, for a future corpus of seminal educational scholarship which will be more directly discussed in the next chapter, it is significant to note that until his retirement from the Board of Education in 1910, Holmes' only published interventions in relation to education had been relatively minor and non-controversial (assisted by their anonymity). We have already seen for example in his *Inspection Reports* his reluctance to fully condemn disciplinary approaches in schools – particularly in light of surrounding social upheavals which he implicitly addressed – whilst the tenor of these publications, although hinting at a range of existent problems, never sounded above a mild rebuke. We have likewise observed how, in his early collections of poetry and *Sursum Corda*, Holmes had marked himself out as one who wore his influences – T.H. Green, Matthew Arnold and the Romantics in particular – very much on his sleeve through his commitment to the not mutually exclusive traditions of both pantheism and Idealism and the themes of love, faith and nature worship which occupied his verse.

Throughout his time (36 years) as an Inspector it was indeed such *poetry* that made up the bulk of Holmes' writing and it is implicitly clear from his own published statements that it was this genre which he regarded as perhaps his most important and long-lasting literary contribution. This belief was motivated by Holmes' strong conviction in the 'inspired' nature of its construction and its subsequent expression allowed, according to its author, for privileged insight into the nature of spirituality and of demonstrating access to a 'stronger and subtler sensibility' (Holmes, 1900, 10). This attempt to both explicate and establish the power of poetry as a genre owed much to the earlier pronouncements of Shelley whose seminal essay *A Defence of Poetry* (1821) had marked out the role of the poet as being one to both channel and communicate feelings of sublimity and images of beauty as well as being a rooted foundation stone of many of the other creative art forms. For Holmes, as for his illustrious forebear, the poet had a particular gift which permitted him privileged insight into humanity: 'The poet's imagination does more than give him insight into human nature. It gives him insight into the heart of cosmic nature, into the very "soul of things"' (Ibid., 36). The poet thus became elevated to the role of special kind of genius who had access to the 'hidden truth' (Ibid., 35) and by so doing could untangle the complex interconnectedness and *vie profonde* of life.

Undoubtedly his first two earlier collections, as well as the volumes which emerged later – *The Creed of my Heart* and *Sonnets to the Universe* which were published after his retirement – attempted to fulfil that aim in providing for a coherent set of beliefs and principles drawing heavily from the depths of Holmes' soul and instinctive creative impulses. They thus reflected Holmes' own dictum, following Wordsworth, that poetry was the 'expression of strong and deep feeling' (Ibid., 2) which was (more than often) to be experienced spontaneously and joyfully. This is hinted at within Holmes in two main ways; first the very sporadic nature of his poetic composition whose 'fits and starts' – there are significant intervals between volumes – indicated possession by a muse which itself was the impetus for intense bursts of activity. His autobiography suggests for example that his last sonnet sequence was written within the course of a week. Second, many of his best early poems are those set within very real locations and geographies, – his 'Sonnets to the Atlantic' sequence from the west coast of Ireland where he visited as a boy for example – which thereby reflected observation, immersion and sensitivity toward his surrounding landscapes to which he had a close affinity.

More pertinently even than its direct subject matter, Holmes' poetry can be seen to both mirror and echo the changing concerns of his philosophy and the topography of his intellectual thought as it evolved across time. As an example, his first two collections were primarily concerned in the pantheist sense with the worship of nature with frequent exhortations made to the power of the elements, particularly the sea and the ocean which he imbued with great spiritual force calling it, 'dark and mysterious as an evil dream' (Holmes, 1879b, 'Light and Shade'). This was in keeping with the idealism (in both senses!) of his Oxford youth which had argued for the existence of some form of higher sublime power which existed beyond the simplified material world and which was embodied for Holmes initially as a spirit within Nature.

Moving away from this immediately external world, Holmes' third and fourth volumes – entitled *The Silence of Love* (1899) and *The Triumph of Love* (1903) respectively – and published later although still whilst he was an Inspector – were addressed 'to Psyche' and dealt with his own inner responses to an imaginary muse and his articulation of the feeling of idealized love. This was a move broadly in line with his own explorations of feeling, emotion and the soul which preoccupied, as we shall see, his religious writings of this time. Further, in pronouncing that love as perfectly embodied would be 'silent, unrequited, unconfessed' (Holmes, 1903, 'XXVII') and that its triumph would be achieved by recognition of its eternal qualities rather than as bound and shackled by earthly carnalities, Holmes was here reflecting his nascent exploration of Buddhism and its attendant ascetic lifestyle which he saw as a counterweight to many of the materialist earthly impulses that served to stunt self-realization. Finally, in the remarkable *Sonnets to the Universe*

(1918) sequence, Holmes sought to bring these two realms (the external world of nature and the internal condition of being) together and this fascinating, almost liturgical sequence of 21 poems served as a paean to the pantheist 'oneness' of the Universe, Nature and Man which was the focus of much of Holmes' later endeavours with the Quest Society and his deeper investigations into the philosophy of the East and its greater inclination toward a belief in the concept of 'Wholeness'. This in itself was a logical extension of Holmes' previous rejection of much of the prevailing spirit of Western-style religions including Christianity which he saw as placing restrictions upon Man's freedom through the imposition of a legalistic and constricting doctrine.

This intellectual journey embodied in his poetry, whilst only touched upon here, was however one explicitly and more deeply acknowledged by Holmes in his autobiography, aptly entitled it will be remembered *In Quest of an Ideal*, in which he argued that true self-realization, spiritual high attainment and the apogee of human development was to be attained by cultivating the virtues of *disinterested devotion* and *self-loss*. This loss and escape from self was ultimately to be achieved in three ways: 'The love of "nature", being intrinsically unselfish, is one way. The love of the beloved...is another way...the third way [is] the way of human love, the way of love of man as man' (Holmes, 1920a, 114–115). One can thereby observe the various phases of Holmes' poetry (nature, love and the universe) as providing a road-map for his spiritual growth and personal transformation as it became generated in the wellspring of his wider reading.

In addition it is worth therefore noting here, in passing, the wider and more immediate significance of this poetry as for many contemporary readers perhaps unacquainted with Holmes' educational endeavours and (to that point) mostly anonymous writing this would have been the sole way in which his name was disseminated and recognized within the public domain. Surprisingly given how it has today all but disappeared from view, it was this which served to cement his burgeoning literary reputation; contemporary reviewers praised for example his verses for their 'command of stately rhythm and of sustained elevation of thought' (*The Athenaeum*, 20th December 1902) as well as its 'quite uncommon beauty and distinction' (*The Times*, 6th January 1899). Its significance for Holmes himself can be attested by his frequent references to the importance of the discipline in a range of different and wider contexts and not merely for the spontaneous and divine insights he felt it afforded him. In writing of its place in schools for example he was to frequently refer to the value it could hold for children even encouraging the teachers in his district to take it 'in preference to any science or foreign language' (Holmes, 1883, 359). More grandiosely Holmes was to argue that, 'it is the descent from poetry to prose...that tests the worth of a creed' (Holmes, 1905b, 85) and when considering the poetry found within the words of Christ he was to make clear his position on the role of poet as a shaman:

> the poet, if sincere, always speaks with an air of inspired conviction, he is content to deliver to men just so much truth as each man in turn is able to

assimilate…it belongs to the essence of poetry to be all things to all men, and yet to give to each man no more than he can claim as his own.

(Ibid., 100)

Although all poetry embodies truth, in Holmes' case it did so by virtue of being a vehicle for his own very particular ideas about the universe, God and the place of Man in relation to these. His was not, in the main, poetry of character, tales, narrative or conversation and virtually all of his verse is *subjective* through its use of personal pronoun – I, me, mine and so on and often addressing either himself or his Beloved ('you'). In rejecting these more dominant and traditional forms, much of what he wrote instead represented a personalized response to an external reality by using verse as a vehicle for bigger ideas and beliefs about the spiritual condition of the world. Whilst three of his volumes were explicitly sequential and deserve to be read and appraised in that light, almost all of his poetry (and there are a little over 230 individual poems in his canon) was thereby a means to convey a very particular philosophical message or messages. In addition nearly three quarters of these poems are in sonnet form which, whilst on the one hand suggesting stylistic limitation, is less surprising when one considers how its structural and schematic restrictions necessitate distillation of a particular idea in extended metaphor and, in the Shakespearian form[1] which Holmes used more than any other, a denouement within the final two lines. Arguably, this was the form which suited him best and it is in his longer sonnet sequences where he seeks to articulate his philosophy of love and how it should be most appropriately expressed that his poetry is at its strongest and most consistent. Whilst, as has been mentioned, its explicit Romanticism betrays obvious debts, his particular exploration of pantheistic and Eastern themes makes it unique within its time and it appears refreshingly untouched by contemporary trends. For example although a little less than four years separated Holmes' last volume in 1918 from T.S. Eliot's *The Wasteland* they could hardly be more different in either form or content. Similarly there is little connection to the aestheticism of the Decadents, the earlier long narratives or character pieces of Browning or Tennyson or even the more straightforward rambunctious expositions of Kipling, Newbolt and Masefield all of whom formed the surrounding literary context of which Holmes as a practicing poet would have been fully aware.

Nonetheless for all the originality of voice, posterity has done Holmes' poetry (and its enthusiastic reviewers) few favours; save for a handful of facsimile reprints, it is only as recently as 2016 (80 years after his death) that any proper scholarly edition has been made of this poetry and there are few, if any, publications addressing its significance.[2] As with any advocacy of a minor poet, it is of course easily possible to overstate its case; some of his sentiments for example are simply too bland and derivative and appear as generic by comparison. His use of archaisms – 'O', 'thou' and the like – can seem, even by the late Victorian standards of the time, anachronistic, and the few poems in which Holmes' persona is not present are undoubtedly weaker and unconvincing in their adoption of a different voice. Likewise, one encounters the inevitable problem when dealing with the sonnet sequence, and especially one driven by its own overarching *idea*, which is that of repetition and this creates difficulties when trying to isolate and pinpoint individual poems for praise and recognition. This may explain perhaps why Holmes was, to the best of the author's knowledge, only once anthologized[3] and why it has been his educational work that has remained his greatest and most discussed legacy. However, whilst his poetry can on occasion be so criticized stylistically, and may anyway not fully interest those whose business is education, it remains an important and hugely significant part of his *oeuvre* and in combining traditional form with esoteric and non-conventional ideas gives us a particularly distinct corpus within the poetic canon which offers much and remains impossible to overlook when attempting an appraisal of Holmes' life and work in which the different genres of his writing conspire together to address common concerns. It was after all his friend and fellow educationalist R.W. Macan who was to presciently point out that, 'Holmes was at once less and more than a philosopher *von Fach*: he was a Poet, a philosophic poet…Moreover his prose composition, where he is dealing with philosophy, is essentially poetic' (Macan, 1937, 9).

For all of its merits however it was really in this 'middle' period – after his early poetry yet before his major educational writings – that we start to see Holmes emerge too as a *prose* writer of some distinction and it is this which provides the basis for beginning to explore more directly his educational ideas which is, after all, the central purpose of this narrative. Drawing on the theistic impulses of his earlier verse, this stage of his life (which we could put roughly between 1890 and 1910) was characterized by writings on *religion* and the publication of three important books – *A Confession of Faith by an Unorthodox Believer* (1895), *The Creed of Christ* (1905b) and finally *The Creed of Buddha* (1908b). These books and the theological perspectives adopted therein were to be inexorably intertwined with much of his later thinking on schooling and pedagogy and so similarly cannot be overlooked when attempting any form of assessment of Holmes' educational philosophy and legacy. Indeed it is worth noting that the opening chapter of the later treatise *What is and What Might Be* concerned itself with reiterating many of these theological arguments perhaps for a readership – teachers, educationalists and pedagogues – who may not previously have come across them. It is also pertinent to point out that these religious works were published anonymously, perhaps indicating (and there is no correspondence relating to it but it seems a reasonable assumption) a desire not to offend colleagues and those in his profession by espousal of unorthodox opinions. Although this was not the first occasion on which Holmes had valued his privacy and he was clearly – as his shock at the leaking of the Holmes-Morant Circular indicates – a humble man reticent within the public spotlight, given his ascendency within the ranks of the Board of Education at this time he may have felt that it was inappropriate to be seen to be advancing contentious points of view, particularly given the expected neutrality and essential functionary quality of civil servants.

There is also the possibility – and one that McDonald (2008) in his analysis of Holmes' intentions within *The Creed of Christ* has alluded to – that in choosing to criticize the centralizing and quasi-bureaucratic aspects of Judaic Christianity, Holmes was drawing an implicit parallel with developments at the Board of Education at the time as its leading administrator Robert Morant sought to consolidate control of the various departments under the auspices of the Central Office of the Board. As Neil Daglish (1996) has diligently charted, these changes were particularly controversial especially those manoeuvres which sought to bring the elementary inspectorate under the control of other departmental branches. On this Morant had earlier found himself challenged by Cyril Jackson – Holmes' predecessor as Chief Inspector of Elementary Schools – and a man who saw the power of his own department as being threatened by plans to move his best and most able men toward this new branch. In an undated note to Morant, Jackson had made clear his antipathy toward these new plans: 'You know how very strongly I feel the absolute necessity of retaining the full responsibility of H.M.I. [His Majesty's Inspector] for all the reports of his district' (ED, 22/4, Cyril Jackson to Robert Morant). It could then be argued that this strength of feeling and concern was here being channelled by Holmes who would have been fully aware of the implications such policy would have had on his own administration particularly his having now inherited much of Jackson's legacy. Although originally published anonymously, it seems certain that Morant too as a confidante would have known anyway of the *Creed's* true authorship and Holmes may well indeed have felt able to appeal to him ideologically, not least as Morant himself had previously dabbled in these ideas. This is made evident within the papers of Michael Sadler[4] who in a long biographical sketch wrote of Morant that, 'He had about him a dim halo of Buddhist austerity. He had broken away from Christian orthodoxy and felt the power of Oriental mysticism' (Sadler Papers, Eng., Misc. c.550).

At the very least, even if we refuse to accept that Holmes' intentions here were politically motivated, the case he was to make as we shall we see stood in opposition to many of the prevailing and more orthodox Victorian theological views and, in his views about God and the 'spirit', he was to find himself implicitly siding with many of the more radical groups such as the Theosophists and, more significantly, the Froebelians whose doctrines, as Joachim Liebschner (1991) has shown, were gaining ground in England around this time with a mass increase in Society membership[5]. This was often very much in contravention to the will of the Board of Education whose resistance to the Froebel Society's efforts to have its Elementary School Certificate recognized have been well charted and characterized as a 'long struggle' (Liebschner, 1991, 70) with little solution forthcoming. Given therefore the centrality of religious writing to his world-view and how it was to intertwine with his educational beliefs, it is to exploring this aspect of Holmes' thought that the book now turns.

Holmes, Christianity and Western religion

Holmes' interventions in religion came at a time when theological schisms were emerging which threatened to overturn the dominance and hegemony of the established Church. As early as the 1860s whilst Holmes was still a schoolboy, the easily accepted sets of beliefs of the earlier part of the century seemed to be coming under repeated challenges from a range of different directions. Although, as Ieuan Ellis (1988) amongst others has pointed out, the tangible impact of these threats were often more imagined than real, following Charles Darwin and his theory of evolution as outlined in *On the Origin of the Species* (1859) various commentators and critics had certainly been left challenged over their belief in the traditionalist conception of an omniscient being and divine creation. As a result many churchmen had therefore responded by putting 'much ingenuity and effort…[into] harmonizing Genesis and geology, and [by] reinterpreting the 'days' of creation' (Ellis in Thomas (Ed.), 1988, 64). Such reconciliation formed the basis of the work of those such as the clergyman Aubrey Moore writing in the influential tract *Lux Mundi* (1890) who began to skilfully resolve the budding conflict between evolution and theology by arguing against a more literal interpretation of the Old Testament and in particular the book of Genesis in which the origins of Creation were to be found. Others, such as the firebrand Thomas Henry Huxley, went even further and turned their questions upon the very figure and divinity of Christ himself: 'What did he really say and do; and how much that is attributed to him in speech and action, is the embroidery of the various parties into which his followers tended to split themselves within twenty years of his death' (Huxley, 1894, 229).

This line of thinking was a direct descendent of the remarkable earlier essays of J.R. Seeley (*Ecce Homo* and *Natural Religion*) which themselves had sought to humanize Christ and question both the place and necessity of the supernatural in religion. Seeking to justify and maintain the position of the organized established Church some even argued instead that complex scientific theories *increased* rather than diminished the greatness of the Christian God; after all who but for an omniscient, all-knowing and ultimately all-powerful being could have created a system of life so complex that it took humanity nearly 2,000 years to uncover its rules? Holmes' work and ideas were thus contributing to a debate into the substance of Christianity and established faith that had been going for at least forty years. This maelstrom was being further accentuated by the formation of alternative sources of spiritual nourishment; 1907 for example marked both the foundation of the Buddhist Society of Great Britain (whose ideas as we shall see attracted Holmes) as well as that of the United Methodist Church from its various splinter groups. In a similar fashion, the Catholic Church had gained long-sought and hard fought legitimacy following the recreation of the diocesan hierarchy in 1850.

Although toward the end of his life moving more down the path of nascent Theosophy through a commitment to wholeness, soul-growth and spiritual integration in which even Huxley's potentially woolly term *agnostic* became seen positively as an 'unceasing quest of the ideal' (Holmes, 1921b, 436) there is evidence, certainly earlier on in his writing, of Holmes following the trend of the aforementioned Aubrey Moore, Charles Gore *et al.* and actively seeking to reconcile science and religion rather than merely attempting to promulgate the traditional dichotomy and downplay one in respect of the other. As a School

Inspector required to oversee and adhere to the expanded 1861 Codes which included branches of pure and applied science and in addition being a well-read intellectual with an interest in theology it seems but inevitable that Holmes would have had familiarity with these continuing debates over the role and nature of God. In any case, he understood all too well the utility of the new discoveries being made by science and happily admitted that the methods and practices of (as an example) the medical field with its measured and specialized procedures and attempts to understand even the minutest interrelationship between organs of the body should be reflected in a pedagogy which more fully sought to understand the intricacies of human nature in the classrooms. These types of pedagogy formed part of what Adrian Wooldridge has defined as' the quest for a science of teaching' (Wooldridge, 1994, 53) which was being developed by more forward-thinking educators of the time. It is not unsurprising to note that the later New Education Fellowship, for whom Holmes was to be a seminal figure, included in its ranks many psychologists and pseudo-biologists for whom science was to provide an empirical foundation for the discipline of education.

Science and the challenges it posed were therefore to be equated for Holmes with notions of development and progress although unlike other contemporaries he did not use it to support any aspect of the *status quo* by attempting to intermesh it with existing theological doctrine or by using it as evidence for the hitherto unknown complexity of God. On the contrary he argued more radically that its properties and characteristics were very much distinct from traditional religious thinking which relied on isolated and unexplained supernatural phenomena such as miracles and visitations. These events – whose power and reverence relied precisely on their inexplicability – stood very much in contrast to the field of science and its quest for empirical global truth and which sought to understand the universe as 'an organic whole' (Holmes, 1905b, 109) bound by universal laws and increasingly complex layers and infinite levels of being. In that way, Holmes was to promulgate the belief that science was a way of demonstrating the flaws inherent within prevailing religious viewpoints and, instead, served very much to support his earlier idealist case which went against the notion of the transcendent God: 'With the gradual development of Science and the gradual spread of the scientific tone of mind, the sphere of the Supernatural has been and is being constantly restricted' (Holmes, 1898b, 7).

As we shall see, this more scientific way of thinking was one which Holmes believed could, and indeed should, be applied to the soul and the natural law of the soul's growth thereby explaining his early attachment to the scientific method which sought to bring both the knowable and unknowable world under some aspect of unity and regulation. Unexplained and isolated phenomena of the type revered by religion therefore not only defied logic – a similar manifestation of Arnold's *aberglaube* – but also contributed to a fragmentation of life which went against Holmes' instinctive impulses toward harmony many of which stemmed from his earlier attachments to Idealism and the existence of an ethereal Absolute. Discoveries in his lifetime of various sub-atomic particles and structures were to give further substance to Holmes' belief that there were new realms of hitherto unknown existences which themselves indicated not merely the presence of overarching laws and principles (the existence of such invisible particles relying on inference derived from scientific theory) but also that these transcended simple knowable external realities.

This contextual backdrop is important to appreciate as it allows us an entry point to not only understanding what made Holmes' religious ideas distinctive in their own right but also how they were to provide an overarching framework which would serve in time to explain what he saw as many of the dominant features of education. After this fashion, Darwin's theory of evolution thereby became seen as a precursor for the charting of another dimension of human growth: 'The idea of evolution, re-discovered and elaborated by Physical Science, will gradually ascend to higher planes of existence, and will at last be applied to the world to which it essentially belongs, — to the world of the soul's inner life' (Holmes, 1905b, 199). Holmes' believed strongly – and here we begin to observe his originality – that the human soul was as much capable of evolving as the physical body and that its end-point would be at the stage of *self-realization* in which Man recognized that his soul was one with the soul of the Universe. In the same way that science had indicated how physical appearances and characteristics were not fixed with animals and plants improving, adapting and reconfiguring themselves to changing circumstances over centuries so, in the same way, the human soul was capable of infinite levels of growth and development the end-point of which (if indeed there was an end-point) we were unaware. This was to prove an important and enduring theme to Holmes' writings; nearly 20 years later for instance he was to state hopefully that 'Slowly but surely the idea of evolution is undermining the foundations of orthodox Christian theology' (Holmes, 1923h, 227). Whilst this quotation was itself part of an article arguing more widely and abstractly for the idea of God as 'Eternally One' (Ibid., 228) it still reinforces how Holmes saw science as supporting his convictions in opposing established Christian beliefs and its more fixed 'Supernaturalist' view of the division between God and Man.

In this, as Alan Blyth points out, Holmes was standing up not merely to seemingly immovable religious doctrine but also, more widely, those within the contemporary educational world in particular the followers of the German philosopher and pedagogue Johann Friedrich Herbart[6] whose understanding of the relationship between individuality and character formation 'appeared particularly well attuned to the prevailing economic, political and social circumstances' (Blyth, 1981, 77) of the mid- to late-nineteenth century when his ideas held sway and when concomitant concerns over democratic ideals were at their highest. In particular Herbart believed that whilst children had individual potentials which could be instilled, these were only successfully expressed when they were seen as making an active contribution to society as productive citizens. To reach that desired end, children thus had to be 'transformed by education in accordance with...the accumulated values of civilization' (Ibid., 70).

In making these assertions Herbart had been keen, when thinking about individual development, to subsequently distinguish between humans and other 'lesser' organisms, in other words to reject any attachment to theories of education which were analogous to plant growth and therefore, in Holmes' eyes, to get left behind by recent advances such as those made by the Child Study movement which had better charted the processes of growth of the human mind and body. Such organic discourse it will be remembered had served as the cornerstone of Romantic ideas about schooling from Rousseau and Froebel onwards and in seeming to oppose them Herbart embodied that more rationalist and instrumental view of education that saw a 'successful' child as one who could contribute directly to the economic well-being of their society and not perhaps as one who had moved to fulfilling latent spiritual potentials. David Hamilton (1989) has implicitly touched upon this in his seminal work which explored the transformation of the large schoolroom into separate 'batches' or classrooms (akin to factory production lines) with the resultant view of the child as an economic unit. Such units were to have corresponding levels of social exchange value as they became *commodified* hence the link to a form of instrumentalism within education which saw schooling as having a particular social purpose. Holmes may not have thought in quite these terms but the impact of such changes may well not have been lost on him throughout his Inspection career and the unsuitable conditions of many schools for the purposes of an education designed to foster growth of the spirit alongside the body.

The contention therefore of the neo-Herbartians – whom Holmes was to later lambast brilliantly in the first chapter of *In Defence of What Might Be* – rested on the belief that non-human life had a pre-determined form unlike that of humans whose appearance and character, prior to birth, was unknown. Although naturally receptive to the principle of the potentially vast configurations of human life, Holmes was troubled by what he saw as a theory stemming from a false analogy; plants he argued – on the surface very unlike humans – also have the capacity to change over periods of time depending on the prevailing environmental and climactic conditions and even in any large field of apparently identical plants there will always be subtle levels of variation thereby belying the idea of uniformity. There was also, by extension, the troubling issue of the implied separation between Man and Nature with the former being seen as different and therefore, by extension, as superior to the latter. This clearly went against any suggestion of unity which, as we have mentioned, was a significant part of the Idealism then influencing Holmes' thinking.

Most significantly of all though, whilst correct about the need to carefully nurture the growing child, the Herbatians placed too heavy an onus upon the role and responsibility of the teacher and what for Herbart became the need to fill the child's mind with 'thoughts, feelings and desires it could not otherwise have obtained' (Holmes, 1914, 43) for Holmes represented instead attempts to both impose on the child externally and to do so contrary to the laws of *inward* nature and natural human development. The ideas of Darwin had demonstrated for him that growth was not merely about fulfilling latent potential through the metaphor of the builder's yard – that is by simply providing the raw materials for growth and being a 'soul builder' – but instead by being more organic and sympathetic to the child's natural inclinations as 'men began to realize the unity of life…the idea of growth…began to apply…to whole orders of living things…and at last to the Cosmos conceived as a living whole' (Ibid., 32). By contrast, Herbart's theories led ultimately to a belief concerning education that was both pre-Darwinian and functioned to 'repudiate the authority of Nature…refuse[s] to utilize the expansive forces that are at work in the child [and] which dooms him to a life of receptiveness and passivity' (Ibid., 56). In light of subsequent recent psychological research which has indicated how much sense and meaning the child can make of their world such comments seem surprisingly prophetic.

By using the theory of evolution in this way Holmes was further implying not only that there was a more or less common unity between all living organisms within the Universe and that every species had the potential for unlimited development but also that crucially the gestalt capacities which made up an individual (what he was to term *racial* characteristics) were innate and did not need to be as strenuously mediated by society – another difference between himself and others who saw the child as needing close guidance and instruction in order to fulfil their potentials. One thinks here of John Locke's earlier empiricist notion of the *tabula rasa* and the need to therefore imprint and fill up the child with information they could not otherwise obtain, a view which Holmes had indirectly touched upon and condemned in his earlier *Inspection Reports*. Why after all should it be the case that adults held a monopoly on Truth? The numerous examples of democratic living and experimentation within those schools of the New Education Fellowship (most notably Summerhill) should serve to illustrate the pervading influence of that idea! It was clear then that education was for Holmes one of the key sites in which such spiritual growth and development of potentials took place and so the school took on a level of added significance beyond its more obvious function of knowledge transmission. In alluding to its transformative potential, Holmes was to comment that the role of the teacher was primarily to encourage the 'build up of a social world of their [the pupils] own inside the school' (Holmes, 1921a, 82) thereby allowing them to learn from each other and from their own natural impulses.

Further to his allusions to Darwin, attempts to balance the empirical with the spiritual and advocacy of science more generally, in his critique of the existing Church it should be stressed once again that Holmes was never to dispute the existence or indeed the essential 'divinity' of its fundamental figure – Christ – and indeed was to the end of his life to explicitly refer to himself as a Christian. For Holmes, the point about Christ was that he represented, in an unconventional take on his holiness, the perfect embodiment of a life lived according to the principle of soul-growth through self-realization embodied through his ultimate sacrifice upon the Cross. Given how such an interpretation stood in direct contrast to more conventional theological understanding (Christ as the infallible Son of God and purveyor of miracles) it was no surprise to find Holmes arguing that the message of Christ had become distorted across time and, as a result of such false construal and interpretation, had led to a curtailing of Man's freedom in particular that of the spirit which was regarded as its most important manifestation. Although then his subject was the person of Christ, his was not the Christ as classically represented by the Gospels and whose words had for centuries been taken literally by the Church and its followers. Instead, the starting point for seeking to ingeniously reinterpret the position of Christ was through arguing that many of the sayings attributed to him and written down as verbatim in the New Testament were either falsely ascribed or, more often, wrongfully understood. As he put it, 'the Western World has paid a superstitious reverence to the letter of what Christ is reported to have said, and has made no sustained attempt to interpret *its spirit*' (Holmes, 1905b, 2, italics added).

This is an important utterance for it strikes at the heart of Holmes' analysis of Christianity and, for that matter, organized monotheistic religions more generally; whilst Christ through his teaching and moral message was a figure to be hugely admired, Holmes cautioned against following the pronouncements of those who sought to interpret his meaning often for their own dogmatic ends. This was particularly the case for those sayings which Holmes classified as being 'unintelligible' (Ibid., 5) but to which the authors of the Gospel accounts had given literal sense and which were couched in the discourse of truth and the action of obedience. The power and importance of Holmes' Christ therefore stemmed not from his being the Son of God (which he would have denied) but instead through the way in which he articulated a philosophy that was wholly antithetical to prevailing and constraining ideology:

> It is quite clear that Christ was a 'prophet' in the widest sense of the word; that he was possessed with large and far-reaching ideas of a more or less revolutionary character, and that he was therefore, speaking generally, in revolt against the tendencies of the age in which, and the people among whom, he lived.
>
> (Ibid., 7–8)

Going back to the very first pages of his debut collection of poetry written nearly a quarter of a century before he addressed these issues so explicitly in *The Creed*, Holmes had articulated this general view in a handful of thought-provoking verses which tackled head-on the nature of the divinity of Christ. Almost as if laying out his doctrine for his earliest readership, Holmes even here was keen to stress that Christ's significance was in acting as a conduit for the idea that God was not transcendent as posited by orthodox religion bur rather *imminent* and located within the very heart of Mankind: 'In Christ God stoops to earth, through Christ man/ climbs to Heaven' (Holmes, 1876, 'What Think Ye of Christ?'). This fusion of Man and God was equally well articulated in the succeeding poem in which Holmes identified the role Christ was to play in delivering Mankind from its previous worship of a God who was both distant and perceived as judgemental. It was only through the intervention of Christ that there entered into human consciousness a more earth-bound understanding of the role of the divine: 'Be near – be with us – so we can/Tread in the path Thy footsteps trod,/Oh! Godhead stooping down to man-/Oh! Manhood reaching up to God' (Ibid., 'Cur Deus Homo'). Although explicitly religious themes were not the main focus of Holmes' poetry and his conception of the immediate God was expressed more broadly as that found pantheistically within *nature*, these writings nonetheless had laid down an early marker by implying that Holmes was prepared to reject much of the established thinking on religion which he argued placed undue emphasis on unthinking ceremony and ritual which was antithetical to the spirit of Christ himself.

These notions of theological infallibility and obeisance were crucial to Holmes for equally central to his world-view was the idea that, through the misinterpretation of the spirit of its founder, Christianity had taken a form more in line with post-exilian Judaism whose essence was 'devotion to a divinely given law' (Holmes, 1905b, 29). Handed down through the Commandments given to Moses and facilitated by both the legalism of the Pharisees whom Holmes devoted much time in various works to discussing and condemning as well as the highly efficient bureaucracy of Rome, Christianity thus became skewed toward a framework of legalism, directives and the letter of the law which 'established itself at the expense of the *spirit*' (Ibid., italics added). Under this code, Man's actions and their moral worth were judged not by the intention inherent within them (deontological ethics) or their consequences but simply whether 'they complied or failed to comply with the letter of the Law's enactments' (Ibid., 36). Holmes was not of course the first to make the connection between organized theology and the imposition of particular inflexible forms of decree which impacted more broadly upon social behaviour. Indeed, this philosophy of what may broadly be called Legalism had its roots very much in the ancient East in the Qin state of China and, as the recent edited collection by Dresch and Scheele (2015) has shown, its branches can be traced further afield including the proto-democracies of both Rome and Greece. Nevertheless, whatever the precise historical origin of the concept – and ultimately whether of course one agrees with the way Holmes was to use it – by both attacking prevailing Western religions and, later, by linking this framework to aspects of the modern world including crucially education Holmes was offering a completely fresh and innovative critique of contemporary society which found its origins within a much older set of values.

Holmes, externalism and dualistic thinking

In therefore acknowledging that such religious behaviours were capable of being observed, recorded and quantified, Holmes was to coin the term *externalism* which was his way of explaining how even those processes and actions which were traditionally considered internal and of the soul could be reduced to the level of outward materialism. It was those forms of behaviour which could themselves be rendered visible and apparent that therefore allowed for religion and, in other contexts, different sources of authority (for example a school teacher) to establish their hold and control over individual minds through being able to lay down rigid codes of practice. An obeyance of these codes therefore became a matter of individual personal choice but one constantly mediated with the commensurate threat of risk and reward often involving theological and divine judgement. Perversely, despite its intention of seeking to preserve moral order through clear codified instruction, Holmes argued that such a framework had the opposite effect with criticism of other's moral actions becoming more commonplace and people feeling less inclined to address and challenge their own personal ethical development happy as they were to obey un-problematically what was laid down before them. Typically, this example filtered down from the very top: 'There was nothing in the bearing of the Pharisees that incensed Christ so strongly as their intolerant dogmatism, their censorious attitude towards their fellow men' (Ibid., 58).

As we shall see in the following chapter, this concept, although emanating in a very different time, had huge implications within more contemporary society and particularly for its *educational* practice as it served to explain and underpin Holmes' withering critique of a schooling system driven by similar unthinking obedience in the classroom. For now though, such behaviours were repeatedly sustained, according to Holmes, by elements of more contemporary scholarship and activity which continued to delineate that profound misunderstanding and misrepresentation of Christ's spirit. In a later essay for example considering a recently published scholarly work *The Beginnings of Christianity* Holmes, whilst not denying the intellectual rigor of the research on show, broadened his argument to take a sideswipe against those writers who maintained adherence to the Judaic elements of Christ's divinity through, once again, literal interpretation of his words. Exemplifying his belief in the need to more truly determine the *spirit* of Christ, Holmes was to write:

> I have contended that when we are trying to determine the religious beliefs of a great teacher, the words which he used about God are not our only available source of evidence; [that] there are other sources at our service which have even more to tell us.
>
> (Holmes, 1921c, 62)

Despite then those earlier attempts at a re-characterization of the persona of Christ by the likes of Seeley and Huxley and the questioning of the inherent nature of his divinity, Holmes still saw little progress in either academic scholarship or religious practices that served to provide a better and truer understanding of the real meaning of his philosophy. Whilst the former could be easily evidenced by an analysis of contemporary writings – with which he would have been familiar – the latter was embodied in such ancient and, for Holmes, antiquated practices as communion and baptism in which young children were influxed with the supernatural external God as it appeared to enter their bodies at the moment of blessing. Such notions not only implied the sense of an overarching external (and by inference, judgemental) God but also went against the more humanist and immanent interpretation of Christ which Holmes strove to put forward.

This concept of externalism whilst therefore serving to both create and maintain a false interpretation of Christ was also inherently bound up with the aforementioned procedural legalism as it relied heavily on the codification of both actions and behaviours which were most readily referenced and monitored through relation to a written word. Classically, within Christianity, this encompassed missives like the Ten Commandments, prophecies and parables but also sermons and dogma as spouted from the priestly pulpit. Hand in hand and underpinning this was a deep held attachment to the long-established Doctrine of the Fall[7] which meant that Man was viewed under an aspect of sin and untrustworthiness. Although much ink had been previously spilt discussing the precise nature of Man's sinfulness – was the guilt Adam's alone or to be equally shared by his descendants for example – there was, even amongst those more moderate Church scholars and believers, a recognition that Man's mortality both distinguished him from the eternal 'perfect' God and tended him toward concupiscence. Being bound to accept this meant that he was, as a species, *a propos* destined for damnation and pre-ordained toward sinful behaviour which could only be overcome by achieving salvation through '*doing* God's will' (Holmes, 1911, 15, original italics) and acting in an appropriate fashion as laid down by those in authority. Embodied perfectly in the personas of the Pharisees or Roman administrators, often this authority consisted of those who were the arbiters and interpreters of spiritual texts and writings and who, by virtue of their supposed learning, acted as mouthpieces for the Divine thereby collectively reinforcing the need for accepted behaviour in deference to a higher power.

Belief in Original Sin was once again, as we shall see in the next chapter, to have more serious ramifications in relation to classroom practice but, in the context of life in its broadest sense, Holmes believed that it immediately predisposed Man to a narrow path of being through having to be told in detail what he was to do and, more importantly, how he was to have to do it in order to achieve later redemption. At work operated a crude 'carrot and stick' scenario in which fear of eternal damnation was counterbalanced by the hope of salvation and which was based upon 'correct' external action which could be both observed and monitored. This was a view reinforced by such important and seminal thinkers as John Wesley whose burgeoning Methodism and its attendant sermons used a medical analogy to imply that religion was a way – perhaps ultimately *the* way – of healing the diseased soul inherent within Mankind. Given that Wesley himself had been a noted schoolmaster[8] this further reinforced the link between religious dogma and educational practice – a connection that was to so irk Holmes.

Having a social system therefore based on these premises provoked, according to Holmes, two responses. First, and most straightforwardly, it meant that man's freedom was restricted and given over to the rule of law. Here, Holmes did not solely have in mind laws in the civic sense (although through the Ten Commandments this was still manifest) but instead freedom to pursue ideals, to judge the merits of legal frameworks, to question motives, think abstrusely and so on. The critical qualities which led to the growth of the soul as it sought to cultivate and develop were thus quashed with a result that Man's spiritual growth was either banned or, more commonly, side-lined as unnecessary. This impinged too upon his conscience and imagination; after all if the Law could lay down so precisely how Man was to act then where was the freedom to imagine alternative possibilities, actions or points of view? Indeed, one of the recurring themes of Holmes' writings on education – itself heavily prescribed – was his bemoaning of the lack of opportunity for the use of the imagination even within the most creative of subjects.

Above and beyond however regulating Man's actions, the rule of law meant second the evolution of a *dualistic* way of thinking between 'the world of Nature which is fallen, ruined and accursed, and the Supernatural world, which shares in the perfection and centres in the glory of God' (Holmes, 1911, 14). Holmes saw this as an entrenched and widespread process which encompassed not merely opposition toward divine force but also, 'mind to body, spirit to matter, good to evil...the Creator to the visible Universe, the Supernatural to Nature, God to Man' (Holmes, 1914, 81). Such a belief had an additional two implications; first it effected a binary division between particular components of life and served to segregate potentially harmonious elements as humans continually thought in opposites and polarization. In much of Holmes' work we therefore see his actively attempting to mitigate this by multiple mentions of the concept of 'Unity' between on the one hand both God and Nature but also, more profoundly, between the human soul and the Universe. This was very much of course in keeping with his devotion to Idealism. Second, dualism served to debase notions of a Creator, Nature and Man who were all in this scheme brought down to the level of materialism and ephemera standing as they did in opposition to the belief of the Divine in Nature and the Divine Spirit in Man. Later on in his work, particularly within the pages of *Self-Realization* (1927a), Holmes was to explain how this dualism was apparent not merely within traditional Christianity but also further back in the Stoics and Epicureans of Ancient Greece. Despite representing very different intellectual traditions in place and time the point remained that, 'Both philosophies degraded Nature to the level of what was ultimate in their analysis of its material content. Stoicism never got to the soul. Epicureanism never professed to do so' (Holmes, 1927a, 61).

Established Christianity was therefore, in its way, an inheritor of these movements. By choosing both to localize God in Israel as per the reading of the Old Testament (thereby ignoring the rest of the civilized world) and, as well, assuming that the will of God, rather than being able to be discerned by Man, was only to be apprehended through the diktats of law-makers, Holmes was indirectly arguing that Christianity had given itself over to a form of *atheism* which had prised apart God and humanity. Even the recent claims of Protestantism, which allowed for the individual to discern his or her own understanding of God, still clung to the idea of a transcendent entity separate from the material world of Man. The will of God not being found in Man's heart was for Holmes tantamount therefore to *dis*belief and there was something of a perverse logic in the way in which he saw literal and unblinking belief in God as equating with its exact opposite. This process was further compounded through people retaining hope that the gap between the two polarized worlds (spirit and flesh) was not indivisible which allowed, where perhaps behaviours warranted it, for the possibility of miracles, revelations and occasional prophetic visitation – that is, events which were solely to be explained by the existence of another greater and distant power whose mysteries were unknowable by the human mind. Such events – long elaborated in established Christianity over many centuries and often drawing on stories of the Old Testament as example – served the purpose of reinforcing to Man his general unworthiness, the need to be subservient in the eyes of God and his general absence of any divine, supernatural or spiritual qualities. Nor was such division equated solely with the unexplainable and the extraordinary – there were parallels to be drawn too with the everyday practices and ceremonies of the established Church. We have mentioned already how events like baptism and communion were seen to go against the spirit of the teachings of Christ however, more profoundly, they reinforced the idea of an inherent separation between Man and God predicated as they were upon the presence of an external spirit entering into the body of the child following an act of ceremonialism.

Giving added piquancy to Holmes' writing was the disturbing influence that the Christian conception of morality continued to have in the nation's *schools*. Although one of the provisions of the supposedly 'neutral' 1870 Education Act had been that the newly founded Board Schools were to be un-denominational without an act of daily collective worship, there nonetheless existed – as scholarship from N.J. Richards (1970) onwards has shown – a series of controversies and arguments between the various Church of England factions many of whom were continuing to vie for control over local administration. As Peter Gordon and Denis Lawton (1978) have pointed out, it would be a mistake to think that these struggles did not impinge upon the nascent state sector and indeed some of these powerful groups did indeed retain an influence at the local level. In some cases – such as that within Joseph Chamberlain's district of Birmingham – the Act's strictures were simply ignored and religious instruction and Bible study were imposed in the schools at the behest of the predominantly Anglican majority.

Even closer to home, as Tony Taylor (1993) amongst others has demonstrated, organizations such as Lord Cranbourne's (later the Marquess of Salisbury's) hard-line Church Party had acted to strengthen the position of the Anglican Church through the Voluntary Schools Act (1897) and, latterly, the 1902 Education Act which served to counteract the more general state-approved trend toward secularization through ensuring that religious voluntary schools were subsidized by rate payers. Although this was a remit outside of Holmes' elementary school background his proximity to Whitehall and its key figures (including Robert Morant who was a key architect of the 1902 Act) as well as the headline controversies generated by its passing meant that Holmes' religious writings were overlapping, albeit indirectly, with many prevailing educational concerns. Whether these were conscious links on Holmes' part or not remains hard to ascertain although it nevertheless seems a reasonable point to make that his critique of religion carried associations with developments happening within his own known field in which military-style drill and obedience amongst young children were prevalent. Certainly, as Holmes' intellectual scope became wider at this time, the role of Western religion in seeking wittingly or otherwise to affect a profound dualistic way of thinking became enhanced to incorporate not merely behaviours but also language, morality and the fundamental nature of being. The link therefore between Holmes' religious ideas and his wider philosophy of life cannot be overstated.

Whilst then it is right and proper to place Holmes' writing within that spectrum which sought to re-orientate contemporary understanding of Christianity it is perhaps worth noting as well the similarity between his broad critique of religion and the ideas of Friedrich Nietzsche (1844–1900) with whom he appears to share significant philosophical comparisons. This is not a connection that has previously been explored – and neither was it explicitly addressed by either author – however in seeking to stake a case for the timelessness of Holmes it perhaps does us well to seek to locate his thinking in conjunction with one of 'the giants' particularly as both seemed equally scornful of aspects of modern society. Although Nietzsche's relationship to Romanticism has been debated – and leading scholars like Walter Kaufmann (2013) have been keen to distance themselves from such a reading – it is nonetheless evident that the dominant themes of his writing were passion, the physical world, awe, and life as an aesthetic experience, all of which overlapped with the traditional concerns of the Romantics who inspired Holmes. Even if Nietzsche himself was not a Romantic *per se* and decried the use of this label, this aspect of his thought was undoubtedly felt by those claiming his influence. The composers Richard Strauss and Gustav Mahler for example both constructed huge orchestral works drawing on his writings and, in the former's sublime *Alpine Symphony* (1915), we find encapsulated a breath-taking vision of landscape in which the overwhelming grandeur of Nature could easily be construed as pantheistic.

This feeling of awe and supremacy within, and in the face of, Nature comes through equally strongly in Holmes' own writing but particularly his poetry; in addressing the mountain of Snowdon for example he refers to the 'White lipped moanings of the eternal deep' (Holmes, 1879b, 'Snowdon') whilst elsewhere much of his early verse sought to address the relationship between Man and his surroundings in particular the overwhelming authority of natural phenomena such as the lashing sea of his Irish boyhood. In reflecting on its depths and power in which 'all things seem[ed]/ Dark and mysterious as an evil dream' (Ibid., 'Light and Shade') he was – in the same vein for example as Shelley's observations of Mont Blanc – indicating a force which was both terrifying in its spectacle and aspect yet, for Holmes at least, intimately connected to humanity through the eternal spirit which bound together the human soul and the natural world.

Although the work of Nietzsche was distinctly *Germanic* (perhaps *Teutonic*) in tone it nonetheless overlaps still further with Holmes who long held a fascination with Germany and its particular schemes of education. This was initially manifest through his engagement with the work of those such as Fichte, Schelling and Froebel who sought an underlying unifying force in Nature and whose ideas had helped hone the currents of Idealism he had encountered at Oxford. In addition, as Richard Hinton Thomas has shown, the *Wandervogel* ('Wandering Birds') youth groups[9] – who had arisen 'as a protest against the same features of society with which Nietzsche had found fault' (Thomas, 1983, 96) – shared with Holmes concerns over the vitality of nature and a broad sense of anti-industrialism. Their proximity to the outdoors and emphasis upon countryside-based activities such as camping were to form a strand of later New Educational Fellowship thinking which sought to celebrate the outdoors and Nature. Whilst Holmes drew ultimately more upon Eastern ideas designed to promote the growth of the spirit rather than the body there are still distinct ideological similarities. Indeed, Holmes' active love of nature was reflected, as we have earlier mentioned, in his own life in which mountain climbing (from 1876 he was a member of the Alpine Club) and fishing were significant relaxations and in which he developed considerable skill. His engagement with the outdoors in this very physical and masculine way was then clearly influenced by more Germanic ideals.

Crucially however, the relationship between Holmes and Nietzsche was not confined merely to the aesthetic. In Nietzsche's last work *The Antichrist* (posthumously published in 1895 the same year as Holmes' *Confession of Faith*), he made a convincing case for the disconnection between established Christianity and the person of Christ, a situation brought about he believed by the authorities of the former having distorted the original message in order to exert social control within the burgeoning Roman Empire. In an unconscious pre-shadowing of Holmes, Nietzsche asserted that, 'The great lie of personal immortality destroys all reason, all naturalness in instinct; – all that is beneficent, that is life-furthering, that pledges for the future in instinct henceforth, excites mistrust' (Nietzsche, 2004, 110). Nietzsche's point here was that Judeo-Christian morality and the doctrine of salvation had been both manufactured and manipulated by St. Paul which had therefore led to the creation of a master-slave duopoly. Holmes too, although less conspiratorial and more inclined to blame Man himself for his spiritual decline, saw in established religions the root and origin of much of the contemporary educational and social malaise.

Although the shades may thus have differed, in both writers' cases it was clear that the failings of society originated from the systems of thought of the weak. Nietzsche's critique of contemporary *fin de siècle* Europe for instance stemmed from a conviction that the dominant slave-morality forbade the exceptional individuals (the *ubermensch*) from shining and he called upon them in his moral writings to assert themselves and follow their own convictions. Under a similar aspect, Holmes argued that the decay of Western civilization had arisen because 'we have allowed the *average man* to make and unmake our philosophies and our creeds. The *average man* instinctively takes for granted the intrinsic reality of the outside world' (Holmes, 1920d, 15, italics added). In both cases, there was a clear argument that the faults of Western civilization arose from the preponderance of a 'weaker' and inferior form of morality which could only be averted through changes to the existing order of thought.

Whilst Nietzsche may not have desired – despite his choice of nomenclature – to judge one morality (the 'slave') as inferior to another (the 'master') he nonetheless associated the former with the characteristics of hatred, denial, and a singular evasion of present realities – what he called *ressentiment*. Similarly for Holmes, his use of the term 'average man' is one deployed metaphorically throughout his many writings in order to elaborate the prevailing more commonplace way of thinking about the world which equated the knowable material external reality with the totality of immediate existence: 'The plain average man unhesitatingly takes for granted the intrinsic reality of the material or outward and visible world... he instinctively bases his philosophy on this fundamental assumption' (Holmes, 1924c, 35). This more static conception – static for it conceived of the world as knowable because it was fixed and *vice versa* – ultimately negated the spirit and the need to look inward at the soul to appreciate that the inward and outward universes could be bridged in a vision of unity.

If then, Christianity – and by extension other 'organized' religions and creeds – were premised upon the idea that 'salvation was to be won by obedience to a formal Law' (Holmes, 1908b, 90) where did Holmes ultimately locate the divinity of the faith itself? After all, it would be a mistake, as was alluded to earlier, in viewing him as being wholly antithetical and dismissive of the orthodox Christian Church. Rather, his was a criticism which was premised on the idea that whilst its core spirit remained sound, its key tenets had been misinterpreted across time. This was a theme he was to address brilliantly in a paper read at Manchester in 1919 – a time in which his concerns over the future shape of modern society and the place of religion were at their highest. Although explicitly concerned with addressing religious *instruction* within schools, as he had hinted at within his earlier poetry, Holmes here found the significance of Christ as lying in his doctrine of *unselfish love*: 'The love which Christ had in mind was to be free from every taint of self... Unselfish love, disinterested devotion and service is the only knowledge that really counts' (Holmes, 1923e, 191–192). Speaking as he was under the shadow of the First World War, which he believed had come about through failure to adhere to his prescribed moral path, this providential caveat was all the more powerful as it alluded to the greatest of all loves which transcended more simplistic notions of human community. That love was not loyalty to a nation, a tribe, a collective or an organization but instead manifest through recognizing that Man, Nature and Spirit were ostensibly indivisible and that human relations had to therefore be thought of in that more unified way.

Whilst this is a theme that will be more widely addressed in a succeeding chapter which considers more broadly Holmes' *political* beliefs it is worth noting here as it suggests both his theological unorthodoxy and also why he came ultimately to pledge closer allegiance to philosophies of the East which he saw as offering a more genuine path for self-development. This authenticity stemmed both from their greater appreciation for Unity but also through their more nuanced recognition that salvation was not simply a tawdry result for being seen to be doing good: 'a Heaven which can be so cheaply earned is scarcely worth striving for' (Holmes,

1908b, 10–11). It is significant then that having established for himself that Christ, through his teachings, had rejected any hint of a dualistic way of thinking and its attendant transcendent God, Holmes was now to locate other global manifestations of this philosophy which could better act as a blueprint for his developing system of beliefs. Significantly, its antecedents were to be found in places very geographically and spiritually separate from the heartlands of Christianity and it was this exploration that was to be the driving force behind much of his later writing, thinking and acting.

Holmes and the solution of the East

Given Holmes' distrust of conventional Western styles of religion which he so originally and eloquently dismantled, it is perhaps unsurprising to find that he turned to what may be broadly considered 'the East' as an alternative and yet also complementary source of spiritual salvation and as one which might better explain the mysteries of eternity and the spirit. It was after all orthodox Christianity's dogged adherence to the ideas of deliverance and damnation in relation to the afterlife that for Holmes so embodied both its controlling and dualistic aspects. Clearly distrustful too of the emergent doctrines of atheism (having no belief was as bad as it being un-wilfully corrupted) this turning was therefore envisaged as a very personal solution to the world's problems yet as one that through its creed, commitment and tone was to bear all the hallmarks and characteristics of a faith. In much the same way then that Holmes could be seen as contributing to continuing debates around the role and position of Christianity in times of theological turbulence and the Victorian 'crisis of faith', so too was he an important figure in both endorsing and raising domestic awareness of these ancient religions and creeds. Although the image of the starch-collared Chief Inspector appears somewhat incongruous when set against esoteric ideas more at home within the liberal 1960s, Holmes nevertheless became one the foremost proponents and promoters of Eastern mysticism.

As we saw in an earlier chapter, Holmes' interest in Buddhism had been stirred whilst a School Inspector in Kent by a reading of texts such as Mabel Collins, *Light on the Path* (1885), A.P. Sinnett, *Esoteric Buddhism* (1883) and, later, Rudolph Steiner, *The Way of Initiation* (1908). Despite at the time these works being seen as comparatively novel and as having a limited readership Holmes' decision to begin these explorations was perhaps less surprising than we might initially think. As W.J. Mander's (2011) exemplary work has shown, the doctrines of *Idealism* which Holmes encountered at Oxford continued to be widely promulgated by a new generation of thinkers and there is a logical overlap between its tenets and those beliefs held within the East. In particular it was the Idealists who had begun to think speculatively not only that reality differed from appearance but also that no amount of simple recourse to common sense (*a la* established religious doctrine which spoke in simple dualisms and which was supported by explicit empiricism) could mitigate this. In discussing, for example the world of knowledge, the Idealists, 'insisted on its essential underlying *unity*, arguing that all ideas were systematically linked together into one whole with no fundamental divisions' (Mander, 2011, 3). This talk of unity – which was not merely confined to the realm of ideas but also the social world in which human beings were not viewed as separate fractured entities to be considered independently – clearly resonated with Holmes and his developing view of the essential Oneness of the universe particularly that between Man, the Spirit and God.

Conversely, it is worth also noting that Holmes' interest in Buddhism was concurrent to the growth of a small yet significant national movement within the United Kingdom which concerned itself both with importation of new ideas and works and disseminating the spiritual possibilities they could offer. Much of the success of this spread of Buddhism, as Ian Oliver (1979) has shown, stemmed from the work being carried out by the academically oriented Pali Text Society (founded in 1881 by Thomas William Rhys Davids)[10] which widened access to English translations of ancient texts with a consequence that, by the time of Holmes' publication in 1908 of *The Creed of Buddha*, there were additional visible signs of organized Buddhist activity. We have already noted earlier on for example the foundation of the Buddhist Society of Great Britain and Northern Ireland of which Holmes himself may have become a member and this strand of more spiritually attuned understanding was to inflect the thinking of other groups including the neo-Romantics, those attached to the Arts and Crafts movement as well as figures such as Edward Carpenter[11] and the mystic poet Lewis Thompson.[12] Likewise, although journals such as *Mission Field* and *East and West* were concerned more with the conversion of Buddhists towards the Christian viewpoint than they were with propagating Eastern ideas they nevertheless gave a window on these notions to a prospective readership. Holmes' beliefs then did not originate in an intellectual vacuum and he was clearly neither the first nor the most prominent figure to espouse adherence to such tenets. However where he was so original was the way in which he began to explore how these ideas were not just to be directly applied as a set of guiding personal principles but as they could inform his later analyses and discussions of education.

However, in spite of these developments one must be wary of viewing Holmes simply as a conventional Buddhist; although the *Creed of Buddha* offers his own particular interpretation of that belief system and served broadly as a panegyric to its founder, Holmes ultimately was to develop a relatively idiosyncratic quasi-religious philosophy which was to borrow as much from wider developments in Ancient India as it was from anyone else. As he was succinctly to put it, 'The problem which Greek philosophy grappled with, but left unsolved, had, as it happened, been solved in India centuries before; solved in the realm of ideas by the sages of the Upanishads, solved in the realm of conduct by Buddha' (Holmes, 1927a, 52). Whereas however the devotees of the Upanishads[13] had been content simply to theorize, it was left to the Buddha to 'elaborate that nucleus into a comprehensive scheme of life' (Holmes, 1924e, 77). In real terms, this consisted, as per what could be termed 'conventional' Buddhist interpretation, of leading a comparatively ascetic lifestyle free of the need for materialist possessions and desires: 'It is desire for the things of earth that draws man back to earth; and desire for the things of earth is generated by belief in their reality' (Holmes, 1908b, 34).

This was an important principle for Holmes as it stood in contrast to what he characterized as the more decadent Western way of thinking which, as has been earlier elaborated, was materialist and, as a consequence, carried with it two significant implications. On the one hand, when taken literally, this meant the glorification and desire for material objects as ends in themselves. Second, and very much connected to this, materialism as a term was used to describe an unconscious way of thinking – often found within the average man – which regarded what was present in the material universe as both 'real' in itself and therefore as constituting the totality of reality. This was an endemic byproduct of the division between the supernatural and the earthly which prized Man away from seeing any unity between God and the Spirit. Attachment to materialism therefore served to ground Man, somewhat pessimistically, very much to the real world with its consequent follies and lack of spirituality. In commenting on the teachings of the Buddha for instance Holmes was to explain,

> It is certain that he urged men to enter and walk in the path in order that, by extinguishing all desire for earthly things, they might win deliverance from the earth-life, with its attendant suffering, and attain to that blessed state of being which he called Nirvana.
>
> (Ibid., 63)

Whilst sentiments like this were in themselves noble and undoubtedly acted for Holmes as a moral blueprint and way of actively living his life, in drawing too from the earlier tradition of the Upanishads he was to further posit that any such state of blissful being achieved through freedom from earth-bound desires ('Nirvana') was in itself unobtainable and something therefore to be continually striven for. As an example we can see this belief filtered through his aforementioned love poetry, much of which was composed around the time of his preoccupations with religion. Here he argued that it was necessary to move beyond the earthly conception which embodied it physically in the carnal act (literally earthy lust) and which could be easily understood and discarded but instead to view it eternally through denying its fulfillment thereby preserving it as an obtainable ideal. In this way, Holmes was not merely promulgating asceticism through denial of lower order pleasure (sensuality) but also conceptualizing a key component of life as eternal and as a quest to be continually sought in the realm of the infinite. This language of the 'eternal' and the 'unobtainable' was to percolate much of his writing and were to be constant themes in many of his subsequent religious and philosophical writings. In so doing they thus presented an obvious contrast to the supposed dogmatism of the West in which notions of God and religion were more 'fixed' and couched in quantifiable action and language.

These discussions of love within his poetry from the turn of the century were though mere precursors to his later prose works which sought to widen this perspective on the eternal and which were far more explicit in explaining where it was such ideas found their genesis. In particular, denial of the reality of the material world was seen ultimately to depend upon transcending the self/ego by recognizing its place in relation to what Holmes came to see, broadly speaking, as a wider community of souls. Once more relying on good conduct, finding one's true self relied on 'suppressing egoism, with all the desires and delusions on which it feeds, and breaking, one by one, the fetters of the surface life and the lower self' (Ibid., 99). Perversely, this process of recognizing one's place within the wider canvas of the Universe and other beings relied initially upon going deeper into one's individuality through self-examination, reflection, realization and contemplation – things as we shall later see that Holmes saw as bound up in the role of the school and its need to promote self-expression and imagination. After all, the interrogation of the individual Self could surely only be best achieved by a system of education which had at its heart space for the child to interrogate their own interests and development – what could loosely be called child-centredness. So far then so Buddhist and there was nothing perhaps in these ideas concerning bodily denial that would have surprised many of those who were influenced by the same writings as impacted upon Holmes particularly in their stress upon denying the primacy of the ego and moving away from the bondage to Self.

However, Holmes' religious and moral philosophy was to ultimately advance this precept and, nearly 20 years after the publication of his initial discussion of the Buddha, he was to embroil these ideas with those drawn from Ancient India and the example of what he termed the 'mystics' who were the 'pioneers, the leaders of Mankind, in a great adventure, in the quest of God' (Holmes, 1928a, 13). It had been these men and their pantheist beliefs that Holmes saw as amongst the first to recognize and articulate the outwardly (for him at least) very simple truism of the One in the All – in short the essential unity of *all* things. This was a level of unity beyond that of the traditional understandings of Western pantheisms which were often limited to the totality of the current *material* universe rather than all aspects (both material and spiritual) located across both time and space. In order then for those in the contemporary world to be able to achieve the same state – in other words to realize that level of spiritual attainment and in the process defy their religious tradition and inheritance – meant undertaking the not inconsiderable task of breaking down the surface of reality by changing their fundamental perception of the external world and the Self within it.

By so doing the intention was for Man to move from viewing reality as a *state* to a *process*. The former (and dominant) way of thinking was framed very much by orthodox Western theology which placed the unknowable aspects of life – soul, spirit and the like – in a state and position of direct opposition to what could be known. Christianity (and for that matter most widespread monotheistic faiths) had it will be remembered worked on the assumption that, 'the existent is the real, and that there are no degrees in reality. What is not real is unreal, and what is unreal is pure illusion: it has no existence' (Holmes, 1927a, 33). Life was thus conceptualized as static and dualistic – hence the link with his earlier pronouncements on organized religion – and ran counter to what Holmes was now embracing as the need to view every aspect of being holistically and within the confines and providence of human experience.

Clearly, given its rejection of theological absolutes, Holmes' understanding necessitated more cryptic foundations of faith and so a very important dimension to his way of thinking was the concept of the *infinite* – another term which recurs within much of his writing. In calling upon Mankind to recognize both unity and Oneness Holmes believed that this allowed for a greater widening of the soul's possibilities – after all it was no longer limited to the easily knowable and obtainable – and so had the potential to access unlimited levels of untapped potential. The educational implications of this, as we shall see, were of course overwhelming but from a philosophical standpoint it meant that, 'The Absolute, the Transcendent, the Infinite are not ends to be achieved, but vanishing points of our adventurous thought and our insatiable desire' (Holmes, 1928a, 75). Such writing belied both a complex philosophy and one which seemed, to the casual reader at least, difficult to enact in an everyday setting.

However, in contrast to the 'fire and brimstone' dogmatism common to traditional religious and social ways of thinking which laid down conduct and behaviour in tablets of stone, Holmes was to proffer a clearly apprehendable alternative whose basis was, simply, *love*. This most modest of ideas was for him at the heart of Reality and, therefore, the ultimate aim in the search for the ideal. Perhaps explaining why so much of his earlier poetic preoccupations had been with this emotion, love was seen as significant in two ways. First, at the more intimate level, it was seen as embodying the personal transformation of an individual as two people in love added to one another thus affecting a form of particular growth and development which was the foundation of Holmes' philosophy. More significantly however, love (and here Holmes was talking more generally) was also seen as a way of breaking down the barrier between the self and the material world: 'In and through love the distinction between subject and object is effaced for a while, and knowledge...is superseded by a more intimate relation of what is known' (Holmes, 1921d, 100), By not seeing people as ends in themselves, and acting with the commensurate *disinterested devotion*, meant therefore ceasing to think of emotional responses in material terms thereby serving at a stroke to undercut the supposedly dominant way of viewing the world. In conjunction with the need for self-realization – stemming from a recognition and even a devotion to the ideals of the East (in particular the Upanishads) – meant therefore a scheme of life governed by a new set of ideals and principles and one which, as we shall see, informed much of the rest of Holmes' writings including those concerning education.

It is for this reason that Holmes' religious writing, far from condemning Man for his supposed weakness, is laced with sanguinity and continually offers the reader a sense of optimism by appealing to the innate benevolence, wisdom and good sense of human nature all of which has been stunted and prohibited from flourishing by a particular dualistic and – by extension – materialist framework. Whilst it is possible to disagree with much of what Holmes said – and as we shall see the idea that it painted to what amounted to a caricature of religion was a point to be later raised by his critics – his work nevertheless offers thought-provoking reconsiderations of Christianity (whilst not denying its essential spirit) which became both inflected and overlaid with tenets from a radically different spiritual source. In its own way this was both novel and original and, if nothing else, is a vital floor stone in seeking to understand the spiritual dimension at the heart of this most unique of thinkers.

Notes

1 The Shakespearian sonnet form is comprised of three quatrains of four lines each and culminates in a couplet. The rhyme scheme is abab cdcd efef gg.
2 For the only critical edition of Holmes poems see *The Selected Poems and Prose of Edmond Holmes* (2016), Farleigh Dickenson University Press edited by this author.
3 These were to come in the *Oxford Book of Mystical Verse*, published in 1917 and edited by Daniel Howard Sinclair Nicholson and Arthur Hugh Evelyn Lee.
4 Michael Sadler (1861–1943) was a British educationalist, historian and university administrator. In 1895, he was appointed to a government post as Director of the Office of Special Inquiries and Reports, resigning from the Board of Education in 1903. In 1917 he was appointed to oversee a commission investigating Indian education.
5 According to Joachim Liebschner, membership of the Froebel Society increased 'from 562 in 1899 to over 2600 members by 1910, and to an ever-extending programme of consultation with the Board of Education, Local Education Authorities, education societies, training colleges and schools' (Liebschner, 1991, 61).
6 Johann Friedrich Herbart (1776–1841) was a German philosopher and a man credited with founding pedagogy as an academic discipline. His work explored the connection between individual potentials (which Herbart believed were not innate) and the contribution these could make to future society. His work continued to enjoy popularity and excite debate in the United Kingdom even in the years leading up to the First World War.
7 This refers to the idea, deriving from an interpretation of the Book of Genesis Chapter 3, of Man 'falling' from a state of innocent obedience to God to one of guilty disobedience. For many Christians, this first sin committed by Adam was thus to be transferred to all of his descendants.
8 John Wesley (1703–1791) had founded Kingswood School in 1748 near Bristol ostensibly for the sons of itinerant Methodist ministers. It was noted for its adherence to strict discipline and ascetic conditions.
9 *Wandervogel* was the name adopted by a popular movement of German youth groups from 1896. The name can be translated as wandering bird which reflected their ethos of shaking off the restrictions of society and getting back to nature and a form of spiritual freedom.

10 Thomas William Rhys Davids (1843–1922) was a British scholar of the Pali language and founder of the Pali Text Society. Controversially he was to suggest that the Aryan races and the Buddhist peoples shared a common ethnicity.
11 Edward Carpenter (1844–1929) was an English poet, writer and social activist who was a close friend of Rabindranath Tagore.
12 Lewis Thompson (1909–1949) was a little known British poet and mystic who lived in India from 1932 until his untimely death from the effects of sunstroke.
13 The Upanishads, which number in total around 200, are a collection of spiritual texts which contain the central philosophical concepts of Hinduism, some of which are also shared by Buddhism and Jainism. Within these texts are statements which followers believe contain the truth as to the actual nature of reality (*Brahman*).

Chapter 4

What is and the key educational works

Introduction

As has been made explicit throughout the previous chapters, the publication of *What is and What Might Be* in 1911 marked a watershed moment in Holmes' life and career. It was the first of his major extended pieces of educational writing, the first publication of his retirement (although nearly all of it had been composed whilst still at Whitehall) and ultimately it was destined to be the one work upon which, for many educational historians and thinkers, his reputation has rested. As R.J.W. Selleck for example has rightly indicated such was the subversive and *exposé* nature of the book that it both 'startled, stirred controversy [and] stung the enemy into action' (Selleck, 1972, 47). So successfully did it do so that Holmes was forced three years later to publish *In Defence of What Might Be*, written as both a riposte to its critics and as a response to the controversy which the original text had generated. Such was both its combative tone and character (a polemical diatribe in the very best sense) it can truly be considered to have been one of the most radical texts ever written about education. Perhaps because of its uncompromising nature, reviews of the time were, in the main, unsympathetic to the points being raised. In part such negativity was to stem from Holmes' earlier involvement with the infamous Circular which precluded some from taking wholly seriously his credentials as a champion of liberal and child-centred education. As one anonymous commentator of the time put it, 'If Mr. Holmes were charged before an intelligent jury with being illogical, inconsistent, and muddle-minded in this particular, we fear the verdict would be "guilty"' (ED 24/101, *The Schoolmaster*, 17th June, 1911).

Notwithstanding such contemporary critical opprobrium (some of which bordered on the outright hostile and which focussed as much on the persona of the author as the contents of the book), equally important to its status as a *succès de scandale* was its impact upon those educators who were to be thinkers and torchbearers for these ideas later in the century. 'Like many other young teachers,' wrote J.H. Simpson,[1]

> I found this book both fascinating and challenging, if only because it was in such sharp contrast not only to the principles which had informed my own

school education, but also to the theory…and the practice of the elementary schools which I had visited as a young inspector.

(Simpson, 1954, 106)

Correspondingly, E. Sharwood Smith[2] was to fulsomely assert, 'I know that, when I read it in 1913 it was like the discovery of a whole new world' through acting 'like a fresh breeze blowing through a stale and jaded world' (Sharwood Smith, 1935, vi). The personal impact it rendered upon these particular men was therefore significant and was further replicated in the biographies of many others including Edward O'Neill, Caldwell Cook, A.S. Neill and Norman Macmunn all of whose names were to become famous later on and who in their diverse ways were to be transmitters of Holmes' subversive spirit.

Nonetheless, whilst the fame and notoriety of *What is* was undoubtedly well deserved such an impact has, perversely, done Holmes' historical reputation few favours. Indeed such was the long shadow it cast upon educational thinking down the years (whether this was always acknowledged or not) that it has tended to overshadow many of the other key books produced by its author. Holmes therefore has borne the unfortunate distinction – common to certain poets and novelists – of being remembered primarily for one *tour de force* work and little else. Whilst this is understandable given its peculiarly wide scope and savagely biting critique of schooling, the consequent ignorance of his other writings is unfortunate given how they were to build upon that earlier book and develop and reinforce certain of its fundamental ideas. Indeed, after that fashion, it is impossible to disassociate *What is* from, in particular, the two volumes which succeeded it – *The Tragedy of Education* (1913b) and *In Defence of What Might Be* (1914) – as well as a small number of supporting journal articles and pamphlets many of which sought to supplement and supplant the original thesis.

All of these works are crucially therefore inter-dependent and help to contribute both toward understanding Holmes' mature educational beliefs but also how these tied into his broader understanding of the condition of contemporary life. These were brought together in his contention that particular historical developments and currents of thought – many of which we have previously explored in relation to religion – had given rise to contemporary education systems in which the natural growth and development of the child was stunted, a process which in turn was then repeated cyclically and *in perpetuity* by those children as they became adults and educators. In thus seeking to appraise and understand Holmes' educational philosophy it is prescient to remember that one cannot and should not consider his texts in isolation from one another. Indeed, what is noticeable when tackling the corpus of works is how often the same concepts and terms – 'growth', 'nature', 'freedom' and 'soul' to name but a few – continually recur and themselves form the basis of both a coherent philosophy and grand world-view. Without wishing to labour the point, such is Holmes' longitudinal and all-encompassing perspective that he should not be considered as one whose interests lay 'merely' in education; for him this was but a lens – albeit an important one – through which he could explicate many deep-seated historical processes and changes. It is this overlaying of education with theological and philosophical thinking or, to view it another way, the incorporation of education into a much wider thesis exploring the condition of humankind that therefore makes Holmes a truly unique and innovative thinker.

What is equally conspicuous in the works of this period of his life, beyond their grand ambition, was their clear advancement from the earlier educational writings and initiatives alluded to and mentioned in the previous chapters. There Holmes had set about observing and identifying first-hand many of the (as he saw them) negative symptoms of the British educational landscape notably a lack of relevance and interest in the curriculum for the child, the continual presence of testing across the sector and narrow and prescriptive programmes of study. Likewise, in his two most important religious texts from that earlier time-frame – *The Creed of Christ* (1905b) and *The Creed of Buddha* (1908b) – Holmes had convincingly articulated the ways in which Christianity had departed from the original spirit of its founder and allowed its message to be distorted in the process. Because of this failing of the established Western religions, humanity could only find spiritual salvation, freedom and 'truth' by turning its gaze Eastward. As Holmes moribundly put it:

> It is to India then – the India of the Upanishads and of Buddha – that the West must go for the ideas, both central and subordinate, which shall rescue it from its embarrassments and restore it to a state of spiritual solvency.
> (Holmes, 1908b, 249)

These observations, whilst in themselves insightful and often drawing on his own direct experiences of both educational and religious behaviours, merely represented however the most visible and apparent manifestations of much more longstanding human problems, the wider implications of which it fell upon Holmes now to explore. It was in these more developed works that he then set out to combine and advance his twin interests of education and theology by explicating how gradual deviation from Christ's intended principles and the subsequent 'false assumptions of Western philosophy' (Holmes, 1911, vii) had resulted in a distorting of Man's fundamental nature with, as a consequence and of particular relevance here, serious ramifications for his *schooling* in which these flaws were to be ultimately cultivated and reproduced.

Holmes was of course writing at a time in which the impact of new ideas from within a range of cognate fields such as evolution in science, secularism in theology and child-centred psychology in education were beginning to make their mark. Furthermore, as Peter Watson (2001) has explained, the period leading up to the First World War was, more generally, one fertile with new ideas across the full range of the creative arts from the paintings of Kandinsky and Picasso to the music of Stravinsky and Schoenberg and the literature of Eliot, Woolf and Joyce. Much of this sought, often quite deliberately, to challenge established convention by breaking with traditionally accepted forms and through reconfiguring the possibilities offered within the perceived confines of language and sound. Holmes may therefore have been implicitly acknowledging this wider cultural context when referring to what he called the 'clamour for a new order' (Holmes, 1923d, 175) in human relations which had the potential to usher in an era he christened 'the Kingdom of Heaven' (Ibid., 189). Regardless however of his wider intentions, Holmes' own iconoclastic writing was tied to this spirit of insurrection and he espoused a desire to, in Ezra Pound's pithy phrase, 'make it new' by attempting to draw upon these emergent ideas to challenge conventional pedagogic assumptions and practices. We have already seen for instance his active and fulsome praise for the work being carried out in Montessori schools as well as his energetic participation in nascent theological debates and those pertaining to new forms of spirituality. All of this was indicative not merely of Holmes' originality but also the way in which he sought cross-fertilization of different intellectual disciplines.

Despite these broader advances, Holmes nonetheless remained, for now at least, generally *pessimistic* about the state of Western humanity and his important writing was heavily predicated upon the belief that particular religious ideas (those driven by assumptions of sinfulness) were – despite what various later chastened critics amongst the more liberal and enlightened theological fraternity contended – still deeply entrenched within the peoples of developed societies and continued correspondingly to inflect many wider aspects of their lives often to their considerable detriment. Having thus identified at a more general level these malaises it now fell upon Holmes to link them to what he perceived as the concurrent failings within the organization of national *schooling* and to crusade against these wrongs by attacking contemporary methods of teaching and instruction. In so doing, he was clearly attempting to provide a bridge between his earlier preoccupations with practical educational experiences and his idealistic religious philosophies.

This avowed desire to both critique and deconstruct the education system did not of course make Holmes immediately unique. Indeed, it had long been standard practice amongst those educators within the so-called progressive tradition to point to the defects inherent within pedagogic systems of their own time and even, on occasion, to similarly link these to corresponding failings within parallel social and political structures. Jean Jacques Rousseau had alluded to generally within the pages of *Emile* (1979) for example to the corrupting effects of what could loosely be called civilization on the upbringing of the young and, as Matthew Simpson (2006) amongst others has argued, that whole book has been seen by some as a broad satire of prevailing bourgeois mores and foibles. Similarly, nascent Marxists and social reformers such as Robert Owen of New Lanark had pointed to disparities in income and circumstance as being the root cause of social inequality and educational underachievement. Owen himself had even identified the importance of developing character and generating enjoyment in the classroom at the expense of rote learning and punishment – the latter of which being common enough practices at the time particularly within the Scottish Calvinist tradition of 'Original Sin' found within parts of Scotland.

However, although in his way part of this dissenting child-centred tradition, Holmes' writing proved itself to be exceptional in two ways. First he saw educational problems as intertwined with the declining condition of the human *spirit* as it became adversely influenced by both religious doctrine and adherence to a world seen materialistically and not idealistically. Second, he was to write about these problems with a detailed and learned understanding of theology and the wider tides of philosophy in a way that set him far apart from many others in his field. Even the equally voluminous A.S. Neill, whose ambition and educational vision were undoubtedly the equal of Holmes, lacked, at least in print, his level of scholarly erudition and reads as simplistic and homespun by comparison – not perhaps that Neill would have minded that. In the process though of his own scholarship, as shall hopefully become clear, Holmes sought to challenge many accepted notions and beliefs not merely those pertaining to teaching and pedagogy but also wider social assumptions concerning the nature of childhood and what it meant to be a child.

The origins of the educational malaise

At its heart then, the purpose of Holmes' mature educational writing was to attempt to delineate and give better articulation to the long-term origins of the maladies he had previously witnessed during his tenure as an Inspector. A declamatory passage at the start of *What is* provides both an initial flavour of the manifesto-like quality of the text as well as an authorial *mea culpa* signalling to his readership Holmes' feelings of guilt for having been blind for so long to the failings of the system in which he had been working:

> the *externalism* of the West, the prevalent tendency to pay undue regard to outward and visible "results" and to neglect what is inward and vital, is the source of most of the defects that vitiate Education in this country…[It] had many zealous agents, of whom I, alas! was one.
>
> (Holmes, 1911, v–vii, original italics)

This was not new ground for Holmes who had previously mentioned the idea of externalism in relation to established religious practices, seeing it as a consequence of ancient forms of worship dating back to the pre-Christian era in which the processes of legalism had conspired to codify the spirit and impacted upon many aspects of civilized life. However, it says much for the growing assurance in the power both of his convictions and the system of beliefs that underpinned them that Holmes now felt confident enough to state that he saw through the smokescreen which propagated this degradation of morality. After that fashion, in referring to the 'inspired teacher whose thoughts are all poems' (Holmes, 1908b, 95) who was able to 'purify and spiritualize the conception of a personal God' (Ibid.) rather than 'the average man [who] is quite sure to debase and externalize it' (Ibid.) it is tempting to view this less as the intended commentary on the Buddha but instead as the figure of Holmes himself who now felt able to take more of an active and vocal role in 'combating the generations of debasement to which religion had been subjected by the tendency of the "average man"' (McDonald, 2008, 167). Having therefore set himself against this paradigmatic way of thinking, Holmes was to now begin to explore *how* precisely this impacted upon, and translated to, schooling and the more micro aspects of human life.

In some ways the approach advocated by Holmes can be thought of as comparable to classic Marxist theory in which economic relations (the broad 'base') have a bearing upon all other areas of human relations (the wider 'superstructure') for example family, religion, schooling and the like. In Holmes' case however this model was based not around the inequality of economic relations but, instead, via a *spiritual* poverty which had served to lower the condition of humanity through encouraging dis-unified, materialist and therefore debased and amoral forms of thinking and perceptions of the world. Nor was this connection to the radical left one about which Holmes was unaware; indeed, the materialist determinism inherent within traditional interpretations of Marxism was in fact criticised brilliantly in his 1912 paper to the Fabian Society in which he argued that the creeds and diktats of socialism and the nationalized socialist state were merely replacing one system of control by another and would not lead to spiritual salvation until Man changed his more fundamental philosophical outlook on life. By so doing, Holmes was implicitly acknowledging both a sympathy for the communality inherent within the diktats of the left – 'What [interests and] attracts me about Socialism is its instinctive recoil from separatism and its unswerving trend towards unity' (Holmes, 1923a, 34) – but also more importantly the ways in which his thinking diverged from these older models in particular their aversion to any religious aspects in the widest sense of that term.

This legalism and the externalizing of actions which Holmes saw as such a dominating feature of society was to have one significant consequence – that Man came to see himself as only capable of being saved through correct and appropriate dutiful and visible conduct. Thus the doctrine of 'salvation through obedience' came not only to be fostered but also correspondingly reinforced through human agency and was to be an implicit and unthinking way of life for many. For Holmes this was embodied primarily in the codes and declamations of the law-makers and (in a more ancient context) of the Pharisees whose 'fearless logic and [a] fixed tenacity of purpose' (Holmes, 1911, 19) had led to Man's actions being judged purely by his outward observable forms and modes of behaviour. It was after all only through these that an individual's moral worthiness and thus hopes for salvation could be ascertained, considered and ultimately judged. Although rooted in ancient theology, this was a more important point for education than may first appear for two central reasons; on the one hand the system of risk and reward appealed, according to Holmes, to Man's basest and most primitive instincts which was little different to, 'the lash of the whip that punishes the lagging race-horse, or the lump of sugar that rewards his exertions' (Ibid., 23). Human activity and sense was thus reduced to more atavistic forms of motivation and feeling which were antithetical to the more refined and higher planes of spirituality and soul. Given that there were still high levels of apparently unjust corporal punishment in schools at the time of writing, this was, as Jacob Middleton (2005 and 2008) has indicated, a prescient issue and one which would have been evident to Holmes through his school inspections and knowledge of the sector.

Second, the need to have to account for, and be judged by, outward action (the aforementioned externalism) was set firmly at odds against what Holmes considered to be higher level *inner* growth which, by its very definition, stood in contrast to that which was visibly measurable and obviously apparent. If therefore it could be argued that inner growth was of a natural type, externalism was surely wholly adversative to the laws of nature and, in the organic discourse characteristic of his beloved earlier Romantics, Holmes used science to support his case:

> nowhere in the whole range of physical nature do we find an organism being built up from without, instead of from within... An outsider can indeed supply the building materials that are needed... But Nature forbids him to play the part of the mason or the bricklayer; and he must therefore leave it to the organism itself to build up the fabric of its being.
>
> (Holmes, 1913b, 43)

To further paraphrase one of his own examples, the new-born infant could thus be compared to an acorn in which is contained the potential for growth into a fully fledged tree and which, following the laws of nature, 'will struggle unceasingly to evolve itself' (Holmes, 1911, 241). Such an idea had its origins both in Darwinian science but also the Germanic Idealists – Kant, Fichte, Schelling *et al.* – as well as their greatest disciple Friedrich Froebel whose general contention had been that at birth Man was everything he was destined to be via a series of latent potentials which were to be nurtured, like a plant, by both the school (the greenhouse) and its teachers (the gardeners). If however, some form of external imposition was allowed to dominate the life, it would serve to both distort and quell the inward impulses toward growth and halt development. Indeed, under the pretext of Original Sin, this suppression was often actively to be encouraged for if the child's nature was held to be innately sinful it would be unhelpful, dangerous and illogical to encourage its independent development.

Following from that premise, Holmes was therefore to argue that mainstream education was both repressive and, through this repression, unnatural in that it served to suppress ordinary natural impulses toward growth including, in particular, those childhood instincts of creativity and self-expression. More widely, forms of discipline meted out in schools were seen to break the will of the child and, by so doing, preclude his escaping from the Self. Through his explorations of the philosophies of the East, Holmes had come to regard this letting go of Self as intrinsic to the process of out-growth and a precursor to genuine freedom and, by focusing solely on external realities and measures, the outcome of schooling (inadvertent or otherwise) was to stunt the child as it reached maturity: 'The reality of life is to be measured, not by outward results, but by inward intensity' (Holmes, 1914, 283).

Underpinned therefore by a series of beliefs that limited children's behaviour and knowledge to simplified dichotomous choices (often obedience or disobedience to the will of the teacher or else as having right or wrong answers to set questions) made education akin to the static world Holmes believed was promulgated by supernaturalism and which therefore 'rob[bed] the [child] of its vital elasticity, and so either weakens it into brittleness or stiffens it into sullen obstinacy' (Ibid., 303). In either case, the child ended up as both broken in spirit and arrested in inner growth through being forced to be rigidly compliant or else given to resent and reject his schooling.

Although ultimately these processes of externalism and obedience found obvious embodiment within the punitive and corrective measures enacted in schools, Holmes' ingenuity lay therefore in first locating them within large-scale and historical moral frameworks which established religion had done much to spread over the centuries. Indeed, the first chapter of *What is* was devoted to explaining in quite brilliant fashion this specific connection with an intention perhaps to alert an unaware *educational* readership (who would most likely not have read his religious tracts) to his general thesis. Within this section, Holmes made it palpably clear that the desire to exalt words, texts and the need for correct external action over and above encouraging the growth of an independent inner spirit had caused Man to become both intellectually docile and inactive. This was a flaw found not only in the more ritualistic and longstanding elements of Catholicism but also in the recent individualistic strands of Protestantism in which Man's distrust of his own higher nature meant he still placed undue faith in obedience to other supernaturally inspired external sources – in this case the Bible and specifically the Gospels of the New Testament. Cognisant too of the rise of secularism, Holmes also understood that *lack* of faith in God also served as detrimental to the spirit. Indeed, hostility and apathy to organized religion and increasing disavowal of established doctrine had merely created instead a new form of spiritual anomie: 'the absence of a central aim in human life has never been so complete as it is now. Most men are content to drift through life...neither knowing nor caring to know why they are alive' (Holmes, 1911, 33).

This influence had proven itself to be particularly nefarious in ensuring that humanity continued to think in terms of artificial dualisms with populated much religious (and educational) rhetoric – supernatural *or* nature, head *or* heart, immortality *or* damnation and so on. The upshot of this had been that Man failed to see the essential unity of all aspects of his existence including the (for Holmes) self-evident truism that as there existed easily apprehensible outward natures so too was there commensurate inward nature both of which constituted a unified Whole. This form of binary thinking was one roundly condemned by Holmes and, as Peter Gordon and John White (1979) were to faintly suggest, was later surreptitiously echoed in the work of John Dewey in particular through his seminal tract *Experience and Education* (1938) from which derived the important concept of 'Either–Or' which was an attempt to explain why educational (and human) thinking had too long been driven by a refusal to recognize 'no intermediate possibilities'

(Dewey, 1938, 1) in its search for absolutes. Although Dewey's immediate concern was the cleavage between progressive/ vocational and traditional/ academic education and the detriment that carried for the emergent American nation which had urgent need of frontier physical skills, it was nonetheless marked with a whiff of that earlier Holmesian spirit:

> The history of educational theory is marked by opposition between the idea that education is development from within and that it is formation from without; that it is based upon natural endowments and that education is a process of overcoming natural inclination and substituting in its place habits acquired under external pressure.
>
> (Ibid.)

Such idealist expression – in particular the implication that external imposition was secondary to allowing for the natural development of the child – thereby served to illustrate that there existed important similarities between both Holmes and the incomparably influential educator Dewey. Whilst Gordon and White were of course right to stress that the latter in one sense reflected the 'mirror-image' (Gordon and White, 1979, 148) of Holmes in emphasizing community over religion when thinking about the process of self-realization, there are nonetheless overlaps in the way that for both 'philosophy... remained closely tied to educational ends' (Ibid.) and equally as they attached great faith in the possibility of the limitless mind.

One must of course be wary about drawing too direct a comparison; after all Dewey's was a pragmatic philosophy perfectly attenuated to the American middle ground consensus which served to define its politics, psyche and social outlook meaning it thereby lacked something of the Englishman's otherworldliness and emphasis upon spirituality and soul. The intellectual context was also very different and it would be churlish to compare, for example, the meaning behind a term such as 'freedom' which for both men held widely differing connotations, spiritual and political. Nonetheless, to begin to think in such comparative ways is ultimately extremely useful as it brings sharply into focus the wide and osmotic appeal Holmes' ideas were to have even when (as here) there was no obvious personal connection between the two men. It is also relevant when one considers how education remained for both a *practical* activity and each was to draw upon elements of actual practice as the basis for their theorizing. As an example of this, Dewey's attempts at fostering unity in his Laboratory School in Chicago were to be enacted by structuring school lessons around overarching tasks and projects which could incorporate a range of different subject disciplines. Likewise, Holmes was to both admire and advocate for systems of education which used such creative arts as drama to teach more seemingly academic disciplines such as History and Geography. In both cases subjects traditionally seen within schools as separate and discrete were to be taught in an integrated fashion which served to break down the philosophical and educational boundaries between them.

By so doing it was hoped, at a tangible level, that such forms of learning would furnish pupils with a wider and more three dimensional knowledge of the world and one which had grown from their own inner impulses to delight rather than as being imposed upon them. Teachers and adults could and should guide but they must never coerce. At a deeper level it would also reinforce to children the importance of the concept of *unity* which, for Holmes at least, was a way of combating the inherent dualism fostered by religion and the nefarious stunting of growth which had arisen from it. If, as he believed, the worlds of Man and Spirit were ultimately inseparable so then they had to be somehow equally well connected in the classroom. Holmes' supposition that 'the push of Nature's forces in the inner life of the young child is ever tending to take him out of himself in the direction of a triune goal which I may surely be allowed to call *Divine*' (Holmes, 1911, 201–202) meant that offering encouragement to that inner life became the main purpose behind education. As such inward growth relied on innate desires and instincts to learn and be dramatic, communicative and creative (the processes of which were not discipline-specific) so this had serious implications for the type of schooling that was offered to the child and one quite at odds to that experienced by the majority. It should in that light be evident the way in which Holmes' various intellectual interests were coalescing and ramifying together to offer a particularly provocative critique of the education system and one which found its problems rooted within prevailing religious and philosophical dogma.

Mechanical obedience in schools

Having thereby clarified where the problems inherent within education found their root, Holmes was now in a position to begin to explain in more detail *how* precisely they were manifest within the contemporary landscape. It was this substantive analysis which formed the main critique of *What is* but which also drove much of his other pedagogic writing of this time whose aim was to expose so many of the bad practices he had found in English schools. These fundamental 'defects' in the human condition referred to above were thus themselves embodied through the concept of *mechanical obedience*, a central and recurring term Holmes used to express the exhibited patterns of behaviour within elementary and (particularly) secondary schools which consisted, as he had earlier found, of subservience and docility enacted as responses to particular didactic ways of teaching and schooling. Through carrying out this philosophic dissection, Holmes was thereby able to offer a fuller and more rounded explanation for the sorts of activity he had witnessed during his inspections, in the process repudiating many simplistic contemporary views which saw boredom, truancy, delinquency and underachievement as being the fault of the individual and attributable simply to defects of character.

Whilst much of this represented the logical consequence of an overarching system of theology, equally, as Holmes acknowledged, such views were also explicable through a general ignorance amongst policy-makers and teachers of new scientific ideas and forms of democratic experiment which were currently inspiring an incumbent and burgeoning form of child-centredness: 'For thousands of years education has been dogmatic, dictatorial, disciplinary…repressive, devitalizing. For this there have been many reasons. Patriarchal government…[and] *ignorance of biology and psychology*…are among the influences which have made education what it is today' (Holmes, 1927a, 125, italics added). Even for instance within this apparent new era there remained prevalent still the idea amongst teachers that,

> They think of him [the child] as a unit in a class of twenty or thirty (or more) children, who are all doing the same work at the same time and are all supposed to be in the same stage of mental development.
>
> (Holmes, 1927a, 128)

Not for them what today would be called differentiated learning or encouraging the development of individual interest. Although mostly attributable to a simple lack of psychological knowledge that only came later in the century via Piaget, Bruner and others, the Victorian and early Edwardian view of such matters was embodied in works like that of the Reverend Samuel Smiles' *Self-Help* (1859) whose rags to riches tales and implied rampant individualism (the belief that all one needed to succeed was perseverance and hard work) form the most obvious contrast to the more unifying writing of Holmes. Holmes would undoubtedly have seen such behaviours as failing to recognize any notion of community least of all the very widest which he came to christen the Kingdom of the Ideal which could only be entered through following the path of self-realization.

Much then as later sociologists such as Bowles and Gintis (1976) and Paul Willis (1977) would put 'meat on the Marxist bone' by demonstrating very tangibly how schooling served the ends of a capitalist *economic* base through reproducing its power structures and models of governance, so Holmes was to illustrate how they were comparably entwined with, and inseparable from, *theological* and *philosophical* developments. Whilst this did not entail children being prepared for employment in the labour market through schools replicating class structures or the factory floor (what became known as the 'correspondence principle') or else being oppressed through imbalanced distribution of knowledge (as in the work of Michael Apple), there was still an innate connection between the organization and activity of the school and the broader configuration of Man and society – albeit embodying a spiritual poverty rather than an economic one.

With a prevailing belief in the doctrine of the Fall and Man's inherent sinfulness (which as discussed had led to the path of obedience for his own higher nature was not to be trusted), it followed quite logically that children too were destined to be scrutinized under the same sets of beliefs and assumptions. If anything these were magnified as, by virtue of their age, they were seen as closer to the roots of Original Sin and thereby more in need of punitive forms of discipline and education so as to 'save' them from straying from established paths. This was a perverse inversion of the traditional Romantic idea which had seen children as having greater purity precisely *because* of their proximity to God whose divinity was seen as being at the heart of birth and creation. This more negative of associations was famously adumbrated by the poet Samuel Butler in his epic *Hudibras* (1662) in which he had insisted on the necessity of corporal punishment for children if they were to flourish both educationally and spiritually: 'Love is a boy by poets stil'd;/ Then spare the rod and spoil the child' (Butler, 2005, 126). Although Butler's intention here had been to lampoon and satirize, it was a view that, through the advocacy of those such as John Wesley – whose adherence to particular forms of dogmatism has already mentioned, – had long formed part of the prevailing view of childhood. The historian Lawrence Stone (1977) further supports this by suggesting that until the modern period this Wesleyan understanding was one of four that made up the nexus of thought surrounding the child. These others also included the Lockean notion of the mind as a *tabula rasa* as well as the belief that character was determined at birth. In most cases then, there seemed to be a consensus of opinion against the broad understanding that children could grow and develop from inner impulses as those such as Holmes contended.

All of which meant that, in Holmes' neat phrase, 'In the West men have loyally striven to reproduce towards their children the supposed attitude of their God of Wrath towards themselves' (Holmes, 1911, 45). After all, if Man was considered sinful and could only achieve his salvation through appropriate forms of external behaviour and action was it not therefore logical that children should be subject to the same constraints? Under this aspect, the teacher or adult assumed, by virtue of their use of punishment and mantle of authority, the role of this God by encouraging 'Blind, passive, literal, unintelligent obedience' (Ibid., 50) and by correspondingly seeking to make measurable or *externalize* the child's actions. Such actions, like those of adults, were bound by the system of reward and punishment. One of the consequences of this was that the child was indoctrinated to believe both in their own criminality and to regard as sinful any action which deviated from the teacher's carefully laid-down instructions.

Unsurprising then said Holmes that children who were expected to conform to artificial patterns of behaviour and who were denied the use of their natural instincts, impulses and energies either disobeyed in schools or else channeled their vitalities into other uses. Misbehaviour was a result of confining the child to tasks which did not appeal to their innate interests and not allowing them to dissipate their abundant natural energies rather than by any innate faults of character or their lowly social position. This was illustrated best for Holmes in the striking work being undertaken by Homer Lane in his Little Commonwealth[3] in which the earlier tendency of his supposedly 'delinquent' boys to join gangs and be anti-social was a result of their natural high spirits being repressed by a school regimen that demanded silent and (in Michael Foucault's terms) docile bodies rather than any pre-existing nefarious tendencies. For Holmes, as indeed for A.S. Neill, Lane's work demonstrated that such energies when nurtured properly could demonstrate how 'the spirit of comradeship and loyalty which kept him [the child] in the paths of crime was capable, under favourable conditions, of becoming the chief instrument of his regeneration' (Holmes, 1914, 39).

Much of Holmes' treatise was thereby preoccupied with both revealing and debunking this process of externalism. By so doing, he was giving explicit support to the notion that the child possessed an innate and limitless desire to both grow and learn which was often exhibited as social and sociable tendencies at odds with the expectations of authority. Whilst this was most readily apparent in terms of drill and discipline, more subtly, as Ian Grosvenor and Catherine Burke (2008) have argued in their discussion of the physical space, these were enshrined in the layout, design and overall configuration of the school. This was radical stuff and was a direct descendent of the earlier ideas of Friedrich Froebel. Although Holmes was occasionally critical of what he saw as the Froebelians' undue emphasis upon the role of the teacher, by articulating a belief that the purpose of education was to provide an environment and setting in which the child could fulfil his potential for unbounded and theoretically infinite 'soul-growth' at the expense of merely fulfilling pre-determined patterns of behaviour, he was very much echoing many of the key ideas of his German predecessor. In particular, Froebel's devotion to an 'eternal law' (Froebel, 1898, 1) embodied the earlier Idealist preoccupation with the concept of *Naturphilosophie* (Philosophy of Nature), an all-encompassing term designed to capture the ways in which the constant re-configurations of opposites in nature were attributable to one underlying divine force. Although the context for this was initially much broader, Froebel appropriated it to explain the ways in which schools should teach, 'the relationships which exist in the material world and which link that world and himself [the child] to the ground of all being' (Froebel, quoted in Lilley, 1967, 137). The intimate relationship of Man to nature and the implied sense of the infinite capacity of Man's soul to grow outwardly was a key concept shared by both Froebel and Holmes; indeed the latter freely admitted this by strongly affirming that he was a 'Neo-Froebelian' (Holmes, 1914, 52). In that regard he was hardly alone; as Joachim Liebschner (1991) and Kevin Brehony (2001) have shown, these were ideas which were gaining currency amongst a small yet devoted community in Britain at the time and we have identified how these were, in addition, intersecting with wider developments for example those at the Board of Education.

Although then Holmes was promulgating ideas which had a degree of overlap with those of these burgeoning progressive groups and organizations that did not in any way mean that the power of his damning analysis of Western, and particularly British, education was diluted. For a start, the Froebelian impulse was directed towards the early years with many of the key female pioneers such as Emily Shirreff[4] and Bertha Ronge[5] investing their efforts and attention in the kindergartens of the very young. By contrast, Holmes' anger, of which he freely admitted, was directed more upon the notion of education at the conceptual level but in particular on the *secondary* sector. Indeed, he was to make the point that whilst elementary schools had many prevailing faults 'an excessive regard for outward and visible results [was] not one of them' (Holmes, 1914, 87n). Much of this could be put down to Holmes himself through his pioneering work as Chief Inspector and his reluctance to endorse systems of prescription and surveillance.

As R.J.W. Selleck has further pointed out, infant schools themselves after 1890 were in a 'state of tension' (Selleck, 1972, 23) between the competing demands of not merely the 'progressives' and the 'traditionalists' but also in regards to splits amongst those who saw themselves in opposition to the *status quo*. Elementary education was thus a battlefield in which many progressive factions, including but not limited to, the Froebelians and supporters of Holmes were planting their flags.

At the time of the publication of *What is* however in 1911 these ideas had not yet moved to the older demographic with the progressive schools movement for example still very much in its infancy. W.A.C. Stewart (1972) has estimated that by 1918 there were still only 15 such schools (and many of these were fee-paying) so what impact these ideas had were to only be felt in the succeeding decades after the First World War – a theme that will be addressed in the following chapter. Secondary schooling thus remained at this stage bound to the patterns adumbrated by Holmes with the most clear and obvious manifestation of externalism exhibited via the system of *examinations* and *testing* which were at the very heart of the Western education system particularly when it came to attaining the much-vaunted scholarships and prizes. Whilst the arguments around the validity and equity of testing are today well-established and were becoming so in the early twentieth century through attempts to delineate a more meritocratic system, in Holmes' schema it was not solely their accuracy or fairness that was in question but more their intrinsic *moral* worth. Any curriculum (and Holmes was insistent on speaking generally) which relied heavily on a form of testing and recall was bound to merely encourage and reward particular forms of behaviour and obedience over others, in this case being able to replicate the sorts and types of answers demanded by a particular syllabus and its examiners. Education thus became reduced to a form of what later generations of scholars would term *performativity* in which teachers, pupils and those responsible for testing organized themselves in a pre-meditated and calculative arrangement in what amounted to little more than a strategic instrumental game:

> the teacher will make a practice of studying the questions and putting them [the pupils] up to whatever knacks, tricks, and dodges will enable them to show to advantage on the examination day. In his desire to outwit the teacher, the examiner will turn and double like a hare who is pursued by a greyhound. But the teacher will turn and double with equal agility, and will never allow himself to be outdistanced by his quarry.
>
> (Holmes, 1911, 63)

There is a perverse irony here in that the most 'successful' teachers were considered as those who were to best negate the natural development of their pupils and, instead, relinquish their freedom and autonomy in order to ensure that they fulfilled the wider expectations of the examiners and, more generally, the state!

Clearly then there were pedagogical problems surrounding a system buttressed by regular testing and examination notably through the ways in which the curriculum became narrowed and the purpose of schooling simply became preparation for various forms of assessment: 'His [the teacher's] business is to drill the child into the mechanical production of quasi-material results' (Ibid., 51). Whilst in mitigation those tests administered by the Inspectorate which determined at least initially a school's financial position and academic status (the driving force behind the earlier 'payment by results') had by the time of publication largely disappeared, Holmes was quick to point to the myriad of other forms of testing which still permeated the society of his time:

> The appointments in the Home, Colonial, and Indian Civil Services, the promotions in the Army and Navy, the fellowships and scholarships at the Universities, the scholarships at the Public Schools, the medals, books, and other prizes that are offered to school-children, are all awarded to those who have distinguished themselves in the corresponding examinations, no other qualification than that of ability to shine in an examination being looked for in the competitors.
>
> (Ibid., 73–74)

Although these are common enough criticisms today both in terms of the continuing existence of academic-centred league tables and the 'academy' system which encourages struggle through selection, Holmes proved himself far-sighted in being amongst the first to offer an intellectual argument against regular and repeated forms of testing within the context of a system driven by competition. For every child who succeeded in passing the test, there would be many who would not and so competition served to alienate children who were deemed from a young age to have failed. As he put it, 'while the prize system breeds ungrounded and therefore dangerous self-esteem in the child whom it labels as bright, it breeds ungrounded but not the less fatal self-distrust in the child whom it labels as dull' (Ibid., 76). Even those successful children who had done well within the system were not guaranteed to have done so through love of the subject but merely via seeing the knowledge gained as an instrument for personal external advancement – better money, prospects, recognition and so on – and therefore better able to deploy it in in the appropriate context. This was therefore a knowledge that was both superficially acquired and easily forgotten afterwards and so went against any hope of developing what later became known as 'life-long learners' with an attitude to their study driven by the maxim of knowledge for its own sake. If schooling could therefore do this to those who had been successful 'what may it be expected to do to the child whose school education comes to an end when he is only thirteen or fourteen years old' (Ibid., 77)?

In posing this and other similar questions, Holmes was therefore calling into doubt the fundamental ethos which then underpinned as he saw it much of the secondary sector of schooling. Driven by an innate distrust of both the child and a need to quantify or *externalize* aspects of life meant that education was seen as echoing those features of religion which codified and monitored behaviour and set it on an equally legal footing. Whilst in today's more secular age this religious dimension to Holmes' writing may appear as anachronistic, given the recent proliferation in the sheer number of examinations and tests (even more so than in Holmes' day) there is much to be said for his general critique especially as it prefigures many subsequent attacks on this tendency towards universal testing. Testing of this type therefore led to a propensity to privilege certain kinds of conduct and learning over others – to 'idealize the average' (Holmes, 1911, 106) – and not allow children's creativity to shine or their deeper understanding to come through. Mechanical obedience – on the parts of teachers too who were in bondage to the requirements of the curriculum and therefore pressured to seek certain responses from their pupils – thereby became an inevitable byproduct of this system and one which reflected wider assumptions over the need to control and render invisible the inward.

Wider school culture

Although then testing was clearly a fundamental part of the school calendar, externalism of the type outlined above was not solely confined to the examination hall and, drawing on his experiences as an Inspector, Holmes was to offer a number of vivid sketches as to how it percolated more directly to wider aspects of educational culture through lessons, assemblies, playtimes and so on. Whilst Holmes' earlier writings had observed particular patterns of behaviour in education, in the context of his more fully rounded philosophy they took on a whole new troubling level of meaning with childhood docility seen as not merely representing a straightforward juvenile passivity but instead as embodying the broader state of being of Mankind in which the external knowable materialist world was kept divorced from the inner world of the spirit.

In the third chapter of *What is* subtitled 'A Familiar Type of School' Holmes guides the reader through the various subjects of the school curriculum and indicates how, in more detail, their practices reflected some of these more fundamental ideas. In keeping with his belief both in the mechanical nature of education and the lack of trust afforded to the pupil/ child, a common theme running through his thinking was the recognition that what constituted the bulk of education was simple didactic transmission of knowledge by a teacher to a passive audience of pupils with few attempts to engage them in critical thinking or a more rounded understanding of the subject matter. History represented a good case in point: 'Information as to the dates and names of the English kings, and other historical facts, is easily converted into knowledge of those facts, but it is not easily converted into knowledge of English history' (Holmes, 1911, 90). The same was true both in mathematics in which Holmes observed children following the teacher's instructions in completing simple calculations (imitative in its mechanism of earlier legal frameworks) and, as well, reading and writing in which children often read aloud by rote to the group rather than being encouraged to follow their own interests through independent study. The distinction between 'knowledge' and 'information' was clearly palpable and Holmes was critical of the way in which Western education assumed that, 'to impart information is therefore to generate knowledge, [and] that to give back information is therefore proof of the possession of knowledge' (Ibid., 56). Linking back to his earlier argument around legalistic control, Holmes rationalized this state of affairs by arguing that, unlike information which tended to exist un-problematically on the surface of the brain ready to be regurgitated when necessary, knowledge sinks deep into the child's soul and was therefore to be distrusted as it had the potential to 'escape from the teacher's control' (Holmes, 1913b, 58). Such was to be the fate Holmes argued of any educational activity which could not be quantified or given external measurement. This was most applicable to subjects such as music, art and drama (the so-called creative disciplines) whose end-products were inherently subjective and incapable of being judged by adherence to external objective criteria. Whilst the same point could equally be made in relation to extended, discursive essays traditionally demanded within the liberal arts, Holmes saw this tendency towards externalism as explaining why such subjects were increasingly being oriented more towards simplistic factual rather than perceptual knowledge and against developing forms of critical thinking.

At the centre of this school culture – and the transmitters of these dogmas – lay the activities of the *teachers* who Holmes believed had failed as a *bodypolitik* to take advantage of the potential offered by the earlier move away from payment by results. In part this was seen as an accident of age as 'many teachers who were brought up under the old *regime* have been unable to emancipate themselves from its influence' (Holmes, 1911, 116). Here, Holmes was backed up by statistics with a considerable number of teachers in the profession at the time of writing having been recruited and trained under an older ideology and whose older quasi-Victorian assumptions regarding the character of the child undoubtedly conspired therefore to bedevil the profession. More generally however teachers were loath, or perhaps simply unable, to challenge what Holmes regarded as the prevailing system of educational beliefs stemming from a lack of trust and faith in the ability of the growing infant. As he conceded:

> the one end and aim of the teacher is to do everything for the child; to feed him…to hold him by the hand…to keep him under close and constant supervision; to tell him in precise detail what he is to think, to feel, to say, to wish, to do.
>
> (Holmes 1911, 4–5)

Whilst such a statement echoes many of the situations Holmes had undoubtedly come across during his earlier time in schools, it was only now that he began to link such observations to the wider condition of Mankind. Blaming governments and what Holmes referred to as 'My Lords' (the Board of Education) worked up to a point but that did not in the final analysis go far enough. Indeed such was the hold of this 'wide-spread and deep-seated tendency' (Ibid., 9) toward externalism and the need to measure inward worth by external standards that even those teachers paying lip-service to the idea of education as equating with pupil growth instinctively found themselves acting counter to that tendency chained as they were to a prevailing *zeitgeist*. It was such frustrations that had perhaps led to the damning conclusions reached in the Holmes-Morant Circular. Nor once more was this a tendency solely to be associated with Holmes' own time; there is a parallel too with contemporary developments in which, contrary perhaps to any narratives of practitioner resistance, competition, standards, choice and market pressures has meant teachers focussing increasingly upon meeting management targets and less upon individuals' personal development and broader levels of understanding. Educational 'success' – as it was for Holmes – is often a metaphor simply for improved examination results.

It was easy then to see why Holmes desired all children to engage more in critical thinking and aesthetic appreciation which, as *sui generis* concepts, afforded them the opportunity not merely to develop personally as idealistic thinkers (such creative practices tending to reject a simple material objective standard of reality) but also as it allowed them in the process to challenge accepted dogmas and fixed points of view even as they emanated from those in taken-for-granted positions of authority. This again represents an example of a particularly prescient and prophetic observation on his part and one which has been at the centre ever since of curricula debates whenever the question over testing and knowledge arises. The extent to which examinations and testing should demand simple recall or, instead, ways in which that substantive knowledge can be applied in a range of varying contexts is one of the perennial issues in the arena of test design and in Holmes' case it represented a particularly direct intervention into the regime of examinations which then pervaded many areas of life. These included but were not limited to entry into secondary schools, the Oxbridge Colleges, other Universities, the Great Public Schools and some public service professions. More recently, with the forces of marketization and credentialization shaping the educational agenda, it goes without saying that it is possible to draw a link between Holmes' conception of *mechanical obedience* and the numerous interventions from both academics (such as Stephen J. Ball), media commentators and creative thinkers (Michael Rosen often writing in *The Guardian* newspaper) who have set themselves against this more contemporary agenda.

Whilst such activities thereby represented failings on the parts of the schools to equip children *intellectually* with deep learning so more seriously did particular patterns of action neglect pupil's *spiritual* development. In using theology as an obvious example Holmes both scoffed at the idea of holding an examination in a fundamentally spiritual subject ('scarcely less ridiculous than the idea of holding a formal examination in unselfishness or brotherly love' (Holmes, 1911, 93)) whilst also deriding the fact that by studying the Scriptures for an instrumental purpose as was then common, children risked losing all interest in the beauty and significance of the material under scrutiny. With characteristic cynicism, Holmes argued that such religious teaching was serving therefore to secularize the nation! Nor was this a 'positive' form of secularism free of religious divide and doctrine; instead it was serving to rip the heart out of any of Holmes' ideas concerning inward spiritual growth and the need to move away from the Self, tenets which lay at the heart of his Eastern-inflected interpretation of Christianity.

Taking the spiritual line of argument further still, Holmes was concerned that the competition which was underpinning the ethos of testing led to children developing as both *egoists* and *sensualists,* in other words thinking purely of themselves and their own performance at the expense of the wider community. Classmates came to be seen (often perhaps unwittingly) as competitors rather than comrades and whilst this did not represent any nod on Holmes' part toward fraternal socialism the divisions fostered promoted the primacy of the individual at the expense of the spiritual collective. This represented, for Holmes, a cultivation of lower order pleasures – 'fleshly lust, in its various forms' (Holmes, 1927a, 113) – at the expense of the higher. In his scheme of life, Holmes discouraged the cultivation of lower pleasures as they prohibited full spiritual growth driven as they were by primitive needs of the ego and lacking any consideration beyond the self and the outward material world. Lust in this context was not merely a term signifying the sexual impulse (although it could become so in later adult life) but more as it pertained to a way of seeing the world that was restricted to the limitations afforded by one's physical body and not the mental/spiritual side which was more readily associated with idealism and higher level thought. Schools therefore served as a microcosm of society which

> thinks to magnify self by depreciating others; which values material possessions for the rank and distinction which they confer…which seeks to drive deep and perpetrate invidious social distinctions…which is entirely unscrupulous in its choice of means to its desired end [and] which builds fortune on human misery.
>
> (Ibid., 113–114)

Whilst there is, characteristically, something of the dramatic about this statement it nonetheless reinforces the fundamental importance of education and the school as a setting in which many of these values became transmitted. In particular, Holmes was critical of what could colloquially be called the cult of individualism, an aspect of school culture which regarded the individual as an end unto themselves which thereby encouraged the soul to be in bondage to that Self. Similar in many ways to Immanuel Kant's Kingdom of Ends[6] this idea was to form the basis for Holmes' later writings on politics and morality, although in this context it was to be equally well applied to schools where these wider failings were seen as having their origins. Giving primacy to the importance of the childhood phase Holmes was to summarize, 'The time for emancipation from self to be begun comes earlier to children than we, their elders, are apt to imagine…young children…grow rapidly from their earliest days on all the planes of their being' (Holmes, 1927a, 124). Much as today psychological research has taught us of the importance of the 'sensitive period' of the early years for the learning of language, expression and developing corresponding cognitive motor skills so Holmes saw this time as equally important in nurturing human *spiritual* growth on the path towards self-realization. Clearly there was a conflict brewing between Holmes' self-realization and the instrumental needs of mainstream education.

Very much bound to this, another aspect of school culture that was seen to be discernibly lacking from the establishments Holmes observed were any efforts to promote genuine *creativity* or *self-expression* on the parts of pupils. Whilst this has (once again!) been a familiar refrain since – witness for example the recent criticisms of the Coalition and Conservative Government's abandonment of initiatives such as Creative Partnerships[7] – the originality of Holmes' critique stemmed not merely from it being one of the first to attack government policy in this way but also as it developed from his own suppositions regarding human nature which was, under the prevailing morality which demanded obedience, not to be trusted to its own devices. In seeking to explain for example why there was a neglect of composition (both musical and literary) in schools, Holmes argued that it was because such activity was both hard to measure (and thereby incapable of being externalized) but also because it allowed intrinsically for, 'the sincere expression in language of the child's thoughts and feelings' (Holmes, 1911, 129). Why therefore would these thoughts and feelings be given any value if their progenitors – children – were regarded as inferior and in need of close guidance and attention?

Further emphasizing his commitment to democracy, Holmes was also to make the case that creative talents often resided in those who were not usually recognized by the 'prize system' of schooling which tended itself toward very particular displays of intelligence and knowledge. In acknowledging that 'there are many kinds of capacity which a formal examination fails to discover' (Holmes, 1911, 75) Holmes was echoing – perhaps consciously – the earlier words of Edward Thring[8] the former headmaster of Uppingham School who had famously argued that there was something every child could do well. This is a significant point as the tenor of much of Holmes' writing indicates his connection and association to those forward-thinking public schools who were to later be associated with the New Education Fellowship and whose pioneers – Kurt Hahn, Cecil Reddie and J.H Badley amongst others – were to draw inspiration from the more anti-industrialist and naturalistic elements found within Holmes. Indeed with his references to games playing, scholarships and general support for those ancient atmospheres which he saw as conducive to a range of wide and appreciative learning through debating societies and intellectual peer discussion, Holmes was clearly not ideologically or politically set against private schooling *per se*. What opposition he voiced derived instead from the hot-housing and 'production line' of examinations that schools such as Westminster and Eton prided themselves upon passing successfully as a route to Oxford and Cambridge.

In considering then his vociferous condemnation of this narrow system of learning at the expense of the creative arts one can again tie this to Holmes' wider theories concerning the nature of being as such ethereal artistic endeavour and the very processes of creativity stood, he believed, in opposition to the more direct, simplistic and easily knowable realities posited by knowledge given out within schools. Holmes was, toward the end of his life, to develop this idea into a more complex philosophy using not simply the familiar language of 'materialism' versus 'idealism' but instead articulated as the Law of Contradiction versus the Law of Opposition in which the former worked on the principle of Yes *or* No and the latter as Yes *and* No. In essence, one represented primitive static dualism and the transcendent God whereas the other stood for the more unified way of viewing *in toto* the dialectic relationship of Man to Nature, Nature to (an Immanent) God and God to Man. It was this latter way of thinking which Holmes believed needed to be 'instilled' within children in order for them to fully develop as spiritual beings capable of perceiving the world as an holistic entity.

Holmes' characterization of the child's imaginative and playful actions was similarly echoed by other associated idealists of the time. These included such luminaries as Sir Percy Nunn[9] who was to write that 'play-activity is subject to the general law that spontaneous activity… tends always towards increased perfection of form, to more complete effectiveness, to a higher degree of unity in diversity' (Nunn, 1920, 81). With language such as this it should be easy to see how there was much in Nunn's educational thinking (and in this he was hardly alone) that was therefore indebted to such works as *What is* but which, by contrast, also provided reciprocal support for those earlier ideas. For instance, when thinking about the process of creativity it is unsurprising that Holmes should ascribe it with such importance when, as Nunn was also to point out, it had no real philosophically ascribable ethical value and so was free of the taint of dogma and belief that characterized activities which had as their end-point some sort of pre-fabricated goal such as a moral lesson. If anything, as Holmes (1895) had earlier elaborated, creative practices such as poetry were to be clearly distinguished by their discerning the truth *of* things which stood in contrast to science which told of the truth *about* things. Creativity thus acted as one of the catalysts for stimulating the consciousness to fresh activity which was hugely important for growth and development. Second, the outputs of creativity whether they be a work of art, a story or a musical composition are always left in some way unfinished, incomplete and open to endless interpretation and so supported Holmes' contention within the aforementioned Law of Opposition that there are gradations of reality as life was essentially a *process* and not a *state*. This metaphor worked at another level too as the creative process itself paralleled the course of self-realization which also was a process that was never fully complete and worked toward the irresolvable infinite.

It was therefore clear that Holmes saw mechanical obedience and externalism fostered in all aspects of the school life; this included not only the docile and compliant culture encouraged by syllabus-based teaching but also the lack of promotion or development of the so-called *creative* subjects. This was not to suggest that such subjects were absent from schools; instead Holmes was to find that they were often to be examined or taught in ways little different to the humanities or the hard sciences which included (inevitably!) examination or simple copying of previous example. Nor was this Holmes privileging one group of subjects over another. This would never have done for one driven by the concept of unity besides which Holmes was to argue that subjects were too often taught with recourse to developing particular compartmentalized attributes at the expense of others. In particular this narrow approach applied to the faculties of *perception* and *expression*: 'Perception and expression are not two faculties, but one. Each is the very counterpart and correlate, each is the very life and soul, of the other. Each, when divorced from the other, ceases to be its own true self' (Holmes, 1911, 84). In Holmes' diagnosis these processes were isolated with the sciences and humanities demanding that the child perceive without expressing and the reverse in subjects demanding creativity – that is children expressing what they had not been asked to perceive through being required to simply copy or having the subject of their efforts chosen in advance. Once more then we see evidence of Holmes linking the problems of education to wider elements within his philosophy, in this case the idea that schools had to develop and nurture as wide a range of talents as possible and that the products of these had to emerge from the latent interests and understanding of the child.

Dogmatic forms of control and Utopia

In his discussion of Western education, Holmes then saw the system of testing and its related activities as not merely a way of causing particular forms of obedient behaviour to be exhibited but also as a manifestation of an overall philosophy of control within human relations that he came to later christen within *The Tragedy of Education* (1913) as *dogmatism*. Although he had referenced it tangentially in the course of his earlier writings on Western religion (religions themselves frequently acting as repressive and controlling entities), here it was to be more explicitly defined and elaborated. In so doing, Holmes was to give tacit acknowledgement to the fact that dogmatism was not confined solely to the pupil–teacher relationship but existed in all areas of society: 'Dogmatic pressure emanates sometimes from an individual, sometimes from a corporation, sometimes from a community, sometimes from a class or social stratum, sometimes from a stream of tendency, sometimes from a mob' (Holmes, 1913b, 8–9).

Crudely speaking, this then was a form of control that centred on the laying down and obeying of instruction which in turn depended on unthinking mechanical obedience. This was not however always a malign force and Holmes recognized that in many contexts – he chooses the somewhat incongruous examples of going on an Atlantic liner and taking a train – to put oneself under the dogmatic direction of those in a position of authority is both harmless and sensible. One presumes, for example, that in these cases the ship's captain's instructions as with those of the train guard are designed for the safety and comfort of those under their control. Likewise many laws of 'the State' (from which emanates much dogmatism) which one is compelled to unthinkingly obey are designed to protect the rights, freedoms and well-being of its citizens. However, whilst it might be a good thing to instinctively accept the laws prohibiting such things as taking the life of another or the theft of someone else's private possessions, the problems for Holmes resided in cases where people ceased to question such long-held and taken-for-granted assumptions no matter how ingrained, deep-rooted and 'sensible' they appeared to be. In many ways this foreshadows the argument later put forward by the social thinker Antonio Gramsci (2005) in which class hegemony was maintained not always by direct force or coercion but instead by creating intellectual conditions in which it would seem lunacy to challenge things as they are. Although Gramsci's target was capitalism and the long historical processes which had worked to ensure that it was widely accepted as the most satisfactory political arrangement, Holmes' denunciation of the system of examination and testing and the conditions which underpinned it were similar in that they relied for their rejoinder upon an initial widespread acceptance and mass consensus around the aims and purposes of education. For many people testing and examination was something so intrinsic to school life that it dare not be meddled with. Similarly, in relation to Original Sin (which it should be remembered he saw as the root cause of many of these defects), Holmes pitied the naïveté of those such as one of his chief critics Henry Scott Holland[10] who believed that his 'Modernistic' and forward-thinking approach to Christianity was beginning to overturn the more orthodox literalist approaches to that doctrine. For Holmes, reformers such as Scott Holland, although well-meaning, were in the minority and in no way represented the beliefs of the large number of people who took their own Sin (or at least the need to be controlled) as a given.

Through its more nefarious aspects such dogmatism conspired for Holmes to negate the laws of human nature and development as they served to stunt and repress natural human traits and characteristics. As he put it,

> dogmatic pressure tends to externalize life. For though the dogmatist may seek to control the inner life of his victims, he cannot do more than control their outward action. And so his demand for obedience of heart and soul resolves itself at last into a demand for literal and mechanical obedience, for the production of results which he can weigh and measure.
>
> (Ibid., xxiv–xxv)

This concern with the inner life of the individual was particularly important given Holmes' developing theory of human and child development. In particular, he believed that humans were born with a series of instinctive desires that, when properly cultivated, made for the expansion and elevation of the child's nature which was a key step on the path toward out-growth. These *instincts* (of which there were six) were delineated by Holmes as communicative, dramatic, artistic, musical, inquisitive and constructive. These could be further grouped together into the sympathetic, aesthetic and scientific whose ultimate aims were, respectively, an understanding of and search for *love, beauty* and *truth*. Clearly these were to be best developed in schools and, particularly at the younger age ranges, through *play* which, in being an essentially spontaneous activity, allowed for the child's natural instinctive growth to take place unfettered by adult interference. This was something which had attracted his admiration in the Montessori schools in which *self-education* (individuals learning at their own pace) was the driving force. Nonetheless it would be to do Holmes' overall vision a disservice to assume that these were mechanisms that *only* took place within the time spent in formal education; many of these instincts involved such things as free conversation and reading (communicative), the desire to find things out for oneself (inquisitive) and the need to be constantly self-educating (constructive). When considering society as a whole Holmes therefore believed that there existed many wider social dogmatic pressures which served to demarcate the same stunting effects even into adulthood. We have already identified one of the most important of these as that stemming from religion whose propagation of the doctrine of Original Sin meant a need to have to control the actions of the individual. Others may have included the role of the family in transmitting particular principles across generations or else the authority of the State which sought to promote particular sets of beliefs and values.

However, for all of Holmes' general pessimism concerning the prevalence of this dogmatism there was for him to be one beacon of hope which was Sompting School in West Sussex – an institution already mentioned in the context of Holmes' official life and as being important in shaping his later ideology. Christened within *What is* as 'Utopia' the choice of name, in this context, could hardly have been more appropriate as it was this school, which Holmes visited a number of times whilst Chief Inspector, that was to provide him with a model establishment and blueprint in which none of the problems of mainstream education in particular the desire to control were seen to exist. In that sense it served to embody, alongside the concurrent work being done by Maria Montessori, the 'what might be' of the title. Holmes was therefore throughout to refer to Utopia fulsomely:

> I could easily make a long list of Utopian virtues and graces, but I must content myself with touching on one more typical product of Egeria's philosophy of education, – the joy which the children wear in their faces and bear in their hearts. The Utopian children are by many degrees the happiest that I have met with in an elementary school, and I must therefore conclude that all is well with them, that their well-being – the true end of all education – has been, and is being, achieved.
>
> (Holmes, 1911, 192–193)

Crucial to the ethos of the school was its remarkable headmistress Harriet Finlay-Johnson (the Egeria referred to above); like Holmes her life and influence has been shamefully under-researched – the only comprehensive piece of scholarship addressing her is an excellent historical account by Mary Bowmaker (2002) – and this has similarly served to downplay her influence notably in the field of drama education in which she served as something of a pioneer. Her seminal book *The Dramatic Method of Teaching* (1912) was one of the first works to even vaguely contemplate using dramatic activity as the basis for tackling a range of different subjects and, in its subsequent wide-ranging discussion, adopted a similar starting point to Holmes in that Finlay-Johnson too believed children (or 'scholars' as she quaintly referred to them) had an innate desire to want to learn and be inquisitive and, when left alone, would therefore be active, playful and creative beings. Part of this creativity stemmed from the need to be, in the broadest sense of the term, dramatic (also one of Holmes' instincts) and so much of her work concerned itself with outlining how best to harness this so as to effectively teach wide aspects of the curriculum. Indeed, in using the language of 'integrated knowledge' the 'activity-method' and 'pupil-autonomy' she clearly pre-figured many of the future tenets of the progressive movement; hers was a vocabulary not out of place for example within the 1967 Plowden Report or for that matter many of the more recent attempts to integrate creativity into the curriculum. Discussing her pioneering status Gavin Bolton (1997) is therefore right to say that, 'perhaps more than any other pioneer in classroom drama, [Harriet Finlay-Johnson] can claim the right to that title, on the grounds that she appeared to have no model to follow or surpass, no tradition to keep or break' (Bolton, 1997, 14).

Clearly, as far as Holmes was concerned, the great value of Finlay-Johnson's school was that, despite standing ideologically outside of the mainstream, it allowed for the full development of the aforementioned instincts and propagated an environment which was free from any hint of both dogmatism and mechanical obedience. In so doing it led Holmes to comment favourably on the atmosphere within the school which was driven by both the communitarian spirit and *play* – 'play taken very seriously, play systematised, organised, provided with ample materials and ample opportunities, encouraged and stimulated in every possible way' (Holmes, 1911, 170). The links with creativity should therefore be self-evident and Holmes was to see such activities which included acting out historical scenes or dramatizing literary texts as developing '*Nature's aims* in the child's life' (Ibid., italics added). Only therefore in schools such as Utopia were children allowed to develop their natural instincts from within and fulfil their true inner potentials with none of the dogmatic imposition of the teachers or the State with their potentially stunting consequences. Although at the time of his initial visit, his religious philosophy had yet to be fully conceived and articulated, it was schools such as this that embodied and catalysed the sorts of spiritual transformations towards self-realization discussed in the previous chapter. After all, where better for a child to begin his journey of recognition as to the Oneness of the individual soul of Man with the soul of the Universe than in an environment in which his life was conceptualised as 'one of continuous self-expression; [in which] opportunities for "putting his soul" into what he says and does will often present themselves to him…his outlook on life will widen, and his imaginative sympathy with life will deepen' (Ibid., 191).

Beyond these self-evident educational benefits however, Utopia served equally to move more sharply into focus Holmes' views on the nature of human development. As he admitted later on, prior to his initial visit he had broadly supported the prevailing belief in the congenital (genetic) superiority of the upper classes over the lower orders. Given the *fin de siècle* concern with eugenics and those such as William Bateson[11] – himself cited by Holmes – who were popularizing Mendelian genetics and its impact upon heredity this initial stance was less surprising than one might expect and was to be equally concerning to other liberal thinkers such as H.G. Wells and George Bernard Shaw. Nonetheless, in observing the creative endeavours of children within Utopia as well as in other comparable establishments in the country when Chief Inspector, Holmes became convinced that Finlay-Johnson's school in particular disproved this theory. In using the analogy of the plum he was to write,

> My answer to this argument [Bateson's]…is that plums those children certainly were, and plums of a very high quality, – that the average Utopian child was in fact a better specimen of plumhood than the average product of what we call 'good breeding' and 'gentle birth.'
>
> (Holmes, 1917a, 69–70)

Free of dogmatic control and externalism – which necessitated thinking solely about the self – it seems *all* children regardless of background were able to more fully express their latent potentials and grow and develop accordingly. This was certainly in keeping with that democratic strand to Holmes' thinking.

There were clear social implications for this view; first in the sense that it seemed to disprove those theories which stressed the primacy of genetics and breeding as evidence for educational success and superiority. And second as it was to infringe upon thinking concerning the wider role of the school, notably how, under this aspect, it was increasingly being seen as a setting in which to combat the wider forces at work within society thereby taking on the mantle of what, in today's terms, would be a social change agent. Holmes therefore may have appeared as somewhat pessimistic in his analysis of the world and the effects this was having for education but inherent within was the hope that, following particular examples, true growth (of the spirit) could be fostered and this could lead to a negation of many of the later defects of character which seemed to be of such contemporary social concern. Genetics and nature was an answer for some; for Holmes however it relied more profoundly on a particular form of nurture within schools and society free of any form of outward control.

Debates about Holmes

One of the most noticeable things about Holmes' critique of schooling – and indeed his writing in general – is its rhetorical power and persuasiveness. Its declarative tone both convinces and converts and it is easy to see why there was a sense of discipleship amongst his younger admirers such as E. Sharwood Smith and why *What is* in particular acquired the status for later educators of a pioneering manifesto with its educational idealism and fulsome commitment to a utopian vision. However, in any such discussion, it is important to be aware that there are those who have over time been less than convinced by Holmes' case. In part of course these reactions stemmed from his authorship of the prior Circular which served to characterize him as an elitist reactionary. Beyond such animus (which seems in hindsight much misplaced) these doubts were though perhaps inevitable given the nature of polemics and there were indeed many contemporaries of Holmes who saw his ideal school as unrealistic, took umbrage at his insinuation of widespread malpractice within existing establishments or else were offended by the implications of mechanical obedience fostered seemingly intentionally by orthodox religion.

This latter point was best embodied by the Rev. S.F. Smith (a Catholic priest) who was to ask in an extended and hostile review, 'Will it be too much to expect of our self-confident critic [Holmes] that he should condescend to furnish evidence for these surprising statements' (Smith, 1911, 452)? These 'surprising statements' clearly referred to Holmes' contentious claims that Western education was lingering under a system of doctrinal thinking which had been propagated over two thousand or so years by the established Church of which this reviewer was a devout member. Furthermore, Smith – much in the manner of those who had contributed to debates and columns within *The Schoolmaster* – was to imply that Holmes had besmirched the practice of many existing educators by his suggestion that within the vast majority of schools there continued to exist cultures of repression and dogmatic control. For Smith – as for many others – Holmes' arguments were tantamount to a *reductio ad absurdum* and in no way represented either the views or practices of teachers present or past. Indeed, one could argue that the strength and support shown by many practitioners towards the new progressive ideas – embodied as we shall soon see in the New Ideals in Education conferences – indicate a broader groundswell of sympathy than perhaps Holmes had accounted for.

In a similar vein, another contemporary piece by Mowbray Morris sought to argue that Holmes' vision was unrealistic precisely because it relied too heavily on those like 'Egeria': 'The wisest Department in the world, the best system of examination ever invented, cannot discover many Egerias in this generation' (Morris, 1911, 268). Whilst Morris' contention has to be treated with caution as it embodied that school of thought which felt that 'it is better to remove them [ignorant children] as early as possible from the irksome waste of an education' (Ibid.) and so was, from the outset, ideologically quite distinct from Holmes it certainly raises a valid point about the role of the teacher within Holmes' scheme. His Egeria was after all one capable of working long hours, being musical, dramatic, observant, having an understanding of theory yet all the while overseeing individualized play for a school full of children. It may have been possible for the remarkable figure of Finlay-Johnson but in the hands of less able practitioners how would Holmes' ideas be successfully implemented? This has long been a concern raised in relation to progressive practice and has undoubtedly served as one reason why many subsequent studies in both Britain and America have shown teachers have been too often committed to traditional ways of teaching.

Whilst however the above could be considered *ideological* objections which are, in a lot of ways, impossible to answer given that they arose from those carrying different social and political assumptions as to the purpose of education, it is also worth remembering that Holmes has been seen as guilty too of overlooking particular *historical* changes – both contemporary and ancient – which called into question the veracity of his analysis. For example, in his discussion of the contemporary scholastic context Holmes neglected to mention that the introduction of such examinations into certain areas of public life was as a way of bringing meritocracy into a system that to that point had been riddled with corruption and nepotism. Under the steam of the first Gladstone Ministry (1868–1874) entrance to the Civil Service – based on the earlier Northcote-Trevelyan proposals[12] – and promotion in the Armed Forces now rested on public, competitive examinations and merit rather than simple purchase or personal contact. Although couched heavily in the discourse of efficiency – a term that would have infuriated the anti-bureaucratic within Holmes – this was a deployment of the systems of examinations which was not perhaps quite in the spirit as laid down in *What is* in which they were seen negatively as favouring one class of pupil, fostering competition and, therefore, sensualism and impeding outward growth. Such an example therefore serves as a timely reminder that whilst Holmes' writing was both forceful and persuasive it relies on particular a priori assumptions and it is therefore always possible to identify places where his argument may be flawed and that one contention does not necessarily always follow logically and seamlessly to another. Was it inevitable for instance that developments within wider religious thinking would impact directly upon schools? It was this which has led some critics, in particular David McKenzie (1984), to argue that Holmes' writing was imbued with a sense of caricature regarding the education system which he saw as existing *for no other reason* than to serve the authorities' view over how people should behave at the expense of other factors. As he puts it,

> He [Holmes] gives no recognition to the contemporary need to provide a common standard against which the work of separately controlled schools could be judged, the advantage to poorly-trained teachers to have some set scheme of work rather than no plan at all, and the role of defined school knowledge in promoting a career structure in teaching.
> (McKenzie, 1984, 6)

The same is true of school-based testing (part of the hated Revised Codes of 1862) which – far from being an embodiment of external forms of control – was as J.S. Hurt (1979) and P. McCann (1970) have shown, imbued with another possible function notably facilitating social mobility particularly amongst ambitious and politically aware working class families. In referring to the 1870 Education Act for example Hurt makes the point that, 'Parents who had won the vote in 1867 understandably wanted the schools in which their children were going to be educated brought under a semblance of popular control' (Hurt, 1979, 61). This seems to suggest that such individuals had far more sense of agency than had been given them by Holmes. Furthermore, Hurt goes on to show that the religious strictures so criticised by Holmes as imposing constricting patterns of behaviour were in fact being actively opposed by an increasingly mobile class, itself cognisant of the opportunities offered by mass schooling: 'The reform of education was a political issue that offered radically-minded politically conscious working men the opportunity of breaching, if not eliminating, the Church of England's influence' (Ibid.).

Whilst then developments such as those explored by historians of the period and encompassing the 1870 Act and attendant Codes were part of Holmes' metaphorical Land of Bondage and given commensurately short shrift in his writings, they did seem to have some success in elevating the life chances of working class children and such debates seem more redolent of contemporary unresolved arguments for the justification of the continued existence of grammar schools. Furthermore there is some suggestion too that Holmes' blanket dismissal of the 'payment by results' system was equally misrepresentative and his critique, which argued powerfully that the system had been set up by the authorities to ensure a rigid level of compliance, failed to account for other prevailing factors behind its implementation. These included the need to have a universal system of standards so as to compensate for the weaknesses inherent within a system of schooling heavily reliant on pupil or poorly qualified teachers as well as to make more widely transparent the curriculum and its expectations.

Ultimately, one has to accept that Holmes' writing, particularly as it developed, was predicated on very particular assumptions about the world and its conditions which, if not accepted at the outset, make it easy to admire but difficult perhaps to follow. Like much of the other rhetoric surrounding progressive education it ultimately rests on articles of *faith* in human nature – in this case that the child will display goodwill and civility and a desire to learn not because they have been told or made to but because 'it *is their nature* to do it, because their overflowing sympathy and goodwill must needs express themselves in and through the channels of courtesy and kindness' (Holmes, 1911, 159–160, original italics). Of course such a view neglects the role that external influences may play in developing the character of the child, a point raised by Gordon and White (1979) who stress the importance of social institutions in shaping the growing individual. R.F. Dearden (1968) builds on that contention by suggesting – in a conscious attack on the biological language so common to Holmes and those of his kind – that, 'The growth of a person is something which necessarily takes place in a social group, and in this respect is quite unlike the unfolding of plants' (Dearden, 1968, 33). Indeed, Dearden's argument goes further by suggesting that the epistemological certainty which theorists like Holmes and Froebel placed on the processes of inner growth were themselves misplaced: 'How do growth theorists know the 'laws of growth', or what 'optimum development' is' (Ibid., 34)?

Such points are especially important to note for they were predicated upon philosophical arguments concerning the legitimacy of Holmes' ideas and were not therefore as heavily tainted by earlier political events or personal prejudice. Indeed, the tone of many of these later accounts was to be broadly *sympathetic* to child-centred ideas and − unlike others in the field such as John Darling (1994) and Robin Barrow (1978) − were to be actively cited and deployed by those seeking to justify such approaches towards the end of the century. In that way then it is better perhaps to consider these objections to Holmes under that aspect, that is, more as critiques to be considered rather than as simple denials to be affirmed. Whilst these may well have resonance and strike a contemporary chord − particularly the centrality given to organized religion which seems problematic in today's more secular age − they must not one feels be used as the basis by which to judge or denigrate Holmes. They provoke reconsideration certainly but to use them to dismiss in his entirety such a wide-ranging and diverse thinker as Holmes is to risk losing site of many of the powerful and forward-thinking aspects to his thought.

Notes

1. James Herbert Simpson (1883–1959) was a school inspector whose autobiography *A Schoolmaster's Harvest: Some Findings of 50 Years, 1894–1944* offers an insightful look into the changes that affected English education during that time
2. E. Sharwood Smith was a close friend of Holmes and Headmaster of Newbury School 1902–1924. He was passionately committed to progressive methods of teaching, publishing widely and attending various New Ideals gatherings.
3. The Little Commonwealth was set up by Homer Lane in Dorset in 1912. It was co-educational and designed for the very young to the young adult (the oldest students there were 19 years old). In the role of Superintendent he promoted the ethos of removing forced authority and compulsion.
4. Emily Shirreff (1814–1897) was one of the most important early champions of Froebelian education, writing a number of key articles in the *Education Journal* and latterly becoming President of the English Frobel Society between 1875 and 1897.
5. Bertha Ronge (née Meyer) (1818–1863) established the kindergarten movement in England when she founded the first such establishments in London (1851), Manchester (1859) and Leeds (1860).
6. The Kingdom of Ends is a hypothetical experiment deriving from Kant's categorical imperative. It proposed treating humans and their well-being as the ultimate goal (the ends) rather than as being merely the ends in themselves.
7. The Creative Partnership's programme was established by the UK New Labour Government in 2002 and was intended to build partnerships between schools and creative and cultural organizations. Funding was cut in 2010 and the initiative was abandoned in 2011.
8. Edward Thring (1821–1887) was headmaster of Uppingham School from 1853 until his death. During that time the school reflected his belief in a broad curriculum which should offer where possible a diverse provision allowing for the development of various talents. He also set up the Headmaster's Conference in 1869.
9. Sir Thomas Percy Nunn (1870–1944) was a British educationalist writing mostly in the field of educational philosophy and who was Professor of Education at the London Institute of Education from 1913–1936.

10 Henry Scott Holland (1847–1918) was Regius Professor of Divinity at Oxford who was most notable in his efforts to link socialism and religion. In 1889 he set up the Christian Social Union which was an attempt to reconcile those two seemingly diverse concepts.
11 William Bateson (1861–1926) was a pioneering English biologist and geneticist, noted for his popularizing of the work of Gregor Mendel. By so doing, he was to indirectly give primacy to the role of nature and genetics in determining character, intelligence and the like.
12 Prepared originally in 1854 by Stafford Northcote and C.E. Trevelyan, the Northcote-Trevelyan Report proposed regulating entry into the Civil Service by open examination whilst promotion would be based on merit and not patronage or purchase. This set the tone for turning (in theory at least) the various branches of the Civil Service as well as the Army into a meritocracy open to the ambitious working classes.

Chapter 5

Holmes, society and the later writings

Maria Montessori and the New Ideals conferences

As a result of the popularity of his educational writings in the first decade and a half of the twentieth century – assisted no doubt by the controversy they had generated – Holmes' importance amongst the burgeoning and diverse community of individuals comprising the challenge to the orthodoxy became more clearly felt and established. In charting then the broader dissemination of educational radicalism and progressive ideas in both the United Kingdom and Europe during this time it is imperative to not ignore the persona of Holmes, a development which emerges more explicitly in this post-war period as both his intellectual output increased[1] and as he became more widely known in a range of cognate fields. Whilst previous more dominant historical accounts may have overlooked his contribution in this regard (or else confined their focus solely to discussing the contents and influence of *What is*), it is worth perhaps here exploring the *practical* impact his life was to have as this in itself was indicative of his growing standing not merely as an educational theorist but also as an organizer and, more widely, as a public intellectual. In that vein, much of Holmes' writing following his retirement from the Board of Education was thereby concerned with wider aspects of the world and society as he sought to begin to construct a broader theory of social relations over and above the merely educational. It is this thread then that could be said to percolate this chapter as a whole in which his hinterland widened and he more actively engaged with various communities of practice and world events.

We have already seen that, at the behest of his former employers and just after his retirement in late 1910, Holmes was sent to report both on the recently opened *Casa dei Bambini* in Rome but also more generally on the work of their founder Maria Montessori. Beyond however the published report (1912a) of his impressions for his superiors concerning his travels, this particular line of enquiry was to prove fruitful for two reasons. First, Holmes' emergent interest in these new sets of ideas (which themselves often drew upon a range of varied traditions) was to translate into a more direct contribution by amalgamating many of the more seemingly incongruent progressive groups into a cohesive and unified whole. Second, his admiration for the work being done by 'La Dottoressa' in her 'Child's homes' was to inspire a more widespread social engagement in which his writing came to focus more upon the implications for education in relation to the future shape of society. After that fashion, Sol Cohen has charted Holmes' role in spreading the gospel of Montessori in England going as far as to say that, 'It was Holmes more than anyone else who brought the Montessori Method to England' (Cohen, 1974, 53). This was reflected in part through the publication of Holmes' report as one of the Board of Education's periodic educational missives, a signal perhaps that policy-makers were beginning to be won round to some of these ground-breaking and radical ideas. Cohen is however equally decisive in asserting that Holmes' success emanated too from his unique position as both a traditionalist and innovator who thus succeeded in broadening his appeal through piquing the interest of even those more moderate reformers unable to quite bring themselves to fully support his more iconoclastic and controversial pronouncements. These would have included those such as his former chief at the Board of Education Robert Morant who had previously expressed reserved and implicit support for some of Holmes' ideas through his own intellectual flirtation with both Buddhism and Idealism. It was, after all, not long previously, as we have seen, that Holmes had been a School Inspector and diligent Whitehall servant carrying the whiff of respectability yet simultaneously as one who had effectively retrenched on those commitments in publishing the controversial *What is*.

In many ways, his own mature philosophy seemed ideally tailored to that of Montessori not least through the way in which she too appeared to want to resist the twin poles of both Johann Herbart and Friedrich Froebel whose ideas, as the previous chapter has showed, were simultaneously gaining currency and piquing interest in Britain. Like her, Holmes believed that they and their followers had placed an overt reliance on both the role of the teacher and of nature respectively and were therefore guilty of providing an education that was either too obviously instrumental or else as lacking the support and guidance that should be offered by sympathetic and trained practitioners. In much the same way that Holmes himself had long articulated the importance of understanding Darwinian evolutionary theory, so Montessori too represented that body of opinion which was equally prepared to embrace the new knowledge emerging from within fields such as psychology and who sought to intertwine it with older educational principles: 'Montessori is great, then, because she has re-discovered Froebel's master principle for herself, and in doing so, has interpreted it anew, [first] in the broad and ever-broadening light of modern science' (Holmes, 1912a, 27). Furthermore although he was to be critical of some aspects of Montessori's system – not least its seeming neglect of drawing, games and unfettered creativity – Holmes was still generally impressed with the standards shown by the children in the essential skills of reading and writing:

> The truth is that the Montessori system enables young children to learn reading and writing without mental strain…Whatever else Dottoressa Montessori has done, she has fully proved that reading and writing can be taught to quite young children…without overtaxing their brains.
>
> (Ibid., 17)

This last clause is particularly important to emphasize as it ties closely to a theme of Holmes' writing around this time which concerned itself with the relationship between education, learning and work in its broadest and most prosaic sense. In essence, he was anxious to emphasize that a reason why progressive ideas of the sort advocated by Montessori had traditionally struggled to achieve more common acceptance in England, and were therefore well behind developments on the Continent, was due in part to a prevailing belief that they ill-prepared children for the realities of working life and so lacked something of the exigencies of the 'real world'. Typically then such schools were characterized as all play and no work and suffered from the typical stigmas attached to progressive establishments driven by the ideologies of play, freedom and a non-traditional approach to authority. In a key article tellingly entitled *Drudgery and Education. A Defence of Montessori Ideals* (1917b) Holmes expanded upon this idea and outlined why it was that a system of education which had at its heart a *trust* of human nature – that is, which allowed the child opportunities for their own creative endeavours and trusted them to be self-directed communal learners with innately good natures – would produce individuals who would not see any future work as graft and grind. In particular, the Montessori System with its stress upon self-development through customized personal learning meant that regardless of the mundane nature of the work being undertaken 'the Montessori infant drudges away at what he takes in hand, and finds happiness and even joy in doing so' (Holmes, 1917b, 429).

This argument applied too within the more humdrum aspects of the creative arts; music scales for example – even back then the bane of the young student's lessons – were only found to be boring because the child was frequently unaware of the value they had in facilitating ultimate self-expression through providing a thorough grounding in the landscape of the keyboard necessary for composition. If this was not explained then scales became (as they frequently did) merely didactic exercises in simple memory and motor mechanics with their practice thus becoming resented as routine and dull. Following a similar path, Holmes recounts the tale of a girl placing wooden blocks and cylinders into a frame: 'This was laborious work for a child of three, and it was highly monotonous, but it was not drudgery, for it had a meaning for the child' (Ibid.). Whilst explanations of this type could be construed as unnecessarily instructive because the teacher is seen to be implanting a pre-ordained fixed meaning upon a task, its completion nevertheless stemmed from the desire and enthusiasm of the child and their natural impulses ('instincts') to be creative in their use and configuration of shape and space. In that sense the element of forced compulsion common to many traditional education systems was removed and children 'drudged without knowing that they were drudging, and they thus transformed drudgery into interesting and enjoyable work' (Ibid.).

On the one hand, this strain of thinking can be seen as an obvious extension of Holmes' earlier position which was both to reject any education system that imposed mechanical obedience upon children and, *de facto*, to advocate on behalf of any authority (in this case Montessori) who sought the opposite. As he put it, '*self*-education is the beginning and end of education' (Holmes, 1913a, xx, italics added). Although arguably Holmes here placed too much stress upon the autonomy afforded by the Montessori System – a point later picked up by A.S. Neill who saw its Apparatus as both unnecessarily controlling and rigid – this advocacy clearly extended his previous enthusiasm which had begun via his observations of Harriet Finlay-Johnson's school in which 'the activity of the Utopian child is his own activity…It is a fountain which springs up in himself' (Holmes, 1911, 156). It was these two geographically disparate institutions of both Sussex and Rome that continued throughout his remaining years to embody for Holmes the 'model' educational setting in which the natural developments of the child's instincts were allowed to flourish to their fullest extent thereby facilitating comradeship, love and at a deeper level self-realization and out-growth.

More broadly however, although focussing explicitly upon Montessori, this aforementioned article formed part of an academic engagement with a much wider general concern over the 'state of the nation' in the context of a country then engaged in the multiple privations and hardships of the First World War. Writing here in 1917 it is surely therefore a reasonable supposition to think that Holmes was indirectly attempting to promote his case by arguing for progressive ideas with his readership (who may by this stage have included policy-makers) that even a system as seemingly radical as that of Montessori was not seeking to overturn the existing social order or threaten established institutions and frameworks. If anything, it was implicitly reinforcing it by arguing that young boys and girls, if properly schooled, would be better and more efficient workers by not seeing even the most monotonous tasks as adverse toil and thus given to resent them.

This inference is given further support when one considers other pieces written by Holmes around the War period in which he seemed to tie his backing of progressive ideas to the way in which they could be seen as furthering a wider social utility. In defending his earlier educational polemic for instance Holmes was to write that such radical child-centred notions served as a corrective to the social degeneration – as constituted by 'slackers and shirkers and dawdlers' (Holmes, 1914, 187) – that was perceived as being current within the country at the time. Although subsequent historical accounts notably that of Harry Hendrick (1990) have questioned the authenticity of these contemporary claims seeing them instead as influenced by characteristic scare-mongering around the discourses of nascent adolescence, in nevertheless citing the anxieties expressed by those such as the noted teacher-trainer Geraldine Hodgson[2] over the 'distressing signs of the times' (Ibid., 184) Holmes was explicitly seeking to mould his educational scheme toward encompassing the betterment of the nation through linking it to industry, innovation and the need to foster creative thinking. It was these habits which Holmes considered had fallen into decay as a consequence of the mechanical obedience of the test-obsessed state sector and the rigid discipline of the private. Amid parallel anxieties over the loss of Empire and global prestige, Holmes warmed to his theme by also tapping into this strain of seemingly jingoistic thinking:

The British Empire was built up, in part at least, by the cadets of the county families and the sons of professional men. But nowadays the young men who, in a more adventurous age, would have gone to the Antipodes and other remote parts of the world to 'seek their fortunes' prefer to stay at home.

(Ibid., 189)

Holmes was not the first from the progressive tradition to adopt this line of thinking; we have previously observed for example how Margaret McMillan had earlier spoken of the importance of the imagination to those children who would one day be 'competing with educated workmen of other lands' (McMillan, 1904, xi). Her defence – like that of Holmes – had rested on explaining the connection between child-centred methods and national well-being and how the former with its avowed non-instrumentalism was not in any way detrimental to industrial productivity and the needs of manufacturing. Such concerns were apposite given the Imperial and economic turn-of-the-century anxieties which tied closely into the moral and physical degeneration of the nation which were now finding more fulsome and public expression. In particular, findings from the investigations carried out by those such as Charles Booth and Seebohm Rowntree in York and London respectively[3] had warned, somewhat alarmingly, of the poor physical condition of many young people (in part prompting the Liberal Children's Charter) and it can therefore be argued that Holmes' warnings carried a similar imperative albeit with a focus upon children's intellectual rather than physical development. The references to drudgery in particular were topical during the War as new labour patterns were emerging as a result of the conflict – in particular women undertaking work in munitions and changing apprentice–employer relations via the setting up of labour exchanges.

Although his political viewpoints will be more fully explored in the following section it is worth here mentioning that whilst indicating a sense of patriotism (and as we shall also see in time he was to turn his gaze firmly upon what he saw as the failings of Germany) they also suggest that, unlike his ideas pertaining to education and growth of the spirit, Holmes did not always adhere to more radical sets of social beliefs. In commenting for example on the need for a less dogmatic and more child-centred education system, he was to write that, 'We owe it to our *great Empire*, which would have fallen to pieces long ago if "Do what I tell you" had been our motto' (Holmes, 1915, 969, italics added). In many ways, such language is instructive as it both belies the traditional and convenient association of 'progressive' and 'child-centred' ideas with the ideological left and also indicates that his own political agenda was anything but clear-cut and easily defined. Indeed, for all of his advocacy and espousal of freedom, this freedom was one conceived spiritually and did not by definition necessarily translate into the sorts of liberties being sought by those seeking to challenge social inequality which in England by this time was best being questioned by the socialists and the rising Labour Party. Whilst fit and proper working conditions were one of the key trade union demands would it have appeased, for example, such organizations to hear Holmes justifying the situation of a former Utopian pupil who 'found employment in a large field on the lower slopes of the hills, where he had to collect flints and pile them in heaps… his wage for this dull and tiresome work being no more than fivepence a day' (Holmes, 1911, 193)? Although Holmes' vindication for this state of affairs was that the pupil did not find the work dull nor tiresome as 'he sang his Folk Songs with all the spontaneous happiness of a soaring lark' (Ibid.) this hopefulness seems now somewhat naïve and indicates little desire to seek to challenge the inhering existence of such poorly paid jobs or the greater good (Empire/ nationhood) that they were seen as working toward.

It is then clear that by this stage in his writing career Holmes' preoccupations had moved away from independent and comparatively discrete discussion of religion, idealism and education and was instead increasingly keen to foster a philosophy of *wholeness* (Holmes, 1920c, 167). Although characteristically cryptic, this term referred directly to his new and enduring attempts to bridge the outward material and inward spiritual worlds through encouraging *out-growth*, a process which was designed to lead to a more rounded and fuller appreciation of the whole of existence. This wholeness was to be understood as the Oneness of the Universe in which the divisions of Man, Nature and God and the chasm between the Finite and Infinite were seen as indivisible and therefore capable of being bridged. This could only be achieved, as we have seen when discussing Holmes' educational and poetic writings, when 'the desire to possess had been submerged by the desire to be possessed' (Ibid., 212) and Man's higher orders of thought had been allowed to triumph over the lower which he associated with vice and sensuality. In his verse it will be remembered Holmes had related this to the concept of Love in which its ultimate form was sustained and expressed through denial and, by thus being denied, elevated it above its more carnal associations. Similarly, in education, Holmes had contended that only through the fostering of communal spirit via a form of child-centredness could Man achieve a level of altruism which could further the *disinterested devotion* which would usher in the new era: 'where individuality is duly fostered the spirit of comradeship, being a spontaneous overflow from the wells of happiness, will…inspire…goodwill to others, not only because they are school-fellows but also because they are fellow human beings' (Holmes, 1921d, 97).

However beyond mere classroom practice and its suggestion of unity through communal work and shared childhoods, this integrative idea also had *social* implications and one of the ways Holmes was to embody this wholeness was by his central involvement with the New Ideals in Education conferences and the later New Education Fellowship which, as Kevin Brehony (2004) has shown, were attempts to bring together a range of disparate and occasionally conflicting organizations and groups with different disciplinary and intellectual foci. Driven by the beliefs of pioneering men and women like Holmes, those acting under these banners were motivated broadly by the need to preserve and promote the rights, liberty and voice of the child particularly within the confines of schools in which they saw forms of outmoded oppression taking place. Holmes' earlier admiration for

Montessori was therefore important here for the New Ideals conferences were to be an extension of the four-day conference of the Montessori Society held at East Runton in Norfolk in 1914 and which he had helped organize in conjunction with Bertram Hawker[4] and the Earl of Lytton.[5] These New Ideals gatherings were however envisaged as being altogether grander affairs and, in being deliberately all-embracing and non-factional, were intended to bring together both physically and ideologically all of the various groups adhering however vaguely to the Conference's espoused belief in, 'reverence for the pupil's individuality and a belief that individuality grows best in an atmosphere of freedom' (New Ideals in Education, 1916, Introductory).

In that spirit one of the key features of these gatherings was their non-partisan nature and this was equally clearly expressed in the Conference's statement of aims which declaimed that it did not exist 'to voice the opinions of any particular pedagogical school' (Ibid.). As another key protagonist Norman Macmunn was to more eloquently put it, 'after all, the difference in ideas of Mr [Homer] Lane and Madame Montessori and Miss Finlay Johnson are infinitely less essential than their community of aim' (Macmunn, 1914, 86). On that point of harmony, secondary accounts have also proven also emphatic:

> One of the distinguishing features of the NEF [New Education Fellowship] other than its international scope was that it was a movement that connected lay enthusiasts for the educational reforms associated with the new education with major figures in the developing disciplines of psychology and education, such as Carl Gustav Jung, Jean Piaget and John Dewey.
> (Brehony, 2004, 734)

The echoes with Holmes' own philosophy of unity in this should be self-evident – particularly in the gatherings' avoidance of dogma and fragmentation – and, as the complete proceedings held within the British Library indicate, he was to be a continual and dominant presence throughout the period of the conferences which were to last in various forms up until 1937, the last being held just after his death. Betraying Holmes' influence, and with words which could have been lifted almost verbatim from any of his earlier writings, the 1915 Conference in Stratford-upon-Avon was opened by the then President Lord Lytton who spoke of his disdain for 'all ideas which represent the substitution of the freedom and self-expression of the pupil for the imposed authority of the teacher' (Lytton, 1915, 2).

Anyone and everyone concerned with aspects of educational reform – be it political, philosophical, physical or psychological – were to attend these conferences, a testament perhaps to not only the organizing power of the former Board of Education administrator but also the pull now exerted by his popular and provocative writings whose combative polemic set the tone in envisioning a reconstructed and reconstituted education system. The importance of these gatherings in shaping this confrontational and alternative ideology should not be underestimated and the list of attendees does indeed read as a 'who's who' of educational reformers and rebels; Homer Lane, Michael Sadler, Cyril Burt, Margaret McMillan, Belle Rennie, Percy Nunn and Beatrice Ensor to name but a handful. Within this galaxy of stars Holmes undoubtedly shone brightly – by the time of the 1935 Conference he had been elected as President and was to continually drive the meetings forward both by his own presentations but also as many of the concurrent talks coincided with key themes addressed within his own work. Of particular note was an event called Experiments Day at the Conference of 1917 in which various local practitioners were given a platform to disseminate their ideas and teaching innovations. Introducing the occasion, Holmes called it 'the fulfilment of a long cherished dream' (Holmes, 1917d, 85) and spoke of his vision of 'a clearing-house for educational ideas and experiences' (Ibid.) in which best practice could be shared. Nothing perhaps better summarized the ethic and ethos of this group – and Holmes himself – than teachers drawn from across the land presenting examples of strategies piloted in the crucible of their own classrooms and underpinned by nascent theories of learning and child development.

Whilst of course possible to overstate the importance of these conferences, R.J.W. Selleck is surely right to assert that, 'There was an enthusiasm and vitality about its [the New Ideals] meetings, its numbers increased, its reports sold well; it was possible to believe that the Conference was keeping the light burning in the home country' (Selleck, 1972, 45). Much of this can unquestionably be put down to the efforts and enthusiasms of Holmes who not only presided over all of the conferences prior to his death but acted every inch the *éminence grise* of what now considered itself a genuine intellectual and social movement. Furthermore, he was also influential through his presentation of a number of papers which he delivered with characteristic vigour (many of which were subsequently published elsewhere) whilst he was also in the chair for many notable speakers: 'I think (except for the first meeting of all, at East Runton) he never missed one [conference] in 23 years. Such was his enthusiasm for education and the instruction for education and the instruction and enlightenment of the teacher' (E. Sharwood Smith, 1937, 39). Of greatest personal note was his welcome in 1922 to Harriet Finlay-Johnson (by this point Harriet Weller), whose school had over a decade before it will be remembered provided him with the model of 'Utopia' and its headmistress as 'Egeria'.

It is not perhaps an insignificant detail to note that Holmes' death coincided with the end of these gatherings. Undoubtedly affected by the loss of their greatest champion, by this time (1937) the New Education Fellowship had long superseded the New Ideals as the leading ideological vehicle and, as well, there was a suggestion that progressivism of the Holmesian and New Ideals 'type' had become closer to the established orthodoxy through its capturing of the allegiance of key policy-makers. The Hadow Reports (published between 1923 and 1933) for example had indicated governmental interest in progressive tenets at the level of both theory and practice whilst educational initiatives such as the Dalton Plan[6] continued to be used within classrooms less bound than before by central control. Significantly, the address of Welcome to the 1936 Conference was given by Cyril Norwood who was to be, following the Second World War, one of the architects of the tri-partite structure in which children were placed, so went the theory, into schools which best suited their abilities and aptitudes. Although it would therefore be inaccurate to say education was on the cusp of a new era – and there was much in the late 1930s to be pessimistic about – many of the earlier enthusiasms, experiments and factions had, between the Wars, cohered into a more uniform set of progressive beliefs and procedures. Whilst it would be equally mistaken to attribute this solely to Holmes, his contribution to shaping the discourse facilitated by his wide array of both personal contacts and enthusiasm was undoubtedly important and indicates how that strand of his thinking pertaining to the freedom of the child had achieved wider recognition.

Indeed, much of Holmes' impact came not merely through his ability to act as an organizing champion and motivational force, but also as his ideas were taken up by his contemporaries and there is evidence of overlap between his own educational thoughts and concepts and those being developed by many other important and influential educational groups of the time. One example of this appears when examining the Theosophical movement in Britain in the years leading up to the First World War. Whilst the Theosophical Society had founded its first branch in London as far back as 1878 it took until 1915 for any real inclination to take hold in applying these ideas to education. When it did this took the form of the Theosophical Fraternity in Education which was established by Beatrice Ensor[7] in the aftermath of the New Ideals conference of that year and the glowing reception there afforded to thundering papers read by Holmes and Homer Lane. Their initial meetings were then held at the subsequent Ideals conferences and, by 1920 amid the popularity of their *New Era* journal, they moved to instigate, as has been alluded to, the organization known as the New Education Fellowship whose very name hinted at the more spiritually attenuated direction they wished to take. Although Holmes himself was not an official member of the organized Fraternity many of their ideas and declamations were nonetheless indicative of the osmotic diffusion of his writings and the spread of more Eastern-influenced ideas which he had served to promote. The Theosophists for example believed 'that there was some divinity in every man and woman, and that this power should be drawn out and encouraged wherever possible' (Croall, 1983, 101). Likewise, their calls for self-government in schools, the abolition of competition at the expense of cooperation and the need to promote the child's innate interests chimed with much of the work of Holmes who had earlier spoken of the need to develop the child's natural instincts in an atmosphere of love and harmony.

Although he may well have taken issue with the Theosophist need 'to *prepare* the child to seek and realize in his own life the supremacy of the spirit' (Ibid., 101, italics added) – adult imposition of any kind was usually always unwelcome – Holmes would also surely have supported their advocacy of spiritual development and the need to give full reign to that wide concept. This was often taken, if the influential writings of Rudolf Steiner were anything to go by, in combination with the key principles and beliefs of *science* in whose methods and approaches he saw a way of answering the more esoteric questions of the spirit. Steiner's entire philosophy of anthroposophy or *spiritual science* was after all, crudely, an attempt to delineate experience of what he considered the extant spiritual world by focussing it upon, and mediating it through, inner development. As he himself pointed out, this particular combination of science and mysticism was one that, like Holmes, was seen to have very practical benefits for Mankind:

> All science would be nothing but the satisfaction of idle curiosity did it not strive to raise the *value of existence for the personality of man*. The sciences attain their true value only by showing the human significance of their results.
>
> (Steiner, 1964, xxx)

Though Holmes rarely mentioned Steiner by name in his published writings, when thinking of his promotion of those aspects of evolution which applied to the spirit as well as his conception of the infinite and the need for inner spiritual growth, we can identify additional tangible, if not always explicit, links between them. It is further interesting to note in passing here that it was the issue of the role and purpose of the school that caused in part the rift between the arch-Theosophist Beatrice Ensor and A.S. Neill, the latter of whom complained in a *New Era* editorial about what he dubbed 'Crank Schools' (Neill, quoted in Croall, 1983, 102) and those institutions who maintained any form of adult authority. Quite what he would have made of Finlay-Johnson's Sompting School remains a mystery and evidences not only the broad church of beliefs that encompassed the Fellowship but the ways in which Holmes' ideas, even when indirectly espoused, were open to contestation even amongst his more supportive peers. It will, after all, be remembered that he had earlier given tacit support to discipline in schools when it served as a bulwark against forms of lawlessness and anarchism.

As his writings then served to impact upon a very specific group of spiritual reformers, so more widely were many of Holmes' pronouncements on – in particular – *freedom* and *growth* being reflected in contemporaneous practice and discourse. By now his conception of freedom was one drawing upon the Eastern/Upanishad tradition of internal and potentially limitless soul-growth and its essentially *social* character created by non-competitiveness and selflessness in formation of community, such as he had witnessed within Montessori's establishments in Rome, was to chime with the temper of the progressive schools emerging in England at this time and further into the two decades prior to the Second World War. Many of these had been set up initially as private experiments in order to demonstrate the viability of alternative models of pedagogy in the context of a system in which institutions and their teachers were, as Holmes had continually maintained, still perceived as 'tethered to the examination stake' (New Ideals in Education, 1918, vii). Although their development was patchy and sporadic one thing they had in common appeared to be in offering a direct alternative to the ancient British public school system with both its idiosyncratic language and atmosphere of houses, prefects, discipline and ritual but also its fixation upon academic success and the passing of examinations through deployment of rote learning. The new schools were therefore, as Robert Skidelsky tells us, often reflective of the prior boyhood experiences (both positive and negative) of those such as A.S. Neill, Cecil Reddie, J.H. Badley and others who were to be part of the new vanguard: 'People may leave their school loving or hating it, or both; they rarely leave indifferent to it' (Skidelsky, 1969, 71). In thus choosing to emphasize that democratic aspect – through the absence of competitive games in favour of communal activity or else being run as communities in which there was a marked absence of hierarchy – these schools reflected that key plank of Holmesian thinking which had earlier emphasized the importance of

> a community whose social system, instead of being inspired by that spirit of 'competitive selfishness' which makes 'each for himself, and the devil take the hindmost' its motto, seems to have realised the Socialistic dream of 'Each for all, and all for each'.
> (Holmes, 1911, 210–211)

Nor was this slew of innovation confined to the secondary sector; although by comparison freer of government interference, primary schools too merited special attention especially given the importance for growth that those such as Piaget and Freud (amongst others) had begun to place upon the early years period. Perhaps the most famous example of this was the Malting House School in Cambridge run by the psychologist Susan Isaacs.[8] This was designed, as Philip Graham (2008) and Willem van der Eyken and Barry Turner (1969) have shown, as a laboratory in which not only could children be studied and detailed stenographic records made of their behaviours (many of which formed the basis of Isaacs' key works) but also acted as a means for generating an increased awareness of the *symbolic* importance of their interactions. By therefore beginning to ascribe deeper meaning to basic social behaviours as well as making explicit the methodologies behind them, it could be argued that Isaacs embodied that strand of Holmes' thinking which saw not only the necessity of using empirical science to understand human behaviour but also how there was deeper meaning to everyday individual action. Whilst for Holmes these became overlaid with a particular mystical philosophy, even within the more coldly scientific Isaacs we see evidence of it reflecting general spiritual development and drives towards disinterested devotion. For example one of the key threads in her seminal work *Social Development in Young Children* (1933) is how growing children learn to become socially aware beings, conscious of the need for reciprocity in the course of action. Clearly, this carries with it the pretext that those who do not reach this state have had some form of restriction placed upon their growth which very often emanated from the school or the home – Isaacs after all was equally interested in the role of education as she was in offering advice to mothers. This notion of restricted growth is a familiar one and, like Holmes, Isaacs too placed great import in the pivotal role played by the teacher who was bound to 'respect the child's developing personality and to treat him as an individual, with personal rights' (Isaacs, 1933, 427). Whilst we cannot say for certain that Isaacs and those from scientific backgrounds knew the key works such as *What is* there is still compelling evidence to suggest that much of the case they made ramified with those earlier ideas.

Elsewhere the prevailing notion of freedom as it was being interpreted by many in the progressive movement ran deeper than merely promoting simplistic individuality, choice or licence within the classroom or school setting. Instead it embodied a more global and holistic vision of *spiritual* liberation which can, once more, be traced to Holmes particularly through his descriptions of 'Utopia' which he had represented as a rural arcadia:

> It nestles at the foot of a long range of hills; and if you will climb the slope that rises at the back of the village, and look over the level country that you have left behind, you will see in the distance the gleaming waters of one of the many seas that wash our shores.
>
> (Holmes, 1911, 154)

Harking back almost to a vision of Merrie England, schools such as Tiptree Hall (run by Norman Macmunn), the Caldecott Community in the Kentish hills, the Theosophist schools in Letchworth and Brackenhill, the Little Commonwealth in the Dorset countryside, Neill at Summerhill as well as Dartington Hall represent but a handful of examples in which the outdoors and Nature took on a high level of importance both real and symbolic. Often to be found in isolated rural areas, these establishments were consciously placing themselves outside the more humdrum grind of the modern world and in many of their practices and activities which included gardening, hiking, outdoor lessons and so on we find equally compelling evidence of this ethos. This in itself was a harking back to an earlier Romanticism of the sort practiced by Pestalozzi and Froebel which held that there was some physical, moral and educative power to the outdoors and that children should where possible experience it directly. Indeed, latent and creeping industrialization – which itself seemed such a potent symbol of the modern world – was seen as deforming and impoverishing to the spirit and imitative of the sorts of mechanized behaviours that were equally prevalent in schools. In discussing for instance the working routine of a Lancashire cotton spinner Holmes was to argue that whilst he may carry out his duties assiduously, 'in doing that one thing [he] becomes, as he progresses, more and more automatic, so that the highest praise we can give him is to say that he does his work with the sureness and accuracy of a machine' (Ibid., 275). This mechanization and urbanization of life – associated not just with monotonous toil but with a degradation of morality that T.S. Eliot was to capture so memorably as 'the broken blinds and chimney pots' amid 'the sawdust-trampled street' (Eliot, 2015, 'Preludes') – was therefore seen by many educators as an evil which had to be combated even if it meant simply planting a garden or building outdoor shelters. All who did however, as for so many other elements of their practice, were undoubtedly doing so, consciously or otherwise, through echoing many of the tenets and ideas found within Holmes' far-reaching writings.

Holmes and the Great War

In any discussion of progressivism during the period pertaining to the first quarter of the twentieth century it is both impossible and irresponsible to ignore the First World War. This is because, as we have mentioned above, much of the drive and ambition of the various groups coalescing around the New Ideals gatherings were driven not just by a strong and basic anti-war agenda but because this was expressed more widely as a revolt against the supposed evils of mechanization which was so closely associated with the conflict. Holmes' assertion then that, 'The war has revealed to us the hollowness of the materialistic civilization on which we had prided ourselves' (Holmes, 1923d, 175) clearly spoke for a wide demographic and was perhaps given added prominence by the unique and changing nature of modern combat. In the historian Arthur Marwick's (1988) terms, this was after all an early example of *total war* which entailed the full and frequently direct involvement of large swathes of the population and which was to have a transformative effect upon the social views of the country at large. It was therefore, given the circumstances, almost impossible *not* to have a partisan view on the conflict and all right-thinking members of the intelligentsia (of whom we should class Holmes) were to have some sort of active involvement or, at the very least, critical engagement with the unfolding events.

No less than for anyone else Holmes' involvement was to be both direct and personal; his son Maurice Gerald (born in 1885) served with distinction in the theatres of France, Belgium, Egypt, and Palestine, rising ultimately to the rank of lieutenant-colonel in the Army Service Corps and this would, one imagines, have been a constant source of anxiety and worry.[9] From the wider world of education too and particularly amongst those first wave of New Education Fellowship thinkers born between 1880 and 1890 – many of whom Holmes would have known and admired – A.S. Neill was to serve with distinction on the Western Front as an officer in the army whilst, as was alluded to within the Introduction, Caldwell Cook as a member of the Artists Rifles found time to compose his seminal text *The Play Way* (1917) within the inhospitable atmosphere of the tranches. Embroiled in a slightly different manner, their future comrade in arms Bertrand Russell (who was to open his Beacon Hill School in 1927) represented the pacifist movement opposed whatsoever to any form of fighting and who was to be imprisoned for making inflammatory speeches. On the opposing side, the founder of another key early progressive school Gordonstoun – Kurt Hahn – found himself by 1914 working for the opposing German government advising on foreign policy and strategic decisions.

As in the field of literature where several of the war poets including Rupert Brooke and Charles Hamilton Sorley had just returned from sojourns in Germany prior to the commencement of hostilities,[10] there were in addition deep *educational* links between the two countries now calling each other enemies. The influence for example of Germanic idealism and its attendant Teutonic appreciation of the outdoors and manly pursuits – embodied best in the *Wandervogel* movement – upon such key progressives as Cecil Reddie and J.H. Badley has been well traced by those such as Robert Skidelsky (1969). As for Reddie whose persistently pro-German attitudes were to be the source of much continued criticism and suspicion, so too had the more nakedly Romantic elements to this Idealism struck a chord with Holmes. Much of his early poetry and religious writing were driven by a more primitive naturalism whilst, more recently, it had been such a love of nature amongst the young that had so impressed him in Finlay-Johnson's school. Indeed, much of that particular strand of thinking was embodied within the kindergartens of Froebel which had received reserved praise from Holmes particularly as they sought to develop aspects of the child's spirit in their underlying search for a Divine Law of the Universe. The fact that the War was seen by some as a result of the drilling of (admittedly militaristic) ideals into a docile population may not have been an irony lost on Holmes. Whilst then many progressives including Holmes himself were to condemn Germany for her actions it would have been done with a knowing awareness and sense of regret given her prominent and active educational past.

However despite this transformation of comrades into combatants, the general mood amongst the educational rebels nevertheless remained stoic. Justifying the decision of the organizing Committee of the New Ideals Conferences to continue holding their annual meetings the Earl of Lytton bullishly argued, 'They [the Committee] believed that the holding of the Conference was not only consistent with what was in everybody's mind, but was a duty rendered even more necessary by the fact the country was at war' (Lytton, 1915, 1). The implication here – and one that Holmes would no doubt have agreed with – was that the education and principles of the sort envisaged by the New Ideals grouping had a role to play beyond the mere schooling of young people. Knowledge alone had not after all stopped the world descending into the greatest conflict in its history and so it was other, wider virtues that education had now to be seen to promote. Many of these ramified with the emphasis that those such as Holmes were placing upon *spiritual* and *communal* development, aspects he had so much admired within the *Casa dei Bambini* schools of Montessori. Significantly as we have mentioned, much of the progressive rhetoric of the time was couched as a protest against the wider evils of *fin de siècle* industrialization which was seen to reach its ultimate end-point in the horrors of a different type of war in which men themselves – as in the paintings of C.W.R. Nevinson – became both physical and psychological embodiments of those mechanized machines. This therefore brought a new, sinister and hitherto-fore unforeseen depth to Holmes' conception of *mechanical obedience*, the like of which he had earlier observed as part of the changing pattern of developing adult labour. Given that such processes served ultimately to deaden the appreciative senses and meant men based their existences around cultures of self-preservation and fear (whether of the factory boss or schoolmaster) it was inevitable, according to Holmes, that it would lead to egoism and 'when egoism, which makes each man a law to himself and the potential enemy of his kind, is unrestrained by authority, the door is thrown wide open to anarchy, and through anarchy to chaos' (Holmes, 1911, 207).

Although these words had been penned three years previous, they seemed equally prophetic and relevant amid the tumult of late 1914 and set the tone perhaps for Caldwell Cook's terse assessment that such changes had brought a 'spiritual freshening' (Cook, 1917, 13) to education. There was much therefore to the ideas, idealized communities and hopes of the thinkers allied to Holmes that seemed to be deliberately offering a refreshing corrective to these new developments particularly as they oriented themselves to focusing as much on the development of the spirit and socialization as on mere apprehension of information. As Holmes himself was to so well later put it,

> until the plain average youth can go out into the world with the spirit of comradeship and co-operation and an unselfish devotion at his heart, we shall strive to but little purpose, by means of the League of Nations and other such political measures, to secure international amity and peace.
> (Holmes, 1924a, 16)

These considerations meant that the early New Ideals conferences took place under a marked shadow and general sense that there had to be some future tangible change to the existing educational and social structures. In that light it should therefore be clear why both the conduct and morality of the First World War became so pertinent for Holmes and why the conflict needed to be addressed so explicitly within his work. Not only had he become embroiled at a *personal* level through the direct involvement of family and friends but, in addition, his philosophy with its talk of Utopia, happiness and, most importantly, communality tied closely to many of the concerns within the rising progressive faction. Although they may have initially located much of this community spirit within individual progressive schools which were seen as small microcosmic communities in themselves, so too was that term coming increasingly to be used within a broader context and as emblematic of the need for more *global* harmony. Many of the members of the Fellowship were after all committed to a pan-European way of thinking which drew as part of its tradition upon ideas from across the Continent especially those of Pestalozzi and Froebel as well as from America in the form of John Dewey. Unity and cooperation were key and Holmes – through his Italian sojourns and broad cultural awareness – was all too cognisant of this connection and heritage. As one of the presenters at the New Ideals gathering was to put it,

> The word 'education' dies upon our lips, for are we not engaged in wrestling a foe, whose methods and conceptions of education have repeatedly been held up to us in this country as something to which we should strive to attain.
> (Hutchinson, 1915, 83)

Embodying this sentiment, after 1918, the organs of the Fellowship such as the *New Era* journal were to pay lip-service to the newly formed League of Nations and peaceful attempts at conflict resolution characteristic of the period.[11] Any attempts to therefore disrupt this were bound to be unpopular with those such as Holmes whose more global vision was one based on universal *wholeness* and whose views were, broadly, antithetical to any sort of competition and need to acquire territory.

Given this fact it is then perhaps understandable as to why Holmes came to see much of the burden of guilt for the war as residing with Germany, characterizing her as both an ardent aggressor and as the sole bearer of responsibility for igniting the conflict. Whilst he may have admired those earlier German Idealists and engaged critically and wholeheartedly with their ideas, there was certainly no sentiment spared when it came to attacking the later actions of their country which he was to do with some of his most biting and vituperative prose. More precisely the central focus of Holmes' ire was Prussia who had been the dominant power behind the process of unification in 1871 and whose sabre-rattling *Junker* class embodied for Holmes many of the worst traits of swaggering despotic arrogance and braggadocio. However, even though making his position manifestly clear, his was not a belief driven by the somewhat blind and loyalist patriotism which inspired many of the time but rather a more rational analysis emanating from his identification of the profound flaws found at the very root of German society which had been shaped historically by the sorts of assertive social and educational forces he had made it his business to earlier elaborate. In particular it was the twin evils of *docility* and *dogmatism* which, as we shall see, were the supposed catalysts which impelled Germany toward a position in which both militarism and nationalism became endemic to their way of life and which simmered to the point of needing an ultimate release in the form of state-wide domination. In articulating this vision, Holmes was thereby offering a very direct case-study of where things could go wrong within a country if their system of schooling were allowed to be driven by selfish ends and which therefore rejected his notions of self-realization and out-growth of the soul. As he put it, 'Ultra-docility on the part of the many tends to generate inordinate self-esteem on the part of the dogmatic few' (Holmes, 1916a, 49).

This was not incidentally the only time that Holmes was to use the case-study as a vehicle for outlining his own ideas; another of his many books entitled *The Albigensian or Catharist Heresy* (1925b) was for example to look at the suppression of spiritual freedom in thirteenth-century France. In the case of contemporary Germany however it should be remembered that his writing on the subject was given added piquancy as it was published during the conflict itself and so represented both a strong decrying of her ideals and an equally robust re-affirmation of his own principles which were to serve as a remedy at a time of national crisis. What, one wonders, would the many educational radicals who despaired at a conflict which had effectively pitted two developed educational systems against one another have made of Holmes' thundering denunciation delivered in 1915: 'Germany is military in the fullest sense of the word...its slavishly obedient people are pre-eminently amenable to the discipline of drill...In that school the features of the conventional type of education are reproduced and intensified' (Holmes, 1915, 961). Whilst they may well have shared Holmes' frustration at the more rigid forms of discipline (school and otherwise) inherent within Germany, few if any would have gone as far in explaining how these both reflected aspects of national character and were indicative of an external materialism.

Of course subsequent interpretations as to the causes of the War, including in particular those seminal accounts by those adhering to the thesis of Fritz Fischer (1967) have, since Holmes, focussed in on these factors (especially the militaristic culture within Germany at the time) and given them precedence over more immediate events taking place in the Balkans or the collapsing system of alliances that obligated so many combatants. By therefore invoking these more overarching notions – specifically nationalism, militarism and imperialism – there is an element of the prophetic in Holmes' work. However, unlike those other later writers whose concerns were often explicitly historic, economic or political, once more it is imperative to locate Holmes' response in relation to his earlier writings on *education* and the way in which he saw the failings of German society as residing in particular social pressures and spiritual defects. These failings were particularly well adumbrated in Holmes' major War-period book *The Nemesis of Docility: A Study of German Character* published in 1916 at the mid-point of the conflict and which, as one would expect, drew heavily upon reference to contemporary events to promote its case. In some ways, this is the most disturbing and unsettling work within his corpus for it paints in broad brush strokes a picture of the German people which, to modern sensibilities, smacks of sweeping generalization and occasional racial stereotyping. Such problems emerge from the outset:

> The Germans are the most obedient people on the face of the earth. To say that they obey orders unhesitatingly, ungrudgingly, and punctiliously is to do them less than justice. They do more than obey orders. They wait for them, look out for them, are lost without them.
>
> (Holmes, 1916a, 1)

This most 'slavishly obedient of people' (Ibid., 56) lacking according to Holmes a sense of humour and the ability to self-deprecate came into being through the historical confluence of both tribalism and feudalism and, in tracing these developments across time in Prussian society back through the era of Frederick the Great, he was to explain how it was that contemporary Germany became beset with those twin evils of docility and dogmatism. As we have seen in the previous chapter, within his other educational writings Holmes had spoken in broad abstract terms as to the general assumptions and causes surrounding, particularly, dogmatism but here he was to provide a concrete example in which it – and its mirror image docility – was seen to inflect and persist within an entire culture. Assisted by the process of conscription which meant ordinary men 'would carry back to civil life the habit of mechanical obedience which they had acquired on the drill-ground' (Ibid., 55) the key catalyst in Holmes' analysis was the reification of the State to a level above and beyond its constituent parts, that is, the individuals within it.

In many ways this was bound up with the earlier ideas of that most Germanic of philosophers Georg Friedrich Hegel whose infuriatingly complicated writing on the State had, in essence, raised it to the level of the *objectified mind* and thus commensurate with the two aspects of human will – the subjective and the rational. Or, put another way, as the product of the combination of Spirit, freedom and Reason to become a manifestation of the Spirit (*zeitgeist*) of the population. Taking their cue from this approach although not perhaps its spirit (Hegel's State was divine and benign in equal measure) German university professors and intellectuals, according to Holmes, had developed a 'theory of the State which proves conclusively that meek, *unquestioning* obedience is the first of civic duties and the highest form of patriotism' (Ibid., 71, italics added). This was embodied in the highly regulated level of State bureaucracy in Prussia whose need to externalize and quantify mirrored Holmes' earlier attacks on 'My Lords' at the Board of Education and their mechanisms of testing to determine school grants. Precisely because of this comparatively despotic governance from the dogmatic minority, Holmes contended, German men in their daily lives had been driven to docility and an excessive regard for worship of the State which came to manifest as blind patriotism and a tolerance of the worst excesses of supra-national action notably the grabbing of territory and stirring up conflict in ways that indicated 'inhumanity, rapacity [and] perfidy' (Ibid., 75). In Holmes' schema there were a number of communities which Men were to be part of throughout their life, the greatest of which was that pertaining to Humanity and the totality of the Universe. With the case of Germany however, worship of the State had become the extent of Man's ambition and which, following that premise through, accounted for many of the faults inherent within its society – selfishness, intolerance, lack of feeling and so on.

Nor were such trends confined to her armed forces where unthinking obedience might be more commonly expected – everyday civilian life and particularly *schools* were also key instruments in this process and it is here we see how Holmes' vision of education had by this point widened to integrate other aspects of society. Building on this, in another contemporary article contrasting Germany with Britain, Holmes argued that whilst both nations shared similar ideals in relation to their educational policies – that is systems driven by the need to externalize and a distrust of the nature of the child – 'so far as we [Britain] have an ideal of life, it not merely differs from the German ideal, but is directly opposed to it' (Holmes, 1915, 968). Holmes had long protested the dangerous idiocy as he saw it of attempting to impose (and even examine) such ethereal concepts in schools and the War provided a definitive example of how doing so *in extremis* meant classroom drilling via rote learning thereby created a uniformity of mind which itself contributed to a general docility amongst a population incapable of imagining critical alternatives. This can be tied in with Prussia's longstanding militaristic tradition – they had after all unified via three successful wars[12] – and the prestigious status afforded to cadet schools in which drill of this type was highly prized. At a deeper level, instilling idealism in this way and celebrating the virtue of mass, uniform obedience ran counter to the processes of nature in whose purpose lay 'a general capacity for evolving appropriate senses in….an ever varying environment' (Holmes, 1916a, 114). It will be remembered that the developing of individual natures was not only a key tenet of child-centredness but also antecedent to the development of inward growth of the soul and a recognition of the One in the All. In imposing a 'one size fits all' mentality upon education, Holmes was thus arguing that the Germans were stunting creation of difference and variety which for him was a pre-requisite of a democratic, open and liberal society and not one run autocratically and as heavily centralized as was being opposed by Britain and the Allied powers. This was further reinforced by the aforementioned worship of the State and the militaristic culture embedded more widely within German society and promoted by compulsory national service.

By contrast, the British were more relaxed in their attitude toward each other and the bigger questions of life adopting what Holmes termed a 'Live and let live' (Holmes, 1915, 968) approach rather than necessarily and automatically seeking obeisance toward a State which imposed upon their daily lives and which thereby sought to externalize many of their actions. Indeed, it was that which Holmes assigned as one of the key reasons why Britain was to be ultimately victorious in the War – teaching and instilling patriotism by dogmatic means, as had happened in Germany, caused he contended the inculcation of particular values such as self-esteem, superiority and lack of sympathy which were ultimately to blight the military campaigns and strategy which came unstuck when opponents were arrogantly underestimated. Likewise, in blunting individuality and the ability to think creatively Germany prevented its citizens and soldiery from thinking laterally, resourcefully and above all *instinctively*. Holmes uses the metaphor of a bus driver coming to grief as a result of having learnt to drive solely from a manual which goes against the intuitive nature of the activity in which instinctive decisions in new situations happen on every journey. On the battlefield the blind inclination amongst all ranks to 'merely follow orders' was clearly detrimental and Holmes, in another war time tract this time addressed to teachers, placed an emphasis upon the greater adaptability of the British soldier:

> Since the present war began our army has expanded to ten times its previous strength. How has this been done? By men going into it out of a hundred different callings and learning what was a new trade for each of them...so well has the average Englishman...learnt this new trade...What better proof could be given of the inherent versatility of human nature, of the infinite resourcefulness of the soul?
>
> (Holmes, 1917a, 39)

Although Holmes' point here was more general and concerned with the infinite possibilities of the human being for adaptability it nevertheless carried with it the implicit assumption that this was more likely within a society such as that of Britain. Whilst, as we have sketched out, there were many deep-seated flaws within the British education system particularly at the secondary level where the yoke of examination remained, such poisonous effects tended to subside into adulthood. Unlike Germany there was neither forced peace-time conscription nor the need to impose loyalty to a freshly conceived state – Germany only having become unified in 1870–1871. Of course it is possible here to argue that in offering such praise Holmes seems to be speaking in contravention of some of the critiques made earlier which had spoken of the longstanding detrimental effects of education and which had formed such a central plank of his argument around the nature of schooling. It was after all just before the War that he had bemoaned the lack of individuality, initiative, enterprise and love of adventure within the country at large: 'These are the qualities with which the Englishman of today seems to be less richly endowed than his forefathers; and they are the very qualities which…our elementary schools…would be likely to weaken' (Holmes, 1914, 191). Was Holmes now so caught up in the need to criticise Germany and her threat to the New Ideals project that he was prepared to negate, sidestep and perhaps even forget some of his previous anger? This is quite possible particularly as he too appeared caught up in the maelstrom of propaganda which demonized supposed German war crimes and which spoke of the 'relatively low *moral* of her soldiers, devitalized and mechanized by too much organization' (Holmes, 1916a, 197, original italics).

Holmes' vitriol undoubtedly carried a disparaging tone although it is still quite possible to validate his claims by allying them to arguments developed retrospectively which identified the decline of the German war effort with the increased numbers of crippling strikes, mutinies and revolts as resentment grew against such dogmatic imposition and a weariness accrued around the constant demands of the State. In many ways this later (and perfectly valid) thesis might have garnered Holmes' support as he had previously also argued that these internal ructions, which included a rise in criminal activity, were a natural response to an excessively dogmatic state which had attempted the dangerously impossible task of imposing ideals upon a mind as rigidly as one would impose simple facts. By so doing it shows how Holmes was constantly able to incorporate new events and information into his unfolding and developing thesis concerning both the War and its underlying implications. Perhaps ultimately the two factors are connected; regardless however, it is significant that there was not to be this level of explicit dissatisfaction within the Allied powers many of whose citizenry remained loyal to the greater cause and whose grievances were more readily mediated.

In therefore seeking to chime with the public mood, Holmes reiterated his commitment to virtues not traditionally associated with left-leaning progressive thinkers, and was to make the case for the ultimate futility of a doctrine which sought to impose its ideals upon others in the way that Germany had done:

> We owe it to our great Empire, which would have fallen to pieces long ago if 'Do what I tell you' had been our motto. We owe to it that when the War broke out our Empire rallied round us almost as if it were a single people.
> (Holmes, 1915, 969)

Although ultimately here Holmes' purpose was to level a critique at the hypocrisy and double standards of British life in which there appeared a disconnect between the system of education which consisted of mechanical obedience and discipline and later adult life where 'before he [the child] has grown up we give him freedom and tell him to live his own life and work out his own salvation' (Ibid., 970) he nonetheless appeared to come down heavily against the German way of life with its more heavy stress upon the life-long dogmatic drilling of idealism and associated virtues.

In many ways then the case of the First World War – significant as it was anyway – represented for Holmes a clash of ideologies in which the ideals of liberty, freedom and tolerance were set against those of dogmatism and docility. Whilst this was not atypical of many attitudes of the time which similarly railed against the faults of German citizenry – witness the early propaganda denouncing the beastly 'Hun' for example – Holmes was unique in seeing these as stemming from attachment to forms of education bound to external materialism rather than inward spiritual growth. In this belief he received tacit support not merely from expected quarters but also more Establishment figures such as Robert Baden-Powell, the founder of the Scouts: 'Instruction is not Education. We want to educate the child from within instead of impose instruction upon him from without, and if that can be brought about I believe it will be a very great step in the right direction' (Baden-Powell, 1916, 57). Whilst the militaristic Baden-Powell may have appeared an unlikely bedfellow for Holmes, the Scout movement with its stress upon the outdoors, the combination of self-reliance and team-work as well as the values of respect and loyalty may well have appealed to him.

What this does show however is that throughout the War there was a large consensus of opinion around education which crossed political, social and philosophical boundaries. Often this was concerned with developing an education system which promoted inner growth conducted in an atmosphere of freedom and which was seen as antithetical to the sorts of mechanical constraints and trappings which were now enveloping the world. Much of this naturally led back to the writings of Holmes which had earlier pointed the way in their talk of unthinking and unquestioning obedience in contemporary schools and the need therefore to foster a more 'natural' form of growth. However what marks him out as particularly distinctive is the way in which the War – far from being something to be stoically endured or else seen in the most dichotomous of terms – became instead very naturally subsumed into his much wider viewpoint which equated the social changes in Germany and their results with many of the comparable effects that organized religion and aspects of Original Sin had served to shape. In that way then, we can see that events served to convince Holmes both of the rightness of his cause (there were catastrophic consequences to excessive mechanical obedience) but also that he needed now to turn his attention to looking at how his ideas could be appropriated to exploring concerns more global than education.

Holmes, politics and democratic living

Explicating Holmes' political views is both complex and, at the same time, hugely significant. Complex for in only very few of his published works and utterances does he make explicit his ideological or party-political obligations and yet important for, of these 'political' writings, (many of which emerged at around this period during the War) several betray evidence of his commitment to a form of democracy which transcended the commonly held conceptions and connotations of the term. Understanding this, in turn, not only tells us much about his philosophy as it had been set down in earlier Idealist works but also as it pointed the way toward the last phase of his life and his still greater focus upon inward contemplation. Holmes' view then of democracy was to eschew many of the more overtly politically theorized models relating to participation and right and drew instead upon principles relating to community as linked to *self-realization* which he had earlier insisted should form the basis of a fit and proper system of education. It was therefore schooling – and particularly the lessons he had learnt from Utopia – which came to embody in microcosm for Holmes the future shape of the adult world. This idea had been alluded to through his denunciations of Germany and so one of the reasons why Holmes' political utterances appeared therefore so relevant following the Great War was that he saw this period as a crucial time in the destiny of human relations. In this, he was not alone; from British Prime Minister Lloyd George's rhetoric calling for a Land Fit for Heroes, to W.B. Yeats' portents of doom in *The Second Coming* to the Futurists' earlier clarion call for a sweeping away of the old order by mechanization and technology there was clearly a prevailing mood which suggested a tipping point with the emergence of a new world from the ashes – quite literally – of the old. Writing with the benefit of hindsight in 1924, Holmes was to capture something of this flavour:

> Then came the tragedy of the Great War, which revealed the hollowness of our material prosperity and accelerated the process of its hitherto unsuspected decay. Now…Europe is a weltering chaos of conflicting aims and interests, a whirlpool of selfish desires, of angry passions, of dark suspicions, of jealous fears…The whole social structure is rocking as if in an earthquake…
> (Holmes, 1924c, 216)

This chaotic divide was in essence theorized as a clash between the values of regimented and dogmatic law and order on the one hand and those of adherence to conscience and the inward Self on the other. In characteristic Holmesian language, this violent coming together was not therefore a battle to be fought culturally, economically or even artistically but rather over contrasting systems of belief between advocates of the readily understandable external world on the one hand and those of the internal world of the soul on the other, with only the latter having the potential to fill the vacuum left by the hollowness of the recent conflict. In this, as we shall see, religion was to have a central part to play and in a number of key works published after the War, notably *All is One: a Plea for Higher Pantheism* (1921d) and *The Cosmic Commonwealth* (1920d), Holmes was to make the case for a social reconstruction driven not by economics or politics but instead by the need for a changing conception of God and reality. In many ways this was apposite as the defeat of one power (Germany) who had long relied on a system driven by dogmatic control, feudalism and autocracy ushered in the possibility of root and branch change in Man's thinking in which the vacuum alluded to in the above quotation could be filled. It is perhaps significant to note, after that fashion, that whilst in 1917 Holmes had appeared despondent about the possibility for social change – 'the feudal rather than the democratic spirit is still in the air that we breathe' (Holmes, 1917c, 316) – only a year or so later with the War nearing completion and the Allies looking triumphant he had emerged with a more cautious optimism about the prevailing possibilities. There still remained a plethora of social problems – not least the large numbers of children leaving school early as intellectual wastage – but it seemed that Holmes with a greater focus in his energies now upon philosophy and religion[13] had begun to find something akin to a solution.

In many ways this sanguinity, guarded as it was ultimately to be, stemmed from Holmes' dissatisfaction and suspicion with existing radical political alternatives which he felt had failed to disassociate themselves from those wider and more commonplace maladies in society. One should remember that these years had seen the October Revolution in 1917 which enabled the Bolsheviks to take power in Russia, the Spartacist uprising in Bavaria in 1919 as well as Mussolini's March on Rome in 1922 all of which had been couched in the revolutionary language of change and often taking place in quite abrupt and violent fashion. In one of his best and most polemic pieces of writing (actually a transcript of a talk given earlier to the Cambridge University Fabian Society in 1912) Holmes laid down very clearly where he felt the dangers lay in politicking of the sort most associated with the left. Although admitting a 'small measure of sympathy' (Holmes, 1923a, 3) for the socialist cause through their communitarian system of beliefs driven by the mantra of 'Each of All and All for Each' this was only on the pre-condition that it remained divorced from the official Labour Party and similar organizations whose dogmatism was the equal of anything being put forward by the right. Quite aside from the fact that these groups' conflicting ideologies led to a fragmentation around the meaning of what it meant to be 'socialist', often those such as the trades unions he saw as acting for 'purely selfish purposes' (Ibid., 11) as their actions (strikes, protests and so on) were conceived through the lens of betterment to themselves rather than the collective good in a more holistic sense. In referring for example to the labour strikes – presumably those taking place in the munitions industry during the War – Holmes reported scathingly that, 'the devotion of the strikers to their union [was] as conspicuous as their callow indifference to the well-being of the workers in other industries and the prosperity of the country as a whole' (Holmes, 1921d, 46). Likewise, he scornfully dismissed the Labour Party's call for nationalization which he associated with 'State-despotism of which the capitalists, great and small, will be the first victims' (Holmes, 1920d, 41).

The historically strong devotion of the members of these groups to the creeds and doctrines of (for instance) Marx and other radical thinkers and tracts was well known and both their determinism and fetishization of the economic was for Holmes insufficient and futile in attempting to overturn inequality as it continued to give primacy both to the Self and the reality of (dialectical) materialism. In his aphoristic phrase, 'A change of machinery, without a change of heart, would profit us nothing' (Holmes, 1921d, 139). Whilst the aim amongst those radicals may have been an overturning of the existing social order rather than its preservation, this leftish rhetoric was nevertheless comparable to that behind the attempted imposition in Germany of an ideal which, as we have seen, merely encouraged devotion to the State and a militaristic frame of mind. As then in Germany when such dogmatism had led to the continuance of systems of autocracy, Holmes feared that in failing to first stamp out the intrinsic selfishness of human nature there would remain a persistence of static and unyielding institutional mechanisms within society. He believed (in hindsight probably incorrectly) that workers acquiring the means of production would find the country itself in *more* direct competition with those overseas so entering a period of economic warfare whilst, perhaps more accurately, he argued that a socialist state would need a larger Civil Service many of whom would need to be drawn from the bourgeois class 'which owe their very existence to the stimulus of the desire for gain, and which have made municipal government a by-word for jobbery' (Holmes, 1923a, 21).

Although, as Arthur J. McIvor (2008) makes clear, there was a large increase in trade union membership and thereby risk of strikes at the time of Holmes' writing and frustration at the actions of public-sector strikers as they impacted upon the population at large was presumably commonplace even then, the originality of Holmes' diagnosis stemmed not from an embittered personal or political agenda but more as he saw such actions as demonstrating a fundamental lack of *disinterested devotion* or *unselfishness*, terms which were to be central to his later philosophy of morality and as he came to comprehend the need for reconstructive effort. As we have previously seen in earlier chapters, developing people to think and act in these ways was one of the key points and purposes of education as it was these values which were the basis for self-transcendence through self-contemplation. Preoccupation with the individual self was to be left behind at the expense of the collective. Whilst for many (especially those on the left) this tendency was easily resolved by banding together in organized groups such as unions and fraternities in order to fight for a common good, in Holmes' eyes this was inadequate and seen as a simple response rooted very much in the materialist world from which he desired Mankind to escape. Notwithstanding the self-regard that such organizations seemed to demonstrate by thinking solely of their own group at the expense of the wider community, they also neglected any element of *religion* which for Holmes represented the real site of future change – 'to reconstruct without regard to religion is to build without a plan' (Holmes, 1923d, 176). Leftish thinking – perhaps driven by Marx's characterization of it as the opium of the masses – had long been commonly hostile to the concept of religious orthodoxy and even those such as the Fabians and the earlier Evangelicals who had been driven by a more missionary sense of zeal did so from a paternalistic standpoint which would have been antithetical to that of Holmes. Any attempts at such help were surely to be equated with a dogmatic desire to be seen to 'do good'.

Even when Holmes speaks here of religion, he was not meaning it in the way that the term was conventionally used as encompassing orthodox belief in a theistic God but more euphemistically as referring to a general lack of spirituality in the world at large. Religion there evidently was, however, as Holmes was to make repeatedly clear, these were often the belief systems of the 'average man' (who one presumes would have joined such trades unions) and who also 'unhesitatingly takes for granted the intrinsic reality of the material or outward and visible world, and that when he begins to reflect, in his crudely simple way, on things in general, he instinctively bases his philosophy on this assumption' (Holmes, 1924c, 35). Holmes saw all such political agitation of the time as therefore deriving from the principles of this assumption and as based on a sense of literal as well as metaphysical materialism. Indeed, echoing his earlier Inspectorial observations, he was to reiterate the point that whilst religious studies in schools continued to prevail as a subject it did so under the guise of 'a kind of compulsory extra' (Holmes, 1923e, 192) and, through being so regimented and subject to examination often by rote, was leading to a *paganism* as children both turned their backs on it (through boredom!) or else saw in it the competition which so bedevilled many other aspects of schooling. Either way the end result was to lead to a selfishness which was to place an immovable barrier in way of true soul-growth and which continued into adulthood.

This contention was a clear coming together of the spiritual and the social and so, for Holmes, the void created by the War needed to be filled by a new kind of politics but not one driven by the traditional concerns of politicians such as economics, bureaucratic legislation or modes of governance. Democracy in this context was to spring instead from the human spirit and 'equality of all men in the sight of God' (Holmes, 1917c, 308) rather than the 'caucuses, conventions, unions of democratic control [and] other such contrivances' (Ibid., 316). To therefore avoid any of the self-interest which he saw as endemic within the Western world, rather than suggesting any of the usual targets of reform – housing, welfare, social security, living standards – Holmes built on his earlier investigations into the East to suggest instead that what was needed was for men to aspire toward 'an object so large, so far off, and yet of such supreme magnetic power, as to leave no room for the intrusion of self-interest into the devotion which it inspires' (Holmes, 1920c, 47–48). In using a metaphor appropriate for the time in which pacts, treaties and alliances became commonly seen as a way to foster global cooperation, in much the same way that some form of central strengthening and security (through supranational bodies) was necessary to safeguard European society from being torn asunder by fragmentation and anarchy so Holmes argued the same was true for the human soul which was equally in need of purposeful re-orientation and focussing on a new set of priorities.

The object of Holmes' desire, and the source of this re-orientation, was not then a tangible organization or specific policy or goal but rather devotion to what he was to call the *Cosmic Commonwealth* which was his term for the communal unselfish devotion emanating from a surrendering of attachment to the Self which would in turn be replaced with duty to neighbours and the like. This worldly arrangement was envisaged as one set above the more traditional and prosaic concerns of the State and thus transcended the traditional arrangements of human relations to seek to create a new form of community: 'In and through his membership of that community his communal and his ideal self will merge into one, and the feud between them...will cease to exist' (Holmes, 1920d, 67). It should be evident how the ethical aims of this community – specifically its love of one's neighbour – intersected with many of the parables and sayings of Christ thereby giving credence to Holmes' continuing assertion that he remained, at least in spirit, a Christian and saw in the New Testament teachings not the supernaturalism as traditionally inferred by those ancient interpreters of the texts but rather the first acknowledgment of the principle of self-realization. As he put it, 'Jesus loved to set us tasks which are too hard for us...This, the greatest of all tasks, will never be accomplished...The ideal self will never be found; but for that very reason the quest of it is life eternal' (Holmes, 1927a, 139).

Although the old rhetoric surrounding Liberty, Equality and Fraternity still prevailed after a fashion it was driven by an ultimate aspiration toward a, 'spread of the democratic spirit – the spirit of fundamental equality – among men' (Ibid.). One place in which this could be achieved was in the *school* and in his last two educational works – *Give me the Young* (1921a) and *Can Education Give us Peace?* (1924a) – Holmes had advocated strongly that they should become, 'the central influence of a locality and that if a spirit of comradeship and co-operation was promoted, children should want to devote themselves to the community' (Gordon, 1983, 22). By thereby promoting – albeit indirectly for these were concepts to be lived as much as understood – the notions of self-realization and transcendence from Self within the school community and curriculum, Holmes hoped that these Eastern-inspired virtues would be more widely disseminated within society. As children become happy in school 'they carry their happiness with them to their homes, where the reflected glow of it may light up the hearts of their parents' (Holmes, 1921a, 82). At one level this triangulation pre-figures many of the sentiments of the later Plowden Report (1967) which also argued for a linkage between the school, the home and the local community. Whilst the emphasis here was very different (Plowden being seen as a means to redress prevailing social inequality) undoubtedly the child-centred sentiments of Plowden would have resonated with Holmes as would the idea that education and the school should be the focus both of investment and community life.

Whilst the communal and carefree atmosphere he had previously witnessed within Utopia was clearly to form the basis of his theory of democracy this was now being given a deeper underlying basis as it reflected Holmes' mature philosophical message and was not merely a place where children could simply be happy and take this, or not, with them into later life as was the case for example in schools like Summerhill. If, as Holmes claimed, all men were capable of infinite growth involving the expansion of their instincts surely then this could and should be used as the basis of future societies: 'if every man…had unlimited reserves of potentiality in himself…the claim of the lowliest of men to regulate the affairs of the community to which he happens to belong is as strong as the claim of the mightiest' (Holmes, 1920d, 53). Holmes had earlier made it clear in his key educational treatise that 'it is the presence of the ideal self in each of us which makes communal life possible' (Holmes, 1911, 291) and so this particular evolving understanding of democracy sought to bring these two selves together. In essence, the ideal Self was to be filtered into the communal Self by having the community which it served (the Cosmic Commonwealth) seen as an unattainable ideal thereby moving humanity beyond the trappings of outward materialism and towards the path of self-realization through recognizing the infinite inward capacity of the soul. Materialism of this earlier type was a form of bondage which Holmes equated with insanity through 'drawing to itself more than its share of the man's thoughts and emotions, and so impairing the inward harmony of his soul' (Holmes, 1920b, 511). In fact Holmes was to argue in a contemporary article that many of the issues surrounding such mental instability were partially attributable to the lack of opportunity for true out-growth. Far from intending to trivialize the issue such a point is equally in the spirit of those such as A.S. Neill who sought to explain many contemporary ills by the failings found within the early years and the system which nurtured them.

The underpinning factor then behind Holmes' idealized community and reconstructed world was instead to be *love* which was seen to form the basis of all action. Typically this was not exactly Christian altruism as laid down in the New Testament (and itself a very old precept) but rather as stemming from the idea that it had the power to facilitate deep personal change and moves towards envisioning the unified world: 'love is the centripedal force which makes all things one, the inner harmony which subdues and transform chaos, the mainspring of the Universe' (Holmes, 1929b, 85). This form of love, which was of the sort which was an end itself, was therefore emblematic of the total escape from the Self (given that its object was un-calculating kindness to others) and chimed with Holmes' earlier writing which had been concealed tightly within the cloak of Idealism. More specifically, a life lived according to the precept of love devoid of any taint of selfishness was 'not so much a task to be accomplished as an ideal to be pursued' (Holmes, 1924c, 218). This itself made morality, and therefore the future society which it was seen to underpin, *idealistic* in the sense of pursuing, once more, a goal encapsulated within the infinite. This was a view too associated with a hopeful and *optimistic* way of thinking which Holmes had long connected to aspects of the mind and of the soul, the activities of which were now so central to his writing where the social and spiritual were seen to collide. As he had earlier stated,

Hope – a strong-souled, large-hearted, all-suffering, all-conquering hope – a hope which sees deep into the present and far into the future…it belongs to his nature, it belongs to the world-wide nature which flows in an irresistible stream through his being, to move toward an infinitely distant yet ever-present ideal.

(Holmes, 1898b, 108–109)

It can therefore be seen that in adumbrating this most simple of concepts Holmes was being neither naive or fatuous; in many ways this resembled a return to first principles – like that of Schoenberg to C major – and was thus all the more profound as it carried with it the weight of three decades worth of thought and reflection stemming almost from his first published utterances. As he was therefore in the last years, in something akin to a coda, to postulate more upon life in the next world, it seemed that in the years following the War and in considering the arrangement of life in this one, Holmes had resolved the many threads of his thinking and, through a neat spiritual circularity, found them all for the first time.

Notes

1 In the year 1919 alone he published two books – *The Secret of Happiness* and *The Secret of the Cross* – as well as three journal articles.
2 Geraldine Hodgson (1865–1937) was a schoolteacher and lecturer on education. She was also the author of a large number of works including scholarly editions of medieval theology and literature, textbooks, a biography of James Elroy Flecker as well as four novels.
3 Charles Booth (1840–1916) carried out his most famous work in London toward the end of the nineteenth century. Published as two volumes in 1889 and 1891 Booth's work showed that about 35 per cent of Londoners were living in abject poverty. (Benjamin) Seebohm Rowntree (1871–1954) was the son of Joseph Ronwtree and, inspired by his father and Booth, carried out similar investigations in York. He found that nearly 30 per cent of people were living in comparable poverty challenging the view that such poverty was confined solely to London.
4 Bertram Hawker (1868–1952) was born in Wales to an Australian father and Irish mother. Having worked initially in Australia as a clergyman, Hawker visited Montessori's schools in 1911 (as did Holmes). Impressed with what he saw, he soon set up a *casa dei bambini* near his home in London and served as a tireless promoter of her ideals and of democratic principles more broadly.
5 Victor Bulwer-Lytton, 2nd Earl of Lytton K.G. (1876–1947) was a British politician and colonial administrator. Aside from his interest in education, he had a life-long passion for India becoming Governor of Bengal in 1922.
6 The Dalton Plan was an educational concept developed in 1914 by Helen Parkhurst at the Children's University School in New York and later adopted in the schools of Dalton, Massachusetts. In essence, the purpose of the Plan was to tailor the curriculum to each child's own interests and abilities whilst promoting independence and individuality.
7 Beatrice Ensor (1885–1974) was a Theosophical educator and co-founder of the New Education Fellowship in 1921. Their first conference of that year, held in Calais, was on the theme of 'Creative Self-Expression of the Child'.

8 Susan Isaacs (1885–1948) was an educational psychologist and psychoanalyst who was a pioneer of the nursery school movement alongside publishing various works on the intellectual and social development of children. Between 1924 and 1927 she was head of the Malting House School in Cambridge which was an experimental school that allowed her to develop her nascent theories.
9 During his war-time service, Holmes was mentioned in dispatches twice, and was appointed as an Officer of the Order of the British Empire and of the Order of the Nile, and then received the CBE in 1919. He was created Companion of the Order of the Bath in 1929, and knighted as a Knight Commander (KCB) in 1938. He was invested as a Knight Grand Cross of the Order of the British Empire (GBE) in the New Year Honours 1946.
10 Rupert Brooke (1887–1915) wrote his most famous poem 'The Old Vicarage: Grantchester' whilst staying in Munich. Charles Hamilton Sorley (1895–1915), after a walking tour, had been briefly detained at the German border.
11 The 1920s can be seen in some respects as the decade of diplomacy and there were many such pacts and treaties designed to further peaceful cooperation. Some such as the Kellogg–Briand Pact (1928) were predicated precisely upon using peaceful means as a means of conflict resolution.
12 These three conflicts were the war over Schleswig-Holstein (1864), the Austro-Prussian War (1866) and, finally, the Franco-Prussian War (1871).
13 Between the years of 1919 and 1922 Holmes published one book and four philosophical articles and two books and three articles on religious themes.

Chapter 6

Final years and legacy

The philosophy of his old age

Holmes' death in 1936 produced an outpouring of official and somewhat belated recognition for his considerable achievements. *The Times* wrote optimistically of him in its obituary as one who would 'long [be] remembered for his new ideals in education and as poet and humanist (*The Times*, 16th October 1936) whilst his death also merited a mention in America with the *New York Times* carrying good notice. The following year saw Holmes' old friend and colleague E. Sharwood Smith deliver the inaugural Edmond Holmes Memorial Lecture in which, speaking passionately, he remarked that, 'his influence remains, and will remain, not only with those, who like myself, were his friends and disciples, but with untold generations yet to be' (Sharwood Smith, 1937, 48). In keeping with the spirit of sadness and sense of loss felt by this small yet devoted community, R.W. Macan was apt too in offering a full biographic sketch of Holmes' life in which he made the case for the essentially poetic character both of his writing and persona: 'His prose composition…is essentially poetic…he relies for his premises upon Synthesis, not Analysis; that he is constructive rather than critical, and prefers Intuition to Reason as an organ of Knowledge' (Macan, 1937, 9). Indeed, the proceedings of the 1937 New Ideals in Education Conference of that year from which these tributes were taken and which included papers on the subjects of 'The Religious Spirit in Education', 'Education and the Present Dilemma of Civilization' and 'Discipline – Intellectual and Moral' can be read almost as a *festschrift* to Holmes and his commitment to the democratic ideal (variously manifested) and the child-centred practices that were an inevitable byproduct of this way of thinking.

Not of course that Holmes would have wanted or ever sought such posthumous recognition; his was after all the philosophy in name and deed of *disinterested devotion* and he would have no doubt argued that within all of his endeavours both practical and literary he was seeking to embody an enduring and unending quest for the betterment of, initially, children but later on Man in its broadest sense. Indeed, the quiet, restrained and dignified way in which his death was handled well embodies the intellectual preoccupations of his last years in which his writing became ever more reflective as it sought to both tie together many of the major themes of his life's work but also to look forward with optimism, solace and a degree of contemplation to the plane of existence beyond this one. Despite then finding ultimate intellectual refuge in 'the larger opportunities for spirit-unfoldment which await [him] in the next life' (Holmes, 1932b, 449) Holmes continued to publish works which evinced an increasingly radical spirit in particular through their adherence to particular tenets of the East which still retained a novelty within the established context of the dominant Western philosophical tradition. Even the knowing advent of his own death, which drives many to find solace in youthfully repudiated ideals, found him retaining faith in a positive form of agnosticism which stubbornly repelled the urge to fall foul either of priestly dogmatism or the reassurance of familiar creeds: 'I am tired of certainties – and I am still more tired of orthodoxies; for an orthodoxy which has lost its freshness has lost its truth' (Holmes, 1927b, 490). To the last it seemed, Holmes remained determined to resist finding any salvation and sanctity within the material world and what was typically constituted as the 'real'. What is equally noteworthy as well about these last years is the sheer volume of work and astonishing late outpouring of writing that flowed from his Holmes' pen. Perhaps spurred on by that very awareness of his own mortality – given additional impetus too by the death of his beloved wife in 1927 – between 1925 and 1934 alone he published seven full-length books and twelve shorter articles! Whilst there is inevitably a sense of replication (the articles often contained the genesis of the arguments and ideas that were then transferred sometimes verbatim into the books) by any standards this is impressive not least for a man of his advanced age and the increasing ill health that went with it.

These later pieces appeared almost exclusively in the religiously focussed *Hibbert Journal* (which ran from 1902–1968) as well as three smaller articles found within *The* (Blavatskian) *Aryan Path* (founded in 1930 and published in Bombay as a successor to *The Quest*). The scope and tenor of these journals provide obvious indications as to the direction of this last stage of Holmes' career which was exclusively concerned with themes and concepts more obviously linked to the spiritual and the mystic. By so doing, he was thereby able to give a greater nuance and articulation to his understanding of the ideas of the East as well as more precisely delineating his own philosophy which here found its deepest and most sincere expression and which operated upon its widest canvas. In much the same way as his last educational writings in the years following the War had dealt more abstractly with the importance of community and the role schools had to play within their locality by fostering a sense of comradeship amongst young people so therefore in this final slew of publications did he begin to extend even this idea and conceive not merely of a nexus of inter-connected souls (the so called *Cosmic Commonwealth*) but more the way in which this framework could be translated to ways of thinking and acting particularly when it concerned understanding the structure and composition of the world. Was this world to be thought of as a *singular* entity and in what way could this be understood? What was to be the human condition after death? In what way did the principles of the Upanishads of Ancient India provide more legitimate responses than those conceived within the West?

Whilst these had long been perennial concerns and such concepts had inflected in one way or another nearly all of his earlier writing, it was only now that these types of question were to be more fully answered. As if seeking to initially put his ideological house in order, Holmes was to point to the question over the nature of the Universe which was he said 'the most crucial, for, as man answers it, so will he think about duty and destiny, so will he order his life' (Holmes, 1926b, 404). At its root, as we have seen, this stemmed from a transcendence of the Self (in part through Buddhist self-sacrifice), which became for Holmes the sole way in which many of the problems of the world – itself 'a weltering chaos of conflicting aims and interests, a whirlpool of selfish desires, of angry passions, of dark suspicions, of jealous fears' (Holmes, 1925a, 216) – could be resolved. Increasingly important to this new preoccupation with the ethereal was the idea, in its most global sense, of *unity*. This term had, as with many others, long been part of Holmes' academic lexicon; we have seen in previous sections for example how, in his religious work, he had identified the trend within Western society for the separation of God (the Supernatural) and Man and the pressing need to somehow reconnect these in order to conceive of the 'Whole'. Whilst this division had therefore long been fostered by orthodox Christianity (and it has also been noted the profound implications it had for education), Holmes' portrayal of Christ in works such as *The Secret of the Cross* (1919b) was of one whose very enemy was the individual disconnected Self and the inherent desire to separate it from its material surrounds. As he was to put it, 'Man instinctively separates himself from the world which he looks out upon, and this primary act of separation controls his philosophies and his creeds' (Holmes, 1926b, 404). Now though this separation was seen not merely as a result of the machinations of social institutions (religion, schooling, families and the like) but as embodying more deeply a fundamental flaw in Mankind's current way of thinking, admittedly one facilitated and even encouraged by those organizations and their inherent dogmatism.

This way of thinking was especially influenced by *language* and the way that too often its imprecise uses helped to shape and contributed to wider understanding: 'The pressure put upon human thought by the dualistic constitution of human speech is not easily resisted' (Holmes, 1931a, 256). Whether Holmes was influenced here by any reading of the 'linguistic turn'[1] embodied by those philosophers such as Ludwig Wittgenstein, Bertrand Russell or G.E. Moore remains a mystery but it was clear that, like them and the school of logical positivism which they had previously founded, the symbolic nature of language was of increasing importance, in particular the ways in which its structure embodied far more than merely that to which it directly pertained. In Holmes' case this represented, in a clear and tangible form, that particular way of thinking which reflected and carried with it much wider social assumptions concerning the nature of reality. Indeed, it was these more widespread assumptions which were to bear the brunt of his questioning pen particularly as he became ever more fixated upon the idea of *dualism* and the need to see the Universe as a unified whole rather than as fragmented with elements of it perceived of as indivisible and unbridgeable. This was clearly an idea of central importance: 'In what relation do spirit and matter stand to one another when viewed from the standpoint of reality? Are they both real? Or is only one real? And if so, which' (Holmes, 1927b, 491)? For Holmes, too many previous attempts at answering this, even when emanating from a range of different philosophical traditions, had concluded that it was only really the material realm (matter) which was real. This was an idea very much echoed within the established tradition of British empiricism and its clear-cut claims to truth based on direct sensory experience of an observable world. One implication of this was of course adherence to a belief in the division between Man and God or the known and the unknown.

However rather than merely seeing this condition of being as an extension of an externally imposed religious ethic, in a development which formed the basis of much of his late thinking and which drew on a wider range of concerns, it was instead now to be expressed as the Law of Contradiction. This notion was mentioned *en passant* in an earlier chapter in relation to creativity in schools particularly in the way that such pursuits were seen as antithetical to the view of reality as fluid and not static in that their end-points were always in a state of continual flux – all work to some extent being left unfinished. Whilst however within schools such activities were given comparatively short shrift, more fundamentally it was this Law that Holmes was quick to identify as the guiding principle for his archetype of the average man:

> The rough and ready logic of the people is undoubtedly dualistic. If the average man asks a question which admits of being answered in terms of *Yes* and *No*, he expects the answer to be Yes *or* No. He has no use for "Yes and No." Compromise is abhorrent to him.
>
> (Holmes, 1931a, 258)

Taken from an article entitled *Wanted – A New Logic* (later to be typically expanded into book form) this quotation is an apt summation of Holmes' twilight years and was clearly indicative of how his preoccupations had by now extended away from the activities of schools and even societies to begin to muse on the need for a new paradigmatic way of understanding the world through, in this case, perception and language. Holmes indeed was to caution that 'We have but to read history and look around us to see what disastrous consequences have ever flowed and are still flowing from the dualistic treatment of social, political and economic problems' (Ibid.) and whilst it may appear initially difficult to connect the idea of global ills with that of seemingly dichotomous language, the new logic was seen as 'wanted' precisely because it was envisaged as having the power to transform the individual from one in a state of Being to, instead, one of Becoming.

The flaws within religion which had then in turn affected education were therefore now seen by Holmes as personifications of a much deeper and more fundamental mental malaise affecting the West. Simple blind obedience to an oppressive theology – as outlined in works such as *The Creed of Christ* (1905b) and the first chapter of *What is* – was now seen as a manifestation of that Law of

Contradiction which innately set one thing in opposition to another and led on for Holmes to the Logic of Being in which life as a whole became perceived as static and fixed. In relation to religious systems of belief this meant positing God *or* Man, Nature *or* the Supernatural whereas within schools it was embodied in the language of things being seen as right or wrong or else as having a fixed grade so delineating both their immobile value and position. In the wider context of life it meant simple acceptance of command or law – things were seen simply as right or wrong – with no attempt made to necessarily challenge their veracity or think critically about them. The nefarious effects of competition and dogmatism aside, this way of thinking clearly reinforced the earlier logic and, given the widespread influence of these social institutions, meant a prevailing view of life as delineated by that most dominant of Laws.

Instead, and encapsulating his newly articulated pantheism, Holmes was to put forward an alternative form of thinking about the world that he came to christen as the Logic of Becoming – whose speculative and searching qualities contrasted with the more definite Logic of Being. Attached to this was the Law of Polar Opposition which, once again in contrast to the Law of Contradiction, perceived of reality as a gradation and placed it on a spectrum – 'and' rather than 'or'. This can be seen as pantheist for, in Holmes' schema, humans were either retreating away from or moving toward their own inward ideal – in other words, their ideal self. At no point was this fixed and, conceived as it was within the realm of the infinite, had nothing permanent or definite about it – in effect Man was to always see himself as in the *process* of becoming. How different this appeared to the supernaturalism driving the Logic of Being which, Holmes argued, cared little for such inclinations of character still less when they were incapable of being externalized. As mentioned earlier, Holmes was to further support his case by citing the way in which the everyday use of language often committed people to using antithetical (contradictory) terms – hard and soft, high and low, hot and cold and so on – which themselves failed to recognize those infinite gradations of life. Given the reciprocal relationship language had to the construction of reality (and nowhere was this perhaps more true than in the case of those law-maker theologians whose pronouncements had served to delineate a particular view of Christ) this hermeneutic factor became important in explaining why the Law of Contradiction prevailed. By contrast, the sorts of spirituality in which Holmes found succour were very evidently situated in states of Becoming which were neither one thing nor the other. Returning to his original philosophy for example found Holmes calling for self-loss and self-transcendence as being of the essence of self-identity and, by so doing, he was giving implicit recognition to this state by seemingly incorporating as one two seemingly juxtaposed entities.

It must be pointed out that the later writings in which these ideas are expressed are amongst Holmes' most complex and difficult to understand particularly as they demand of their readership that they agree with and take on faith many of his previously adumbrated tenets concerning the nature of reality and the necessity of self-realization through self-loss. Nevertheless, even the sceptic would admit that what they do achieve is to successfully draw together many of his life's aspects into a theory that exists independent of time or place and which seeks to explain how humans can move beyond the everyday conception of the world and into something more *spiritual*. It should also be very clear from this that these tenets really do showcase the intellectual breadth to Holmes' thinking as he engaged directly with the ideas of another scholarly community and one even further removed from the discipline of education. As an example of this distance consider how initially within the confines of schools children's natural instincts were to have been cultivated 'to foster the growth of [their] whole nature, or, in a word, of [their] soul[s]' (Holmes, 1911, 80). Now though schools and pupils were being asked to go a stage further and, having attempted to shed those trappings of Self, admit and accept a more profound level of unity and the Law of Becoming which underpinned those thought processes. Whilst to modern eyes such ideas may appear as redolent of woolly New Age spiritualism, aside from their striking originality (particularly coming from the pen of one best known for his writings on education) they appeared still as both a logical extension of his earlier thinking but also as a way for Holmes to achieve a philosophical finality as the point and purposes of individual growth with any form of action and thought becoming at this point inseparable from the configuration of the Universe.

It is also worth here remembering that at the time of writing these mystical ideas had not achieved widespread currency and Holmes was right to identify both the paucity of scholarship in the field as well as the limitations of the work of scholars such as Max Muller[2] who, although beginning to explicate their tenets, were not always themselves adhering to them. Indeed it is noticeable, even when at its most complex, that Holmes' philosophy constantly tried to position itself to the practical condition of Mankind – an aspect he saw as intrinsic to the thinking of the Upanishads. In part this was clearly a conscious riposte to those who would seek to criticize nascent spiritualists over how such ideas could be readily adhered to but it was also an expression of Holmes' profound conviction that it was perfectly possible to 'live' this spirituality. In the suitably titled *The World of Self or Spirit: A Scheme of Life* (1929b) as well as various other works written in his last decade Holmes was to therefore delineate a concept he christened *spiritual idealism* which was where he laid out how it was possible, and following the conditions of his Law, to Become. Frequently, this linked back to his earlier explications of the Buddha and values long articulated within ancient creeds: 'Lead the selfless life. Recognize the unreality of what you call self – the separate self, imprisoned in its own individuality, content with its separateness, ready to indulge and enrich, and aggrandize itself' (Holmes, 1930b, 553).

These explanations might themselves have appeared insufficient for those critics of Holmes who saw such ideas as a long way removed from the business of education although to surely indicate what the process of Becoming involved on a day-to-day basis was to force a material foundation upon an aspect of the spirit which was precisely the antithesis of Holmes and what he was seeking to avoid! This was not after all a course in practical ethics! Beyond his discussions around language, Holmes was however clear to point out that it involved generally a rejection of lower order pleasures (sensuality) in favour of the higher as well as acting in ways appropriate to the development of his idealized community: 'It is scarcely an exaggeration to say that all moral evil is resolvable in the last resort into selfishness, and all moral goodness into unselfishness…by unselfishness I mean living to a *higher self* which is ever striving to rise higher' (Holmes, 1924b, 323, italics added). This was really a more abstract expression of those faults that Holmes had earlier identified within other settings, both schools in which competition and egoism prevailed as well as wider society in which Holmes saw reflected some of the worst effects of living according to this lower and more primitive self – dogmatism and mechanical obedience. It was therefore a falsehood to suggest that Holmes had never addressed how these tenets could and should be lived. As we have seen when exploring his work within other genres (education, politics, poetry and so on), all of it was shot through with analysing the faults inherent within the contemporary world and how these could be mediated through changes at the level both of policy and practice as well as within the realms of emotion and democratic structure.

Where however one may find difficulties in these late works is in Holmes' conception of pantheism for whilst there were obvious echoes of earlier Western style pantheism within its tenets, his understanding of the holistic nature of life was really far more closely oriented to that of the *East* and represented his by now full 'conversion' to this scheme of life. Indeed, he was quick to distinguish between the monistic Western view of pantheism and its Eastern cousin; the former (which went back to the precepts of Baruch Spinoza) was underscored by a belief simply in the totality of the Universe's *material* framework and whilst this may have been sufficient for the younger Holmes and his thraldom to the 'God in Nature' by now this had become an expanded vision of reality that meant the All of Being. As he put it, 'It is the synthesis of all worlds, all form of life, all modes of existence, all actualities, all possibilities. It is the totality of things gathered up, as it were, and held together by imaginative thought' (Holmes, 1924c, 16–17). The implications of this way of thinking were clear; if the soul of the individual was bound up with the soul of the Universe then it became an individual's duty 'to find his inmost self, to realise his own unattainable ideal, to actualise his infinite possibilities, to become what he has it in him to be' (Holmes, 1924e, 76). This meant adhering to a life of 'self-discipline, self-transcendence, and self-transfiguration' (Ibid., 77) the conduct of which had been previously laid down by the Buddha.

As he had previously in his writing pertaining to religion, Holmes was to once more draw upon *science* in order to support his case for the general unanimity between Man and the Universe: 'All our sciences – astronomy, chemistry, biology, history – tell us of unceasing and world-wide change' (Holmes, 1926b, 409). Whilst of course, on the surface, echoing many of his earlier pronouncements it must be remembered that Holmes' long life (86 years) straddled a period in which the theories of Einstein had elicited, in Thomas Kuhn's famous phrase, a paradigm shift which served, quite aside from their substantive conclusions, to move science out of the parlours, debating chambers and, to some extent, the Churches. Having therefore grown up amid the gentlemanly, amateur and very Victorian science of Darwin and the ramifications and theological turmoil surrounding the theory of Evolution, Holmes must surely have been staggered by developments in this modern and professionalized age in which elementary understandings over the composition of the Earth had given way to sub-atomic supposition. Specifically, Niels Bohr's modelling of the atom (1913), Rutherford's splitting of the atom in 1917 as well as Paul Dirac's pioneering quantum theory all seemed to give credence to Holmes' theories that the Universe was anything but straightforwardly material and, at levels beyond obvious human comprehension, was constitutive of forces and laws which pointed toward underlying unifying aspects. These aspects – which today encompass the theory of dark matter – were even in Holmes' time becoming ever more unknowable and pushing science and many of its protagonists into closer association with the theological as the veil of perception became lifted. Of course many of these discoveries were very much in the realm of the theoretical and emergent from inference and so Holmes was equally keen to point to the greater accuracy in *quantitative* science which gave tacit support to his Law of Polar Opposition and the infinite progressions within the physical phenomena of reality: 'thanks to the advance of mathematical science, and to the ever increasing perfection of our scientific instruments, we are able to go on measuring gradation in temperature, over a progressively wider range and higher degree of accuracy' (Holmes, 1931a, 262–263).

In many ways the invocation of science in this fashion was apt as the search for new realms and levels of reality was to tie in with Holmes' very last book *The Great Passing On* (1934), described in a private dedication as 'the latest product of my restless brain (Holmes, quoted in Macan, 1937, 14) and which, for one last time, demonstrated that the grand old man had lost none of his power to surprise an audience. This time it was not to be through any thundering denunciation, brash condemnation or violence of language but because it laid bare a very intimate belief in the possibility of communication between spirits of this world and the next – a phenomena Holmes called 'Spiritism'. This was not something new to Holmes – according to his autobiography he had first encountered the work of mediums nearly forty years earlier in Kent – but here it was to be situated in close relation to this body of later work in that it sought to recognize the false distinction which existed between *unreal* and *non-existent*, again an indicator of the Law of Contradiction prevalent within the West. By so doing he was allowing for the continuation of life – and not merely existence – on a plane beyond this one, a point about which he was quite vehement: 'Death is *not* the end of life. It is the opening into a new life; and one which is a *life* and no mere *state* of being, whether blissful or the reverse' (Holmes, 1934, 123).

Intriguingly, the last chapter of this book and therefore the last thing he was to ultimately write, was entitled 'What to Teach the Young' which provides in its way a perfect circularity in that it was education that he was to ultimately see *in the end* as the medium by which all of his other vast and multifarious ideas could be transmitted. He clearly had not – if ever – lost faith in the spirit of the young, acknowledging that they had, 'see[n] through our half-hearted agnosticism and despise it' (Ibid., 174) yet was still prepared to concede that theirs was to be a position of anomie unless in this world, and towards the next, changes could be made to the appreciation of reality:

> the time has come for us to help the young to believe in themselves, to find the Kingdom of Heaven in themselves and claim it as their own. Not till this has been done will it be possible for them, or their children, to found the Kingdom of Heaven on earth.
>
> (Ibid., 182–183)

Maybe after all it was apt that this was to be the end-point of his thinking. For one whose biography from boyhood was educational, whose life (in many senses) was educational and whose very *spirit* was that of education it was appropriate that it should be this which provided the final notes to his life. The many and varied changes to society in Holmes' life – political, religious, economic and educational – may well have conspired to change the type and character of the extant world and his long life straddled the Victorian and Modern periods whose very identities appear in retrospect as almost unrecognizable from one another. And yet ultimately, it was to be education that he was to return to, knowing it not perhaps for the first time but more as a singular thing that had in many ways long underpinned the whole of his thinking. It is perhaps, in keeping with the optimism he himself had long evinced, only to be hoped that he was ultimately to find that which he had long sought: 'God! the One, the All of Being! let me lose my life in thine' (Holmes, 1912b, 'Nirvana').

The legacy

Attempting any appraisal of a man such as Holmes is a complex task and cannot perhaps be carried out according to the standards of other progressives. After all, he left behind no physical bequest in the form of a school or institution, he did not inspire discipleship – as did for instance Rousseau, Pestalozzi or even in the modern age Paulo Freire – nor did his texts become catechistic and used as the basis of either a movement or a faith. How Holmes would surely have deplored such a notion! Likewise, whilst being singularly (and one feels rightly) characterized within many secondary accounts as an *educationalist*, when compiled together the majority of his corpus of writings are theological, philosophical and even poetical in scope and bear few resemblances or give little mention to either schools or schooling. This imbalance would seem to have reflected – if his autobiography is any yardstick – in his own conception of his life in which his long and distinguished educational career was envisaged as part of an early narrative of failure in which for the better part of a quarter of a century he was seen to be little more than an administrative automaton doing the bidding of his superiors. Even upon becoming unencumbered by the constraints of official office, he bore the unfortunate distinction of being part of a generation in which a number of huge talents from within a range of fields (psychology, philosophy, spiritualism) conspired together into a broad educational 'opposition'. He may have been *primus inter pares* but this was not any guarantee that he would ultimately be remembered.

And yet, are these tangibles the sole measures of a man's worth? For one concerned so much with the eternal and connected life of human souls it must surely have pleased Holmes greatly to see the rich and varied contribution made by his *children*. Of the three, and following his successful career in the War and a host of well-deserved honours, Maurice Gerald (1885–1964) was to follow his father most directly becoming Permanent Secretary of the Board of Education and as one influential in developing the 1944 Education Act. How Holmes the father would have received this we cannot possibly say. Despite the rhetoric surrounding the building of a 'new Jerusalem' and the laudable intentions within the report of Sir William Beveridge (1942) to remove poverty, idleness and vice (all in their way manifestations of Holmes' *sensualism*) he may well have seen little fundamental change in the teaching approaches being used. Indeed his concept of mechanical obedience was to be implicitly invoked by those critics such as Brian Simon (2000) and A.H. Halsey *et al.* (1972) who argued strongly that the so-called 'tri-partite' system, contrary perhaps to the intentions of its founders, led merely to a preservation of unequal social hierarchy and continued thereby adding to the intellectual wastage of the previous decades. Conversely, Holmes' radicalism was not entirely of the political kind and we have seen that he subscribed to a view which saw future economic status as subservient to spiritual well-being and satisfaction in carrying out even the most mundane of tasks. Even those 'bastions of privilege' – the middle class grammar schools – were surely more conducive to developing the full range of Holmes' 'instincts' particularly the musical, the artistic and the dramatic than many of the schools of his own generation which were narrow in their horizons and prescriptive in their approach.

Whilst therefore Holmes may have been conflicted over the shape of the post-1944 educational landscape as wrought by his son, he would not have frowned upon Maurice's other successes particularly as he too supplemented his official life by successfully navigating an equally wide-ranging set of intellectual interests and an ability to turn his hand to writing on seemingly disparate and unrelated topics. These included towards the end of his life critical appraisals on the novels of George Bernard Shaw as well as the writings of Captain James Cook. As part of his wider extended family network his nephew Gerard clearly too inherited something of that Holmesian trait of being attracted to the educationally unorthodox and his seminal work *The Idiot Teacher* (1952) was to be an entertaining, enlightening and ultimately sympathetic discussion of the progressive educator E.F. O'Neill and his Prestolee School – something Catherine Burke (2005) has referred to as a 'remarkable and sustained experiment in education...at an unremarkable country elementary school' (Burke, 2005, 263). If this book from amongst his kin would have been especially close to Holmes' heart then even more so would have been the achievements of his eldest daughter Verena Winifred Holmes (1889–1964) who as both an engineer and inventor paved the way for women to enter those technical occupations long thought the bastion of men. Working for the Admiralty during the Second World War, she was influential in advancing the design of torpedoes and superchargers as well as, through her civilian work, pioneering various inventions in relation to the steam locomotive. For one reared in a literary household, this conscious turn to the world of science seems to be a testament to the philosophy of her father who, in surveying what was supposedly the 'best' of the British educational system, had asked disparagingly, 'Why should the boys at our Great Public Schools and the young men at our Universities have to choose between a scientific and a humanistic training' (Holmes, 1911, 262)? The very diverse and active contributions made by Holmes' children to public life indicate not merely a transmission of the key value of *unity* but also a sense of devotion to the larger community. Inevitably, being a Holmes, Verena too was involved in education at the Ministry of Labour, helping train ordinary women to enter the field of munitions as well as later presenting before conferences of professional bodies, often those intended solely for women.

If then Holmes' legacy could be observed vicariously in this way, how was it to be embodied more directly? What links can be drawn between his copious writings and the later developments within British and perhaps even Western education? Some of the answers to these questions have been already insightfully addressed by Colin Richards (2010 and 2011) in which, within the first of these pieces, he identifies four broad areas of educational critique outlined by Holmes – that of the possibility of educational measurement, the practice of examination, the practice of inspection as well as the principle of a centrally imposed curriculum. To those we might also be tempted to add, in light of Holmes' later thinking, the possibility for communal thinking and inward growth and development. To begin therefore to think in these comparative ways across time is to mine a rich seam for, more so than perhaps other facets of history, the history of education is undeniably cyclical with recurring cycles of emphasis in relation to its key areas of power such as policy setting, teacher autonomy and the shape and content of the curriculum. As an example, one only has to observe how this circularity was implied within recent attacks on Coalition educational policy which was popularly dubbed as 'back to the future' and compared unfavourably in various media-related contexts to the more rote-driven learning of the 1950s. Whilst it is of course notoriously dangerous (and perhaps somewhat a-temporal) to draw such comparisons – and in many cases they are often based on false caricatures and generalizations – they do seem more often than otherwise to betray Marx's famous dictum regarding the repetition of history. Whilst the chastened critics of recent policy may be inclined to view these developments more as tragedy than farce they are nevertheless apposite here through the way in which they invoke many of the earlier ideas and contentions of Holmes.

Indeed, this is but one place in which the writings of Holmes have proven extraordinarily prophetic; not only does much of his work pre-date by nearly a century many of those aforementioned critiques but also because his own words, often ignored or shunned in their own time, seem even more applicable to the modern educational landscape in which the neo-liberal agenda has meant a proliferation of examinations, league tables, the rise of competition, summative judgements, rigidity of standards and centrally imposed curricula – all of which would have surely attracted his ire. After all, Holmes' bold assertion then that 'Wherever the teacher looks, he sees that the examination system, with its demand for machine-made results, controls education' (Holmes, 1911, 113) is surely as true now as when it was written. Not only are universal and largely homogenous examinations required of all children but these are proliferating in number and are strongly used as indicators of schools' worth – often to the detriment of those institutions who perform less successfully. With such primacy therefore placed upon examination results and levels of progress, motivation for both pupils (credentialization) and staff (job security and reputation) has become extrinsic whilst wider activities, particularly the creative disciplines which as Holmes rightly showed were in many ways incommensurate with quantification, have become either marginalized or else reduced to subservience in the face of the continued dominance of English, Mathematics and Science. Compounding this, in recent years, these examinations have themselves come under scrutiny for demanding the simple recall of facts rather than any attempt at fostering critical thinking. Holmes had earlier spoken of the 'vulgar confusion between information and knowledge' (Ibid., 53) and once again such words, supported by a whole body of psychological research over learning styles and approaches, carry with them more than a glimmer of truth.

After that fashion, Holmes, psychology and child-centred practice have long remained easy bedfellows with a lot of subsequent progressive practice, rhetoric and policy bearing the stamp both of experimental and empirical support as well as the spectre of the former Chief Inspector. The various Hadow Reports for example, influenced in part by the testimony of those such as Cyril Burt and Susan Isaacs, argued against too heavy a reliance upon intelligence testing as well as for a linear system of education (primary followed by secondary) that had, at its heart, 'activity and experience rather than knowledge to be acquired and facts to be stored' (Hadow Report, 1931, 93). This Holmesian precept was echoed elsewhere in the call for a holistically planned curriculum which sought to recognize not merely the importance of the individual learner but as he/she appeared situated within the confines of a wider community: 'The general aim should therefore be to offer the fullest possible scope to individuality, while keeping steadily in view the claims and needs of the society in which every individual citizen must live' (Hadow Report, 1926, 101). Whilst much educational rhetoric – even down to the recent failed experiments in Citizenship Education – has had discourses of community and living together at its heart, few have done so whilst simultaneously promoting the wide set of spiritual and democratic values found either in Hadow or Holmes. What worth for instance would today be placed upon 'activity, versatility, imaginative sympathy, a large and free outlook, self-forgetfulness, charm of manner, joy of heart' (Holmes, 1911, 231) yet these were the core values enshrined in Egeria's pupils and which Holmes desired to see propagated more widely.

This relationship between Holmes and his successors was unsurprisingly echoed too within the Plowden Report (1967). Unsurprising as, even more than for its ideological forebears, Plowden was underscored by a heavy reliance upon Piagetian theory which, although as Margaret Donaldson (1978) has shown was too prone to viewing the child as egocentric, still celebrated the Sixties spirit of individual difference and the child as 'lone scientist' who was both highly inquisitive and in command of their own patterns of learning. For one so enraptured by the scientific possibilities of understanding the mind, Holmes would have been especially pleased not least as such ideas seemed to support his view of the teacher as facilitator and as one who must 'content himself with giving the child's expansive instincts fair play and free play' (Holmes, 1911, 163). Indeed, such connections could be traced in almost any of the (what could loosely be termed) progressive responses and critiques of government policy down to the *Cambridge Primary Review* (Alexander, 2010) and its associated publications. One central thread of many of these narratives has of course been the increasing encroachment of governments and policy-makers on determining both what is studied and, significantly, how. Largely originating from former Prime Minister James Callaghan's famous Ruskin College speech (1976), such encroachment seems throughout to carry historical echoes of 'My Lords' and the early part of Holmes' professional career in which subjects of study and the contents of the curriculum were explicitly laid down in a series of educational codes. This clearly goes against the ethos of such publications as the various *Handbooks of Suggestions* which were developed by (amongst others) Holmes as a response to such imposition and which sought to liberate practitioners from the narrow confines of official stricture. More significantly, this general tendency seems equally to ramify with his concern over *dogmatism* and those who would argue that, '"Such and such a thing seems good to me; therefore it must seem good to you; in other words you must practise it"' (Holmes, 1914, 8). This tendency has been reflected not merely through the way in which individual policy-makers own life histories, as Gary McCulloch (2004) has suggested, have conspired to influence their decisions but also as such policy is increasingly presented to practitioners and those within the sector as a *fait accompli* and with little to no discussion and consultation. Holmes long ago warned of the trickle down effects of such dogmatism to the classroom – devitalization of life, the narrowing of experience and the demoralizing of character – and with the high prevalence of contemporary discourses around working class failure, mass underachievement and the need for schools to transmit particular sets of values it seems that re-evaluating Holmes' ideas anew becomes ever more necessary.

Even for an instant moving the focus away to more distant settings, we have already identified within an earlier chapter the common thread linking Holmes to John Dewey notably their joint invocation of idealism and the need for schools to reflect that by becoming ever more *democratic*. Assuming then (and it is a fair supposition) that American educational thinking has remained since a long series of responses to Dewey's own voluminous writings, it would be both possible and legitimate to invoke Holmes and his concept of wider community and holistic individual development within this context. These ideas around community and communal learning also formed a cornerstone of the educational philosophy of the Brazilian critical pedagogue Paulo Freire and, once more, whilst on the surface representing a point of extreme contrast (Freire was a deeply committed political animal working in a quite alien landscape) it is possible at a more subtle level to observe points of similarity. For example, Freire's concept of banking education in which educator's 'deposit' knowledge into their students as and when they are needed carries with it something of Holmes' dogmatic forces of control. In both cases, it is external elements which are serving to shape the development of the child and which delineate what will be the ultimate worth or — to pursue the metaphor — exchange value of an individual. Similarly, Freire's concept of *conscientization* (1973), that is to say an understanding that the role of the pedagogue is to develop within their students a belief that consciousness can transform reality, is akin to Holmes' contention that it is only when the long-held assumptions surrounding materialism are broken down will individuals be able to be both spiritually and morally liberated. In fact, the last stage of Freire's process — the development of *critical* consciousness — relies precisely on recognizing the fact that reality and its attendant conditions are not fixed and can be subject to change if accompanied by corresponding changes to individuals' inner understandings and mental states. Whilst it may be the case that Freire was writing in the very particular context of Brazil he, along with other intellectuals such as Henry Giroux and Michael Apple in North America, certainly draw upon the idea of transforming reality and developing pupils to be reflective and critical thinkers who are keen to challenge and contest doctrine and dogma. This may be that of social inequality and not inherited belief in a fixed God but the sense of 'revealing' a hidden truth and going beyond the extant reality is certainly to be found there.

It can, and should, be argued then that the central tenets within Holmes found echo in much subsequent progressive writing and thinking and it is somewhat ironic that the former Chief Inspector should find those ideas considered perhaps too radical by officialdom in his own time being enshrined in later formal, state-sanctioned investigations. Indeed the famous opening declaration of the aforementioned Plowden Report — 'At the heart of the educational process lies the child' (Plowden Report, 1967, 7) — could have been lifted directly from the pages of Holmes over half a century before. Furthermore, whilst it is perhaps to be expected to be able to trace his influence within the 'natural' heartland of Britain, there is also evidence of transmission further afield which well illustrates how his broad range of concerns and powerful aphoristic critiques can be applied in a multiplicity of different contexts. Although few, if any, of those later thinkers and writers would have any awareness or knowledge of Holmes it says as much for his relevance today as it does for the level of critical neglect that has engulfed him. Of how many other progressives could this be said? This is not of course to suggest Holmes was a man out of step with his time and only properly attenuated to our own. Whilst there are undoubtedly similarities between his observations from the early part of the century and those of more contemporary educational thinkers their root causes are very different. The academic language used today for instance to explain these recent detrimental changes in education is often sociological, frequently of the political left and almost exclusively focussed upon the emergence of a distinctly *neo-liberal* agenda and the formation of complex forms of identities.

Compounding this have been widespread technological changes meaning information is now available in ways unimaginable to Holmes as well the emergence of, in Peter Drucker's (1959) terms, knowledge workers and knowledge-based economies in which knowledge has become increasingly seen as a tool rather than a product. All of which is therefore to utilize a discourse and terminology which would have been alien to Holmes who saw the culture of examination, competition and dominant types of learning as originating from the doctrine of Original Sin and the need to foster obedience to ancient fixed belief and its Supernatural God. It is this perhaps which might explain why Holmes has been little cited by those seeking to agitate for educational change. In an increasingly secular age, Holmes' ideas concerning the importance of self-realization, out-growth and Eastern-inwardness somehow seem (unfortunately) less relevant when it is political and social class concerns that abound.

Nevertheless, to reject these profound principles is, as has been made clear, to risk disregarding Holmes' *educational* viewpoint as the one inexorably flowed from the other. However, even accounting for much of the difficulties in translating these spiritual ideas to a different age, there is much within the pages of Holmes that should present salutary reading for today's practitioners. For example, his broad understanding of the term 'growth' encompassed many facets and stands in contrast to the relatively narrow understanding as defined by contemporary policy-makers. To cite a recent example within the United Kingdom, the (aborted) proposal of an English Baccalaureate as well as the subsequent changes to the GCSE examination were driven by a model of education based upon primacy given to a comparatively narrow range of skills – not dissimilar from the culture of examination cited within the works of Holmes. Reducing, for instance, coursework – arguably an opportunity to be a creative and independent thinker – on the grounds that it was both difficult to assess and possible to receive additional help implied both a lack of trust of the pupil but also recognition that what was of greatest significance was quantification. Much of this controversy was attached to a whole host of other recent moves which have seen increased levels of testing at all ages as well as, bureaucratically, a strengthening of control by the Government over schools not seen to be meeting particular pre-set standards. State control seems to be Holmes' dogmatism in another form.

To ignore Holmes is to ignore our own heritage. The amnesia (as distinct from critical disengagement) that has surrounded him has therefore meant that his many and varied works remain unread and ignored which has, of course, profound implications. Quite aside that the utility of the history of education discipline more generally has for illuminating our understanding of problems within the present, Holmes in particular offers us a unique and powerful critique of many of those within our own age. This is undoubtedly enabled by the fact that, in so many ways,

Holmes' time and our own share profound (and disturbing) educational similarities and, were he able to do so, he would have seen one feels little progress since his own days as an administrator. Whilst the broadening of educational opportunity for all and the general rise in the numbers of people studying at higher levels are developments to be welcomed it has been similarly offset by a system which seems to value many of the faculties and traits such as competition which Holmes saw as damaging not just to educational progress but also to moral and spiritual development. Given the broad equation of success with examination performance and the negation of wider understandings of growth and development perhaps now is, after all, an apt time to begin a rediscovery of this most unique and brilliant thinker. Whilst then there are many last words we could allow Holmes, it seems ultimately fitting to heed those written as a response to his sceptics:

> every child ought to be free to develop himself, fully and harmoniously, on all planes of his being...Such a state of things does not exist; and would, I need hardly say, be extremely difficult to bring about. But it is an ideal which we ought to try and realize.
>
> (Holmes, 1914, 129)

Notes

1 The 'linguistic turn' was a term used to describe that development in Western philosophy which had as its focus the relationship between philosophy and language. Often considered to have originated with Gottlob Frege's *The Foundations of Arithmetic* in 1884, it grew to encompass those such as Wittgenstein, Russell and G.E. Moore.
2 Friedrich Max Müller (1823–1900) was a German-born philologist and Orientalist who lived and worked in Britain for most of his life. He was a leading scholar of Indian and comparative religions including a 50-volume set of translations of *Sacred Books of the East*.

Appendix

Board of Education

Memorandum by Mr. E.G.A. Holmes on the Status, Duties &c., of Inspectors employed by Local Education Authorities.

Strictly confidential

1. In June 1908 I sent a Circular (see Appendix 1) to all of the 'E' Inspectors, enquiring, in general terms, which of the Local Education Authorities had Inspectors of their own, what the antecedents of these Inspectors were, what salaries they received, what work they had to do, how they did their work, and whether the Board's Inspectors concerned found them a help or hindrance.

2. The replies received from the Inspectors were summarized and tabulated in the Inspectors' section in this Office. This seems to have been a very laborious process, for the summary tables were not completed till last autumn. I have now summarized these summaries, and have obtained the following results: -

    The County of London employs 24 Inspectors for ordinary 'E' work.
    Of the remaining 49 counties, 16 employ Inspectors for ordinary 'E' work (24 in all).
    Of the 70 county boroughs, 25 employ Inspectors for ordinary 'E' work (71 in all).
    Of the 179 boroughs and united districts, only 4 employ Inspectors for ordinary 'E' work (4 in all).
    In other words, out of 299 Local Education Authorities, only 46 employ Local Inspectors for Ordinary 'E' work. These 46 Local Education Authorities (see Appendix II) employ in the aggregate 123 Inspectors (exclusive of Specialists, e.g., Superintendents of Drawing, of Manual Instruction, of Domestic Training and Cookery, of Needlework, of Physical Exercise, &c.; and exclusive of those Secretaries or Assistant Secretaries who give a fraction of their time – generally a small fraction – to the work of inspection.

3   Of these 123 Inspectors, 109 are men and only 14 are women. No fewer than 104 out of the 123 are ex-elementary teachers, and of the remaining 19 not more than two or three had the antecedents which we usually look for in our candidates for Junior Inspectorships, i.e. have been educated first at a Public School and then at Oxford or Cambridge.

4   The difference, in respect of efficiency, between the ex-elementary teacher Inspectors and those who have had a more liberal education is very great. Very few of our Inspectors have a good word to say for the Local Inspectors of the former type; whereas those of the latter type are, with about three exceptions, well spoken of. In Liverpool, for example, where, out of nine Inspectors, only three are of the ex-elementary teacher type, H.M. Inspector is able to say, 'Their work is well done on the whole, and they are certainly a help;' whereas in Manchester and Salford, where, out of 15 Inspectors, 14 belong to the ex-elementary teacher class, H.M. Inspector says, 'The existence of these Inspectors stereotypes routine, perpetuates cast-iron methods and forms an effectual bar to development and progress,' and he expressly excepts from this general censure the one Inspector – a woman – who has not been an elementary teacher.

5   Apart from the fact that elementary teachers are, as a rule uncultured and imperfectly educated, and that many – if not most – of them are creatures of tradition and routine, there are special reasons why the bulk of the Local Inspectors in this country should be unequal to the discharge of their responsible duties. It is in the large towns which had school boards before the 'appointed ay' that the majority of Local Inspectors are to be found. Thus, in the 12 largest towns – London, Liverpool, Manchester, Birmingham, Leeds, Sheffield, Bristol, Newcastle, Salford, Hull, Leicester, and Nottingham – there are no fewer than 75 Local Inspectors, besides a host of 'Specialists.' In these towns the Local Authorities have inherited from the School Boards not merely a vicious system of local inspection, but also a large number of 'vicious' Local Inspectors. Some 25 to 30 years ago the School Boards in large towns were in the habit of appointing as their Inspectors schoolmasters who had shown exceptional capacity for getting higher percentages in the annual examination, and thereby earning high grants. And these Inspectors were appointed for the express purpose of getting the teachers in their respective areas to pass high percentages and earn high grants. Thus they began their work as School Board Inspectors under the worst possible auspices; and it is not to be wondered at that those of them who survive should still be weeded to the old grooves in which they worked for so many years; that they should look back with fond regret to the days of schedules, percentages, uniform syllabuses, cast-iron methods, and the rest; that they should do their best to keep the teachers in their areas from straying out of the paths of strict routine; and that they should regard any criticism of the existing order of things, and any suggestion that there was room for improvement in the aims and methods of their schools, in the light of a personal affront.

6   We must further bear in mind –
    (i) that many of these Inspectors have worked in one provincial town for 20, 25, or even 30 years, during the whole of which time they have followed in their own footsteps year after year with monotonous regularity;
    (ii) that the teachers, whose prospects of promotion are largely dependent on their favour, have been for the most part as clay in their hands, and have paid them an amount of deference which has confirmed them in their good opinion of themselves and of their ways and works;
    (iii) that the younger Inspectors in the large towns have been trained by them, and have had to carry out their instructions, till they too have become the victims of an evil tradition;
    (iv) that, owing to most of the large towns being greatly overstaffed (Manchester has 12 Inspectors, Liverpool 9, Birmingham 4 plus 10 Specialists, and so on), the Inspectors must, in order to justify their existence, be for ever harassing the schools and interfering with the teachers.

7   Having regard to all these facts, we cannot wonder that local inspection, as at present conducted in the large towns, is on the whole a hindrance rather than an aid to educational progress; and we can only hope that the local 'Chief Inspectors' who are fountain-heads of vicious officialdom, will be gradually pensioned off, and that, if local inspection is to be continued in their areas, their places will be filled by men of real culture and enlightenment.

8   The counties have the advantage over the county boroughs of having started with a 'clean slate.' It cannot, however, be said that they have made the best use of their opportunity. They have been wise enough not to overburden themselves with Inspectors, the greatest number employed by any county being three (Durham, a very populous county). But owing to their being unduly parsimonious, they have not as a rule succeeded in securing the services of really good men. Out of the 24 County Inspectors no fewer than 16 are ex-elementary teachers The salaries offered – 300 £., with no prospect of a rise, is the normal sum – are not good enough to attract experienced men of the Public School and University type. One county has indeed secured the services of a young Cambridge man of great ability, for 300 £, a year ; but he had but recently left his University, and he has taken the post for three years only. It is interesting to note that the two Local Inspectors, about whom our Inspectors are really enthusiastic, hail, one from Winchester and Trinity, Cambridge, the other from Charterhouse and Corpus Christi College, Oxford. Men with such antecedents, provided they possess ability and culture, and are personally fitted for the work, make the best Local Inspectors. For the type of education (in the widest sense of the word) which they have receive predisposes them to take broad views of things, and gives them strength to resist those contracting and corrupting influences which we speak of collectively as 'parochialism.' As compared with the ex-elementary teacher, who is usually engaged in the hopeless task of surveying, or trying to survey a wide field of action from the bottom of a well-worn groove, the Inspector of the Public School and

'Varsity' type has the advantage of being able to look at Elementary Education from a point of view of complete detachment, and therefore of being able to handle its problems with freshness and originality and without paying undue regard to tradition and precedent. If such men are able to enter the services of Local Authorities, they must be liberally paid. But the money would be well spent. The 500 £, which is being spent on one Oxford man in East Sussex, is being laid out to infinitely better advantage than the 900 £, a year which is being spent on three ex-elementary teacher Inspectors in Durham County. Indeed the Durham Education Authority is beginning to realize that its 900 £, a year is being wasted, and worse than wasted, and now that it is receiving full reports from the Board's Inspectors, it is beginning to wonder what use it can make of the three Inspectors whom it has appointed with undue haste.

E.G.A. Holmes
6th January 1910.

Appendix I

Circular sent to each 'e' District Inspector asking for information with regard to local Inspectors

Confidential

H.M. Inspector, Mr.

I shall esteem it a favour if you will let me know which (if any) of your Local Education Authorities have School Inspectors of their own. In the case of those which have seen School Inspectors, will you kindly inform me –

1 How many Inspectors of each sex are employed by each Local Education Authority.
2 What their antecedents have been (social, academic, professional, &c.).
3 What salaries they receive.
4 What work they have to do (please describe this in some detail).
5 How they do this work.
6 How far you find them a help or a hindrance in your own district work.

Appendix II consists of the names of Local Education Authorities which employed Inspectors.

Bibliography

Works by Edmond Holmes

Autobiography

(1920a) *In Quest of an Ideal* (London: R. Cobden-Sanderson).
(1922) 'The Confessions and Hopes of an ex-Inspector of Schools', *Hibbert Journal*, 20 (July), 721–739.

Education

(1879a) Report of the Committee of Council on Education. *General Report for the year 1878 on schools inspected in the West Riding of Yorkshire*, 591–604.
(1883) Report of the Committee of Council on Education. *General Report for the year 1882 on schools inspected in the Ashford District (Counties of Kent and Sussex)*, 351–364.
(1898a) *An Address to the Teachers of the Oxford District. Given at Oxford, at Banbury and at Wantage.* (Oxford: n.p.).
(1908a) *A Village School. A paper read at a meeting of an education club* (Liverpool: Lyceum Press).
(1911) *What is and What Might Be: A Study Of Education in General and Elementary Education in Particular* (London: Constable & Co).
(1912a) *The Montessori System*. Board of Education, Education Pamphlet No. 24. (London: HMSO).
(1913a) 'Introduction' to Dorothy Canfield Fisher *A Montessori Mother*. (London Constable & Co).
(1913b) *The Tragedy of Education* (London: Constable & Co.).
(1914) *In Defence of What Might Be* (London: Constable & Co.).
(1915) 'Ideals of Life and Education – German and English', *Nineteenth Century and After*, 78 (October), 957–971.
(1916a) *The Nemesis of Docility: A study of the German character* (London: Constable & Co).
(1916b) 'Discipline and Freedom', *Nineteenth Century and After*, 8 (July), 88–100.
(1917a) *The Problem of the Soul: A Tract for Teachers* (London: Constable & Co.).

(1917b) 'Drudgery and Education. A Defence of Montessorian Ideals', *Hibbert Journal*, 15 (April), 419–433.
(1917c) 'The Real Basis of Democracy', *Nineteenth Century and After*, 82 (August), 301–325.
(1917d) 'Experiments Day' in *New Ideals in Education: 4th Conference Papers* (1917), 85–86.
(1920b) 'The Psychology of Sanity', *Hibbert Journal*, 18 (April), 509–518.
(1921a) *Give Me the Young* (London: Constable & Co).
(1923a) 'Socialism and Education: A paper read in February 1912 at a meeting of the Cambridge University Fabian Society'. Reprinted in *Freedom and Growth and Other Essays* (London: Dent), 3–35.
(1923f) 'The Recreations of the Spitalfield Weavers', Conference on New Ideals in Education Report. Reprinted in *Freedom and Growth and Other Essays* (London: Dent), 262–275.
(1923g) 'What Joy does for the Young' originally published in *Nineteenth Century and After*, 92 (September) 1922, 389–396. Reprinted in *Freedom and Growth and Other Essays* (London: Dent), 301 – 312.
(1924a) *Can Education Give us Peace?* (Dalton Association).

Philosophy

(1898b) *Sursum Corda: A Defence of Idealism by EGAH* (London: Macmillan).
(1905a) *What is Philosophy?* (London and New York: John Lane, The Bodley Head).
(1919a) *The Secret of Happiness* (London: Constable & Co).
(1920c) 'The Philosophy of my Old Age', *The Quest*, 11 (January), 167–178.
(1921b) 'The Spirit of the Quest', *The Quest*, 12 (July), 433–452.
(1923b) 'Professor Eucken and the Philosophy of Self-Realisation', *The Quest*, 5 (April) 1914, 401–419. Reprinted in *Freedom and Growth and Other Essays* (London: Dent), 37–53.
(1923c) 'Freedom and Growth', *Hibbert Journal*, 17 (July) 1919, 435–452. Reprinted in *Freedom and Growth and Other Essays* (London: Dent), 153–174.
(1927a) *Self-Realization. The End, the Aim and the Way of Life* (London: Constable & Co).
(1928a) *Experience of Reality. A Story of Mysticism* (London: R. Cobden-Sanderson).
(1928b) 'Philosophy without Metaphysics', *Hibbert Journal*, 27 (October), 15–34.
(1929a) 'A Criticism of the New Religion as Expounded by Professor S.A. Alexander', *Hibbert Journal*, 28 (October), 48–68.
(1929b) *The World of Self or Spirit: A Scheme of Life* (London: R. Cobden-Sanderson).
(1930a) *Philosophy without Metaphysics* (London: Allen & Unwin).
(1931a) 'Wanted – A New Logic', *Hibbert Journal*, 29 (January), 252–269.
(1932a) 'The Headquarters of Reality', Hibbert Journal, 31, (October), 129–140.
(1933) *The Headquarters of Reality. A Challenge to Western Thought* (London: Methuen).
(1934) *The Great Passing On* (London: Rider).

Poetry

(1876) *Poems* (London: Henry S. King).
(1879b) *Poems 2nd Series* (London: C. Kegan Paul).
(1899) *The Silence of Love* (London: John Lane).

(1900) *What is Poetry?* (London: John Lane).
(1902) *Walt Whitman's Poetry. A Study and a Selection* (London: John Lane).
(1903) *The Triumph of Love* (London: John Lane).
(1912b) *The Creed of My Heart and Other Poems* (London: Constable & Co).
(1918) *Sonnets to the Universe* (London: A.L. Humphreys).

Religion

(1895) *A Confession of Faith, by an Unorthodox Believer* (London and New York: Macmillan).
(1905b) *The Creed of Christ* (London and New York: John Lane, The Bodley Head).
(1908b) *The Creed of Buddha* (London and New York: John Lane, The Bodley Head).
(1919b) *The Secret of the Cross: A Plea for the Re-Presentation of Christianity* (London: Constable & Co).
(1920d) *The Cosmic Commonwealth* (London: Constable & Co).
(1921c) 'Does Contemporary Scholarship do Justice to the Teaching of Jesus?', *Nineteenth Century and After*, 9 (July), 52–63.
(1921d) *All Is One: A Plea for Higher Pantheism* (R. Cobden-Sanderson).
(1923d) 'Religion as the Basis for Social Reconstruction', *Nineteenth Century and After*, 86 (November) 1919. Reprinted in *Freedom and Growth and Other Essays* (London: Dent), 175–189.
(1923e) 'The Religious Training of the Young'. A paper read at Manchester, November 1919. Reprinted in *Freedom and Growth and Other Essays* (London: Dent), 190–202.
(1923h) 'The Idea of Evolution and the Idea of God', *Hibbert Journal*, 21 (January), 227–247.
(1924b) 'Spiritual Evolution as a Gospel of Salvation and a Principle of Conduct' *Hibbert Journal*, 22 (January), 311–326.
(1924c) *Dying Lights and Dawning. The Martha Upton Lectures, given in Manchester College, Oxford, 1923* (London: Dent).
(1924d) 'Introduction' in S. Radhakrishnan *The Philosophy of the Upanishads* (London: Allen & Unwin).
(1924e) 'Our Debt to the Ancient Wisdom of India', *Hibbert Journal*, 23, Part 1 (October), 72–84.
(1925a) 'Our Debt to the Ancient Wisdom of India', *Hibbert Journal*, 24 Part 2 (January), 207–217.
(1925b) *The Albigensian or Catharist Heresy. A Story and a Study* (Williams and Norgate).
(1926a) 'Tyrell on "The Church"', *Hibbert Journal*, 24 (January), 322–333.
(1926b) 'Two or One? A Defence of the Higher Pantheism', *Hibbert Journal*, 24 (January), 404–420.
(1927b) 'A Last Guess at Truth', *Hibbert Journal*, 25 (January), 490–507.
(1928c) 'The Mystic as an Explorer', *Hibbert Journal*, 26 (April), 427–444.
(1930b) 'The Practicality of Buddhism and the Upanishads', *The Aryan Path*, 1 (September), 549–554.
(1931b) 'Two Conceptions of God. Without or Within', *The Aryan Path*, 2, Part 1, (July), 452–459. Part 2 (August), 528–533.
(1932b) 'Life in the Next World', *Hibbert Journal*, 30 (April), 431–439.

Works about Edmond Holmes

Gordon, Peter (1978) 'The Holmes-Morant Circular of 1911: A Note', *Journal of Educational Administration and History*, 10(1), 36–40.
Gordon, Peter (1983) 'The Writings of Edmond Holmes: A Reassessment and Bibliography', *History of Education*, 12(1), 15–24.
Howlett, John (Ed.) (2016) *Selected Poems and Prose of Edmond Holmes* (New Jersey: Fairleigh Dickinson University Press).
Macan, R.W. (1937) 'A Memoir of Mr Edmond G.A. Holmes' in *Proceedings of the New Ideals in Education Conference*, 1–16.
McDonald, Paul (2008) *An Intentionalist Analysis of Selected Works of Edmond Holmes*, Unpublished PhD Thesis, University of Cambridge.
McKenzie, David (1984) 'The Legacy of Progressivism: Some Reflections on the Writings of Edmond Holmes', *Education, Research and Perspectives*, 11(2), 3–13.
Richards, Colin (2010) 'What Has Been, What Is and What Might Be: The Relevance of the Critical Writings of Edmond Holmes to Contemporary Primary Education Policy and Practice', *FORUM: for promoting 3–19 comprehensive education*, 52(3), 337–348.
Richards, Colin (2011) 'What Could Be – For Contemporary Policy and Practice: Challenges Posed by the Work of Edmond Holmes', *FORUM: for promoting 3–19 comprehensive education*, 53(3), 451–462.
Shute, Chris (1998) Edmond Holmes and 'The Tragedy of Education' (Nottingham: Educational Heretics).
Wilkinson, M.J. (1980) 'The Holmes Circular Affair', *Journal of Educational Administration and History*, 12(2), 29–38.

Archival collections consulted

Archive of the Merchant Taylors' Company and School, Guildhall Library, London.
Archive of St. John's College, Oxford.
Education Department/Board of Education Papers, ED 10, ED 11, ED17, ED 22, ED 23, ED 24, National Archives.
Repton School Archives including *The Reptonian*.
The Bathurst Papers, Institute of Education, London.
The Marvin Papers, Bodleian Library, University of Oxford.
The Runciman Papers, University of Newcastle.
The Sadler Papers, Bodleian Library, University of Oxford.
The Winchelsea Papers, Northampton Records Office.
Wellington School Archives including Edward Wickham's *Headmaster's Report*.

Government publications

Hadow Report (1926) *The Education of the Adolescent* (London: HMSO).
Hadow Report (1931) *The Primary School* (London: HMSO).
Handbook of Suggestions for the Consideration of Teachers and Others Concerned in the Work of Public Elementary Schools (1905) (London: HMSO).
Plowden Report (1967) *Children and their Primary Schools* (London: HMSO).

Publications and periodicals consulted

Blackwood's Magazine.
Hansard.
London Illustrated News.
The Athenaeum.
The Guardian.
The Month.
The Morning Post.
The New Era.
The New York Times.
The School Manager.
The Schoolmaster.
The Telegraph.
The Times.

Other works cited

Alexander, Robin (Ed.) (2010) *Children, their World, their Education: Final report and recommendations of the Cambridge Primary Review* (London: Routledge).
Allen, B.M. (1934) *Sir Robert Morant: A Great Public Servant* (London: Macmillan).
Arnold, Matthew (1873) *Literature and Dogma: An Essay towards a Better Apprehension of the Bible* (London: Smith, Elder).
Auden, W.H. (1962) *The Dyer's Hand and Other Essays* (Random House: USA).
Baden-Powell, Robert (1916) 'The Boy Scout Movement' in *Proceedings of the New Ideals in Education Conference*, 56–65.
Ballard, Philip (1925) *The Changing School* (London: Hodder & Stoughton).
Barrow, Robin (1978) *Radical Education: A Critique of Freeschooling and Deschooling* (London: Martin Robertson).
Bennett, Neville (1976) *Teaching Styles and Pupil Progress* (London: Open Books).
Beveridge, Sir William (1942) *Social Insurance and Allied Services* (London: His Majesty's Stationary Office).
Blyth, A. (1981) 'From Individuality to Character: The Herbartian Sociology Applied to Education. *British Journal of Educational Studies*, 29(1), 69–79.
Bolton, Gavin (1997) 'A Conceptual Framework for Classroom Acting Behaviour' Unpublished PhD Thesis, University of Durham.
Bowles, Samuel and Herbert Gintis (1976) *Schooling in Capitalist America: Educational Reform and the Contradictions of Economic Life* (New York: Basic Books).
Bowmaker, Mary (2002) *A Little School on the Downs* (Bognor Regis: Woodfield Publishing).
Brehony, Kevin (2001) *The Origins of Nursery Education: Friedrich Froebel and the English System* (London: Routledge).
Brehony, Kevin (2004) 'A New Education for a New Era: The Contribution of the Conferences of the New Education Fellowship to the Disciplinary Field of Education 1921–1938' *Paedagogica Historica*, 40(5–6), 733–755.
Burke, Catherine (2005) '"The school without tears": E.F. O'Neill of Prestolee', *History of Education*, 34(3), 263–275.
Butler, Samuel (2005) *Hudibras* (Gloucester: Dodo Press).

Chitty, Clyde, (2007) *Eugenics, Race and Intelligence in Education* (London and New York: Continuum Publishing).
Claydon, Tony and Ian McBride (Eds) (1999) *Protestantism and National Identity: Britain and Ireland, c.1650–c.1850* (Cambridge University Press).
Cohen, Sol (1974) 'The Montessori Movement in England, 1911–1952', *History of Education*, 3(1), 51–67.
Collins, Mabel (1885) *Light on the Path: A treatise written for the personal use of those who are ignorant of the Eastern wisdom, and who desire to enter within its influence* (London: Reeves & Turner).
Committee of Council on Education Annual Reports 1862–1863.
Cook, H. Caldwell (1917) *The Play Way; an essay in educational method* (New York: Frederick A. Stokes Company).
Costin, W.C. (1958) *History of St. John's College, Oxford, 1598–1860.* (Oxford: Oxford Historical Society).
Cox, Gordon (1996) '"The Right Place of Music in Education": Some Ideological Aspects of Music Education in England, 1872–1928', *Historical Studies in Education* 8(1), 15–24.
Croall, Jonathan (1983) *Neill of Summerhill: The Permanent Rebel* (London: Routledge & Kegan Paul).
Daglish, Neil (1996) *Education Policy-Making in England and Wales: the Crucible Years 1895–1911.* (London: Woburn Press).
Darling, John (1994) *Child-Centred Education and its Critics* (London: Paul Chapman Publishing).
Dearden, R.F. (1968) *The Philosophy of Primary Education; An Introduction* (London: Routledge & Kegan Paul).
Dewey, John (1938) *Experience and Education* (Indianapolis: Kappa Delta Pi).
Dickens, Charles, (1992) *Great Expectations* (Ware: Wordsworth Editions).
Donaldson, Margaret (1978) *Children's Minds* (London: Fontana).
Dresch, Paul and Judith Scheele (2015) *Legalism: Rules and Categories* (Oxford: OUP).
Drucker, Peter (1959) *The Landmarks of Tomorrow* (London: Heinemann).
Eliot, T.S. (1915) *The Poems Volume 1,* (London: Faber and Faber).
Ellis, Ieuan 'The Intellectual Challenge to "Official Religion"' 49–72 in Terence Thomas (Ed.) (1988) *The British: Their Religious Beliefs and Practices 1800–1986.* (London: Routledge).
Finlay-Johnson, Harriet (1912) *The Dramatic Method of Teaching* (London: Ginn and Company).
Fischer, Fritz (1967) *Germany's aims in the First World War,* [translated from the German] (London: Chatto & Windus).
Fitch, Joshua G. (1897) *Thomas and Matthew Arnold and their Influence on English Education* (London: Heinemann).
Freire, Paulo (1973) *Education for Critical Consciousness* (New York: Seabury Press).
Froebel, Friedrich (1898) *The Education of Man* (New York: Appleton & Company).
Galton Maurice, Brian Simon and Paul Croll, (1980) *Inside the Primary Classroom* (London: Routledge & Kegan Paul).
Gardner, Philip (1984) *The Lost Elementary Schools of Victorian England* (London: Routledge).
Gardner, Philip (2004) 'There and Not Seen: E.B. Sargant and Educational Reform, 1884–1905', *History of Education*, 33(6), 609–635.
Gordon, Peter (1985) 'The Handbook of Suggestions for Teachers: Its Origins and Evolution', *Journal of Educational History and Administration*, 17(1), 41–48.

Gordon, Peter (1988) 'Katharine Bathurst: A Controversial Woman Inspector', *History of Education*, 17(3), 93–207.
Gordon, Peter and Denis Lawton (1978) *Curriculum Change in the Nineteenth and Twentieth Centuries*, (London: Hodder and Stoughton).
Gordon, Peter and John White (1979) *Philosophers as Educational Reformers: The Influence of Idealism on British Educational Thought and Practice* (London: Routledge & Kegan Paul).
Graham, Philip (2008) *Susan Isaacs: A Life Freeing the Minds of Children* (London: Karnac Books).
Gramsci, Antonio, (2005) *Selections from the Prison Notebooks* (London: Lawrence & Wishart).
Graves, Alfred Perceval (1930) *To Return to All That* (London: Cape).
Green, Andy (1990) *Education and State Formation: The Rise of Education Systems in England, France and the USA* (Basingstoke: Palgrave Macmillan).
Grosvenor, Ian and Catherine Burke (2008) *School* (London: Reaktion Books).
Halsey, A.H., Jean Floud and F.M. Martin (1972) *Social Class and Educational Opportunity* (Bath: Cedric Chivers Ltd).
Hamilton, David (1989) *Towards a Theory of Schooling* (London: Falmer Press).
Hayward, F.H. (1912) *Educational Administration and Criticism: A Sequel to the Holmes Circular* (London: Ralph Holland).
Hendrick, Harry (1990) *Images of Youth: Age, Class and the Male Youth Problem, 1880–1920* (Oxford: Clarendon Press).
Hessey, James Augustus (1850) *A Scripture Argument against Permitting Marriage with a Wife's Sister* (London: Francis and John Rivington).
Holmes, Gerard (1952) *The Idiot Teacher: A Book about Prestolee School and its Headmaster E.F. O'Neill* (London: Faber and Faber).
Hornbrook, David (1998) *Education and Dramatic Art*, (London: Routledge).
Howlett, John and Paul McDonald (2011) 'Quentin Skinner, Intentionality and the History of Education', *Paedagogica Historica: International Journal of the History of Education*, 47(3), 415–433.
Hurt, J.S. (1979) *Elementary Schooling and the Working Classes* (London: Routledge & Kegan Paul).
Hutchinson, Mrs (1915) 'The Montessori Principle in the Elementary School' in *Proceedings of the New Ideals in Education Conference*, 81–96.
Huxley, T.H. (1894) 'Agnosticism' in *Collected Essays, Volume 5: Science and the Christian Tradition* (Macmillan), 209–262.
Hyndman, H.M. (1980) 'Utopia reconsidered: Edmond Holmes. Harriet Johnson and the school at Sompting', *Sussex Archaeological Collections*, 118, 351–357.
Isaacs, Susan (1930) *Intellectual Growth in Young Children* (London: Routledge & Kegan Paul).
Isaacs, Susan (1933) *Social Development in Young Children* (London: Routledge & Kegan Paul).
Jenkins, E.W. (1980) 'Some Sources for the History of Science Education in the Twentieth Century, with particular reference to Secondary Schools', *Studies in Science Education* 7(1), 27–86.
Kaufmann, Walter (2013) *Nietzsche: Philosopher, Psychologist, Antichrist* (Princeton: Princeton University Press).
Kerrigan, Colm (2004) *Teachers and Football: Schoolboy Association Football in England, 1885–1915.* (London: Routledge).
Lawton, Denis and Peter Gordon (1987) *H.M.I.* (London: Routledge & Kegan Paul).

Leese, John (1950) *Personalities and Power in English Education* (Leeds: E.J. Arnold).
Liebschner, Joachim (1991) *Foundations of Progressive Education: the History of the National Froebel Society* (Cambridge: Lutterworth Press).
Lilley, Irene M. (Ed.) (1967) *Friedrich Froebel: A Selection from his Writings* (Cambridge: Cambridge University Press).
Lowe, Roy (2007) *The Death of Progressive Education: How Teachers Lost Control of the Classroom* (London: Routledge).
Lytton, Earl of (1915) 'New Ideals in Education' in *Proceedings of the New Ideals in Education Conference*, 1–2.
Macmunn, Norman (1914) 'Montessori in Secondary Schools' in *Proceedings of the New Ideals in Education Conference*, 78–90.
Mander, W.J. (2011) *British Idealism: A History* (Oxford: Oxford University Press).
Martin, Jane (2010) *Making Socialists: Mary Bridges Adams and the Fight for Knowledge and Power, 1855–1939* (Manchester: Manchester University Press).
Marwick, Arthur (Ed.) (1988) *Total War and Social Change* (Basingstoke: Macmillan).
Mathieson, Margaret (1991) 'The teaching of English in England', *Oxford Review of Education*, 17(1), 3–16.
McCann, P. (1970) 'Trade Unionists, Artisans and the 1870 Education Act. *British Journal of Educational Studies*, 18(2), 134–150.
McCulloch, Gary (2004) *Documentary Research in Education, History and the Social Sciences* (London: Routledge Falmer).
McIvor, Arthur J. (2008) 'Industrial Relations in Britain, 1900–1939' in Chris Wrigley (Ed.) *A Companion to Early Twentieth Century Britain* (Oxford: Blackwell), 319–336.
McMillan, Margaret (1904) *Education Through the Imagination* (London: Swan Sonnenschein).
Middleton, Jacob (2005) 'Thomas Hopley and mid-Victorian attitudes to Corporal Punishment', *History of Education*, 34(6), 599–615.
Middleton, Jacob (2008) 'The Experience of Corporal Punishment in Schools, 1890–1940', *History of Education*, 37(2), 253–275.
Moore, Aubrey (1890) 'The Christian Doctrine of God' in *Lux Mundi: A Series of Studies in the Religion of Incarnation* (London: John Murray, 5th Edition), 55–110.
Morris, Mowbray (1911) 'Musings Without Method', *Blackwood's Magazine* (August), 265–273.
Murray, Nicholas, (1997) *A Life of Matthew Arnold* (London: Sceptre).
New Ideals in Education (1916) 'Introductory' in *Proceedings of the New Ideals in Education Conference*.
New Ideals in Education (1918) *Report(s) of the Conference(s) on New Ideals in Education*, New Ideals Committee (London: Women's Print Society).
Nietzsche, Friedrich (2004) *Twilight of the Idols and The Antichrist* (Dover Publications).
Nunn, Percy, (1920) *Education: Its Data and First Principles* (London: E. Arnold).
Oliver, Ian (1979) *Buddhism in Britain* (London: Rider).
Read, Jane (2003), 'Froebelian Women: Networking to Promote Professional Status and Education Change in the Nineteenth Century' in *History of Education*, 32(1), 17–33.
Richards, N.J. (1970) 'Religious controversy and the school boards 1870–1902', *British Journal of Educational Studies*, 18(2), 180–196.
Richardson, Nigel (2014) *Thring of Uppingham, Victorian Educator* (Buckingham: University of Buckingham Press).
Rousseau, Jean-Jacques (1979) *Emile or On Education*, translated by Allen Bloom (New York: Basic Books).

Selleck, R.J.W. (1972) *English Primary Education and the Progressives 1914–1939* (London: Routledge & Kegan Paul).
Sharwood Smith, E. (1935) *The Faith of a Schoolmaster* (London: Methuen).
Sharwood Smith, E. (1937) 'Edmond Holmes Memorial Lecture' in *Proceedings of the New Ideals in Education Conference*, 39–48.
Silver, Harold (1975) *English Education and the Radicals, 1780–1850* (London: Routledge & Kegan Paul).
Silver, Keith (1994) 'Introduction' in *Selected Poems of Matthew Arnold* (Manchester: Carcanet), 7–22.
Simon, Brian (1972) *The Radical Tradition in Education in Britain* (London: Lawrence & Wishart).
Simon, Brian (2000) *Education and the Social Order: British Education since 1944* (London: Lawrence & Wishart).
Simpson, J.H. (1954) *Schoolmaster's Harvest: Some Findings of Fifty Years, 1894–1944* (London: Faber and Faber).
Simpson, Matthew (2006) *Rousseau: A Guide for the Perplexed* (United Kingdom: Continuum International Publishing Group).
Sinnett, A.P. (1883) *Esoteric Buddhism* (London: Trubner).
Skidelsky, Robert (1969) *English Progressive Schools* (Harmondsworth: Penguin).
Smiles, Samuel (1859) *Self-Help: with Illustrations of Character and Conduct* (London: John Murray).
Smith, Rev. S.F. (1911) 'The Ideas of a Chief Inspector of Schools' *The Month* (November), 449–461.
Steedman, Carolyn (1990) *Childhood, Culture and Class in Britain: Margaret McMillan 1860–1931* (London: Virago).
Steiner, Rudolf (1908) *The Way of Initiation, or How to Gain Knowledge of the Higher Worlds* (London: Theosophical Publishing Society).
Steiner, Rudolf (1964) 'Author's Prefaces' to *The Philosophy of Freedom* (Rudolf Steiner Press) xxii–xxx.
Stephens, W.B. (1987) *Education, Literacy and Society 1830–1870: The Geography of Diversity in Provincial England* (Manchester: Manchester University Press).
Stephens, W.B. (1998) *Education in Britain, 1750–1914*, (Basingstoke: Macmillan).
Stewart, W.A.C. (1968) *The Educational Innovators: Volume II: Progressive Schools 1881–1967* (London: Macmillan).
Stewart, W.A.C. (1972) *Progressives and Radicals in English Education 1750–1970* (London: Macmillan).
Stinton, Judith (2005) *A Dorset Utopia: The Little Commonwealth and Homer Lane* (Norwich: Black Dog Books).
Stone, Lawrence (1977) *The Family, Sex and Marriage in England 1500–1800* (London: Weidenfeld and Nicolson).
Sweet, William (2014) 'British Idealist Philosophy of Religion' in W.J. Mander (Ed.) *The Oxford Handbook of British Philosophy in the Nineteenth Century* (Oxford: Oxford University Press), 560–586.
Taylor, Tony (1993) 'Lord Cranborne, the Church Party and Anglican Education 1893–1902: from Politics to Pressure', *History of Education* 22(2), 125–146.
Thomas, Richard Hinton (1983) *Nietzsche in German Politics and Society 1890–1918* (Manchester: Manchester University Press).

Turner, David (2015) *The Old Boys, The Decline and Rise of the Public School* (New Haven: Yale University Press).
Turnbull, H.W. (1919) *Some Memories of William Peveril Turnbull, one of His Majesty's Inspectors of Schools*. (London: G. Bell).
van der Eyken, Willem and Barry Turner (1969) *Adventures in Education* (Harmondsworth: Allen Lane: The Penguin Press).
Watson, Peter (2001) *Terrible Beauty: A Cultural History of the Twentieth Century: The People and Ideas that Shaped the Modern Mind: A History* (London: Weidenfeld & Nicolson).
Wernham, J.G. (1881) 'Literature for the Young', *Dublin Review*, 63 (October), 354–377.
White, John (2007) 'Wellbeing and Education: Issues of Culture and Authority', *Journal of Philosophy of Education*, 41(1), 17–28.
Whyte, William (2006) *Oxford Jackson: Architecture, Education, Status, and Style 1835–1924* (Oxford: Oxford University Press).
Willis, Paul (1977) *Learning to Labour: How Working Class Kids get Working Class Jobs* (Farnborough: Saxon House).
Wooldridge, Adrian (1994) *Measuring the Mind: Education and Psychology in England, c.1860–c.1990* (Cambridge: Cambridge University Press).
Yamasaki, Yoko (2010) 'The Impact of Western Progressive Educational ideas in Japan: 1868–1940', *History of Education*, 39(5), 575–588.
Yamasaki, Yoko (2013) 'Continuing the Conversation: British and Japanese Progressivism', *History of Education*, 42(3), 335–349.
Young, G.M. and W.D. Hancock (Eds) (1956) *English Historical Documents, 1833–1874* (New York: Oxford University Press).

Index

End of chapter notes are denoted by a letter n between page number and note number

39 Articles 26, 27

Aberglaube ('extra belief') 30, 72
Absolute 28–9, 30, 72, 89
agnosticism 13, 71, 153
Albigensian or Catharist Heresy, The (Holmes) 138
Allen, B.M. 61
All is One: a Plea for Higher Pantheism (Holmes) 145
Ancient India 86, 88, 94, 153
Andrewes, Lancelot 23
Anglican Church *see* Church of England
Anson, Sir William 55, 64n12
anthroposophy 132
Antichrist, The (Nietzsche) 82–3
Apple, Michael 165
Armed Forces: conscription 139, 141–2; examinations 119, 122n12
Arnold, Matthew 13–15, 29–31, 41, 47
Arts and Crafts movement 86
Aryan Path, The 153
ascetic lifestyle 32, 46, 66, 86–7
atheism 24, 80, 85
atoms 159
Auden, W.H. 1
'average man' concept 15–16, 60, 83, 84, 147, 155

Baden-Powell, Robert 143
Badley, J.H. 17, 111, 133, 136
Ball, Stephen J. 109
Ballard, Philip 44–5
Balliol College, Oxford 28

baptism 78, 81
Barrow, Robin 121
Bateson, William 117, 122n11
Bathurst, Katherine ('Kitty') 53–5
Bellamy, James 27
Bennett, Neville 2
Beveridge, Sir William 161
Birmingham 81
block grants 39
Blyth, Alan 73
Board of Education 70, 161; *see also* Inspectorial career
Board Schools 40, 42, 43, 81
Bohr, Niels 159
Bolton, Gavin 116
Booth, Charles 127, 150n3
Bowles, Samuel 102
Bowmaker, Mary 115
Brackenhill 134
Bradley, F.H. 40, 64n4
Brehony, Kevin 104, 128, 129
British Idealism 28–9, 30, 31–2, 66, 72, 80, 83, 85–6, 149–50
Brooke, Rupert 135, 151n10
Bruner, Jerome 102
Buddha 32, 86, 87, 94, 96, 157, 158
Buddhism 11, 66, 85, 86–8, 91n13
Buddhist Society of Great Britain and Northern Ireland 71, 86
Burke, Catherine 4, 104, 161
Burrows, Edward 56
Burt, Cyril 130, 163
Butler, Samuel 103
Butterfield, William 27

Caldecott Community, Kent 134
Callaghan, James 164
Cambridge Primary Review 2, 164
Cambridge University Fabian Society 60, 97, 145
Can Education Give us Peace? (Holmes) 10, 148
Carpenter, Edward 86, 91n11
Casa dei Bambini, Rome 123; *see also* Montessori Schools
Catholic Church 26, 27, 28, 71, 99
ceremonies, Church 77, 78, 81
Chamberlain, Joseph 81
Chief Inspector of Elementary Schools 7, 37, 55, 56–9, 70
child-centredness 1, 2, 44, 56, 88, 102, 121, 126–7, 141, 148, 163–4
children: developing interest of 46–7, 59–61, 102; distrust of 57, 106, 107–8, 140, 166; health 52–3, 58, 64n11; latent knowledge 46, 47
Child Study movement 44, 74
Christ: Holmes on 32, 75–7, 78, 84, 148, 154; Huxley and Seeley on 71, 78; Nietzsche on 83
Christianity: Arnold on 29–31; crisis in Victorian faith 13–14, 70–1; 'high' church approach 27–8; Holmes' attachment to 30, 148; Holmes' critique of 27–9, 67, 69–85, 88–9; Original Sin 11, 57, 79, 90n7, 95, 98, 102, 114, 115, 166; at Oxford University 26, 27–8
Church of England 22, 27, 81, 120
Church Party 81
Citizenship Education 163
Civil Service 119, 122n12, 146
Clarendon Commission 23, 34n3
'Clarendon Nine' schools 22–3, 34n3
class prejudices 15–16, 60, 116–17
Claydon, Tony 20
Clough, Arthur Hugh 13
Coalition Government 7, 111, 162
Cockerton Judgement (1900) 49, 64n9
Cohen, Sol 124
Collins, Mabel 38, 85
Committee of Council on Education 39, 42, 64n5
communion 78, 81
community 51, 100, 102, 137, 144, 146, 148–9, 163, 164–5
compartmentalization of knowledge 47
Confession of Faith, A (Holmes) 52, 69

conscientization 165
conscription 139, 141–2
conservatism: Holmes 12, 13, 22, 34, 45; Oxford University 26, 27
Conservative Government 7, 111
Cook, Henry Caldwell 2, 6, 93, 135, 137
Cook, James 161
corporal punishment 45, 97–8, 103
Cosmic Commonwealth, The (Holmes) 145, 148, 149
Costin, W.C. 26
Counter-Reformation 26
coursework 166
Cox, Gordon 4
Cranbourne, Lord 81
Creative Partnerships 111, 121n7
creativity 11, 98, 111–13, 116
Creed of Buddha, The (Holmes) 69, 86, 94
Creed of Christ, The (Holmes) 52, 69–70, 94
Creed of my Heart, The (Holmes) 66
critical consciousness 165

Daglish, Neil 49, 70
Dalton Plan 130, 150n6
dame schools 42–3
dancing 57–8
Darling, John 121
Dartington Hall 134
Darwin, Charles 13, 71, 159; *see also* evolutionary theory
Davids, Thomas William Rhys 86, 91n10
Dearden, R.F. 120
Defence of Poetry, A (Shelley) 65
democracy 53, 111, 144, 147, 148–9
Deptford 52–3
Dewey, John 4, 99–100, 137, 164
Dickens, Charles 42
differentiated learning 102
Dirac, Paul 159
discipline in schools 12, 43, 45, 97–9, 102–3, 138–9
disinterested devotion 67, 84, 89, 128, 133, 146, 152
distrust of children 57, 106, 107–8, 140, 166
Divisional Inspector post 36, 55
docility 101, 138–43
Doctrine of the Fall 79, 90n7, 102
dogmatism 113–17, 138–43, 145–6, 164, 165, 166
Donaldson, Margaret 164
drama education 2, 56, 100, 115–16

Dramatic Method of Teaching, The (Finlay-Johnson) 115–16
Dresch, Paul 77
Drucker, Peter 166
Drudgery and Education. A Defence of Montessori Ideals (Holmes) 125, 126
dualism 16, 29, 80–2, 85, 99–100, 101, 112, 154–5
Dudley 62
Dunraven, Lord 21

East and West 86
Eastern mysticism 11, 67, 84, 85–9, 94, 153–4, 158; in poetry 19, 68
East Runton, Norfolk 129
Edmond Holmes and the Tragedy of Education (Shute) 3
Edmond Holmes Memorial Lecture 152
Education Act (1870) 40, 81, 119–20
Education Act (1902) 49, 81
Education Act (1944) 161
Educational Census (1851) 43
educational writings 6–8, 9–11, 37, 65, 80, 92–121; anonymity of 57; *Can Education Give us Peace?* 10, 148; critiques of 117–21; *In Defence of What Might Be* 8, 10, 74, 92, 93; on dogmatic control 113–17; *Drudgery and Education. A Defence of Montessori Ideals* 125, 126; Germany and First World War 138–43; *Give me the Young* 10, 148; influence on educational thinking 6–7, 92–3, 123, 129, 131–4; *Inspection Reports* 7, 37, 41, 42–8, 75; legacy of 162–7; on mechanical obedience 101–7; on Montessori Schools 12, 95, 115, 123–6; on national well-being 126–7; *The Nemesis of Docility: A Study of German Character* 139–40; on origins of educational malaise 96–101; on school culture 107–13; on Sompting School 8, 53, 56–7, 115–17, 126, 130; *The Tragedy of Education* 93, 113; *A Village School* 56–7; *What is and What Might Be* 3, 6–7, 8, 69, 92–3, 96, 99, 101, 105–9, 117, 119, 124, 134
Education of Man (Froebel) 1
Education Research and Perspectives 3
Education through the Imagination (McMillan) 53
Egeria 115, 118; *see also* Finlay-Johnson, Harriet
egoism 88, 110, 136, 158

Einstein, Albert 158
Elam, Horace 26
Elementary School Code (1906) 52
elementary schools 101, 104–5, 133; *see also* Inspectorial career
Eliot, T.S. 68, 134
elitism, accusations of 60, 62
Ellis, Ieuan 71
Emile (Rousseau) 1, 14, 95
empiricism 29, 155
English Baccalaureate 166
English teaching 46–7
Ensor, Beatrice 4, 6, 130, 131, 132, 150n7
Epicureanism 80
eugenics 117
evolutionary theory 71, 73–5, 98, 124, 132, 159
examinations and testing 7, 39, 44, 48, 60, 105–7, 109, 114, 119–20, 163, 166
Experience and Education (Dewey) 99–100
Experiments Day 130
expression 112; *see also* self-expression
externalism 77–80, 96, 98–9, 100, 103–7, 108–9, 112, 114, 117, 140

Fabian Society, Cambridge University 60, 97, 145
Fichte, Johann Gottlieb 82–3, 98
Finlay-Johnson, Harriet 8, 45, 52, 56, 57, 115–17, 118, 126, 130
First World War 126–7, 135–43
Fischer, Fritz 139
fishing 21, 83
Fitch, Sir Joshua 14
FORUM: for promoting 3–19 comprehensive education 3
free activity 56
freedom 100, 127–8, 132, 134
Frege, Gottlob 167n1
Freire, Paulo 165
Freud, Sigmund 133
Froebel, Friedrich 1, 10, 47, 74, 82–3, 98, 104, 124, 134, 137
Froebelians 70, 104, 105
Froebel Society 70, 90n5, 121n4

Galton, Maurice 2
games 52
Gardner, Phil 42
GCSE examinations 166
Genesis 71, 90n7
genetics 116–17
German Idealism 82–3, 98, 104, 135–6, 140

Germany 11, 82–3, 135–6, 138–43, 146
Gibson, Charles 26
Gillard, Derek 6
Gintis, Herbert 102
Giroux, Henry 165
Give me the Young (Holmes) 10, 148
Gordon, Peter 3, 4–5, 6, 8, 18n3, 28, 34, 36, 37–8, 47, 49, 54, 59, 81, 99–100, 120
Gordonstoun 135
Gore, Charles 71
Gorst, Sir John 50, 54, 64n10
government grants to schools 39; *see also* 'payment by results' system
Graham, Philip 133
grammar schools 161
Gramsci, Antonio 114
Graves, Alfred Percival 20–1, 51–2
Graves, Charles Larcom 20–1
Great Expectations (Dickens) 42
Great Passing On, The (Holmes) 159–60
Great War 126–7, 135–43
Green, Andy 40
Green, T.H. 28, 30
Gregory, Lady Augusta 20, 34n2
Grosvenor, Ian 104

Hadow Reports 2, 130, 163
Hahn, Kurt 17, 111, 135
Hall, Joseph 26, 35n6
Halsey, A.H. 161
Hamilton, David 74
Handbook of Suggestions for the Consideration of Teachers 7, 50–1
Handbooks of Suggestions 164
Hawker, Bertram 129, 150n4
Hayward, F.H. 62
health, of children 52–3, 58, 64n11
Hegel, Georg Friedrich 139–40
Hendrick, Harry 126
Henn, William 20
Herald, The 62
Herbart, Johann Friedrich 73–5, 90n6, 124
heredity 116–17
Herrick, Robert 23
Hessey, James Augustus 22, 23, 24
Hibbert Journal 153
Hinduism 91n13
History of Education 3
Hoare, Samuel 59
Hodgson, Geraldine 126, 150n2

Holmes, Edmond Gore Alexander: children 45–6, 135, 161–2; class prejudices 15–16, 60, 116–17; death 130, 152; early life and school 19–24; family 20, 22, 45–6, 135, 161–2; historical neglect of 2–6, 63; legacy 160–7; the man 15–17; marriage 45–6; Oxford University 24, 25–33; personal life 45–6; political views 12–13, 45, 127–8, 144–9; racial views 16; relationship to contemporaries 11–15; scholarship on 2–6; teaching posts 33–4; tributes to 152; wife 45, 64n7, 153; *see also* Inspectorial career; writing career
Holmes, Gerard 161
Holmes, Jane 20, 22
Holmes, Maurice Gerald 135, 151n9, 161
Holmes, Robert 20
Holmes, Thomas Rice Edward 20, 34n1
Holmes, Verena Winifred 161–2
Holmes-Morant Circular 5, 59–63, 92, 109, 168–71
hope 32, 150
Hornbrook, David 2
House of Lords crisis 61, 64n14
Hurt, J.S. 119–20
Hutchinson, Mrs 137
Huxley, Thomas Henry 71, 78

Idealism 4–5; British 28–9, 30, 31–2, 66, 72, 80, 83, 85–6, 149–50; German 82–3, 98, 104, 135–6, 140; *Sursum Corda: A Defence of Idealism* 31–2, 60, 150
Idiot Teacher, The (G. Holmes) 161
imperialism 16, 45, 139
In Defence of What Might Be (Holmes) 8, 10, 74, 92, 93
India, Ancient 86, 88, 94, 153
individual difference 44–5, 102, 164
individualism 102, 110
individualized education 51, 125, 163–4
infant schools *see* elementary schools
inner growth 98, 120, 143
in-service teacher training 50
Inspectorial career 7–8, 33, 34, 36–63; as Chief Inspector of Elementary Schools 7, 37, 55, 56–9; disillusionment with 38; as Divisional Inspector 36, 55; Holmes-Morant Circular 5, 59–63, 92, 109, 168–71; initial appointment 33, 36; *Inspection Reports* 7, 37, 41, 42–8, 75; interventions and increasing seniority 48–55; postings 33, 36; retirement 37, 58, 61

instincts 114–15, 116
Instructions to Inspectors 50
instrumentalism in education 10, 25, 41–2, 48, 57, 73–4, 105–6; *see also* examinations and testing; 'payment by results' system
interest, developing children's 46–7, 59–61, 102
Ireland 20, 21, 66
Isaacs, Susan 4, 5, 133–4, 151n8, 163

Jackson, Cyril 55, 56, 70
Jainism 91n13
Jenkins, E.W. 4
Jesus *see* Christ
Jowett, Benjamin 28
Judaism 77

Kant, Immanuel 98, 110, 121n6
Kaufmann, Walter 82
Keble, John 27
Keble College, Oxford 27
Kellogg–Briand Pact (1928) 151n11
Kenney-Herbert, E.M. 55
Kent 36, 38, 42, 43, 159
Kerrigan, Colm 52
Kingdom of Ends 110, 121n6
Kingswood School, Bristol 90n8
knowledge workers 166
Kuhn, Thomas 158

Laboratory School, Chicago 100
Labour Government 2, 121n7
Labour Party 127, 145
labour strikes 145, 146
Lane, Homer 1, 103, 121n3, 130, 131
language 154, 156
Larcom, Sir Thomas 21
latent knowledge 46, 47
Law of Contradiction 112, 155–6, 159
Law of Polar Opposition 112, 156, 159
Lawton, Denis 36, 37–8, 81
League of Nations 137
learning by rote 7, 25, 48, 107–8, 140, 162
Leese, John 50, 52
leftish thinking *see* Marxism; socialism
'Legacy of Progressivism; Some Reflections on Edmond Holmes, The' (McKenzie) 3
legalism 77, 79–80, 96, 97–8
leisure activities: importance of 43–4; outdoors 21, 83, 134, 143; working class 16, 44, 60

Letchworth 134
Liberal Government 5
Liebschner, Joachim 70, 90n5, 104
linguistic turn 154, 167n1
Literature and Dogma (Arnold) 13, 29–30, 47
Little Commonwealth community, Dorset 1, 103, 121n3, 134
Lloyd George, David 144
local authority inspectorate, Holmes' criticisms of 59–61, 168–71
Local Education Authorities 49
Locke, John 75, 103
logical positivism 154
Logic of Becoming 156, 157
Logic of Being 156
London County Council (LCC) 52
love 31, 89, 149; in poetry 66, 68, 87–8
Lowe, Robert 39, 48, 63n2
Lowe, Roy 50, 59
Lytton, 2nd Earl of 129, 136, 150n5

Macan, R.W. 25, 41, 69, 152
McBride, Ian 20
McCann, P. 119
McCulloch, Gary 164
McDonald, Paul 3, 45, 69–70, 96–7
McIvor, Arthur J. 146
McKenzie, David 3, 119
McMillan, Margaret 52–3, 64n11, 127, 130
McMillan, Rachel 52–3, 64n11
Macmunn, Norman 6, 93, 129, 134
Mahler, Gustav 82
Malting House School, Cambridge 133, 151n8
Manchester 84
Manchester Guardian, The 62
Mander, W.J. 85–6
Manning, Henry 27
Marvin, W.S. 58, 61
Marwick, Arthur 135
Marxism 53, 95, 97, 146
materialism 31–2, 60, 66, 77, 87, 139, 143, 147, 149, 165
materialist determinism 97
Mathieson, Margaret 4
'mechanical', Holmes' use of term 44
mechanical obedience 7, 101–7, 109, 112, 113, 118, 136, 161; Germany 138–43; *see also* dogmatism
mediums 159
Merchant Taylors' School 22–4, 26, 27

meritocracy 119, 122n12
Methodism 71, 79
Middleton, Jacob 98
militarism 138, 139, 140
Ministry of Labour 162
Mission Field 86
Montessori, Maria 5, 115, 123–6
Montessori Schools 10, 12, 50, 59, 95, 115, 123–6, 150n4
Montessori Society 129
Moore, Aubrey 71
Moore, G.E. 154
Morant, Robert 5, 18n1, 18n2, 28, 51, 70, 124; Education Act (1902) 49, 81; Holmes-Morant Circular 5, 60, 61, 62–3; on Holmes' promotion to Chief Inspector 55
Morning Post, The 61
Morris, Mowbray 118
mountain climbing 21, 83
Mulcaster, Richard 22
Müller, Friedrich Max 157, 167n2
Murphy Riots 45, 64n6
Murray, Nicholas 30
music scales 125

nationalism 138, 139
nationalization 145
national well-being 13, 53, 58, 126–7
Nature 21, 28, 30–1, 52, 80, 82–3, 134; in poetry 52, 66, 82; in religious writings 30–1, 52
Naturphilosophie 104
Neill, A.S. 1–2, 4, 5, 6, 93, 96, 126, 132, 133, 134, 135, 149
Nemesis of Docility: A Study of German Character, The (Holmes) 139–40
neo-Herbartians 10, 74
neo-liberal agenda 162–3, 166
neo-Romanticism 86
Nettleship, R.L. 28
Nevinson, C.W.R. 136
Newcastle Report (1861) 40
New Education Fellowship 6, 17, 44, 53, 72, 75, 83, 111, 128, 129, 130, 131, 135, 137, 150n7
New Era 131, 132, 137
New Ideals in Education conferences 11, 128–31, 135, 136, 137, 152
New Labour Government 2, 121n7
Newman, John Henry 27
New York Times 152

Nietzsche, Friedrich 82–4
night camps 53
Non-Placet Society 27
Northcote-Trevelyan Report 119, 122n12
Northumberland 36, 55
Norwood, Cyril 130–1
Nunn, Sir Percy 112, 121n9, 130
N.U.T. 60, 61–2, 63

obedience 13; Germany 138–43; in religion 27, 84, 97, 99, 155–6, 166; in schools 7, 11, 12, 28, 78, 99, 101–7, 109, 112, 113, 118, 136, 161; *see also* dogmatism
Oliver, Ian 86
O'Neill, E.F. 4, 6, 93, 161
On the Origin of the Species (Darwin) 13, 71
Original Sin 11, 57, 79, 90n7, 95, 98, 102, 114, 115, 166
Ottley, Henry 26
outdoors activities 21, 83, 134, 143
out-growth 14, 98, 114, 128, 138, 166; *see also* soul-growth; spiritual growth
Owen, Robert 44, 95
Oxfordshire 36, 37, 49–50, 53–5
Oxfordshire County Council 50
Oxford University 24, 25–33

Pali Text Society 86, 91n10
pantheism 21, 30, 31, 52, 88, 156, 158; in poetry 66–7, 68
Parkhurst, Helen 150n6
'payment by results' system 7, 38–9, 41–2, 48, 50, 58, 60, 120
Pellegrini, Carlo 24, 35n4
penny Dreadful genre 47, 64n8
People's Budget 64n14
perception 112
performativity 58, 105
Perse School, Cambridge 2
Pestalozzi, Johann Heinrich 134, 137
philosophy and philosophical writings 4–5, 10, 11, 16, 17, 19–20; British Idealism 28–9, 30, 31–2, 66, 72, 80, 83, 85–6, 149–50; on death 159; German Idealism 82–3, 98, 104, 135–6, 140; *The Great Passing On* 159–60; later writings 144–50; of old age 152–60; in poetry 66–7, 68; science in 158–9; *Self-Realization* 80; *Sursum Corda: A Defence of Idealism* 31–2, 60, 150; *Wanted – A New Logic* 155; *The World of Self or Spirit: A Scheme of Life* 157

Piaget, Jean 102, 133, 164
play 2, 114–15, 116
playgrounds 52
Play Way, The (Cook) 2, 135
Plowden Report (1967) 2, 116, 148, 164, 165
poetry 9, 13, 23, 33, 65–9; *The Creed of my Heart* 66; and Ireland 21, 66; *To the Isis* 31; 'Light and Shade' 82; love in 66, 68, 87–8; Nature in 52, 66, 82; pantheism in 66–7; philosophy in 19, 66–7, 68; religious 76–7; *The Silence of Love* 66; 'Snowdon' 82; sonnet form 68, 90n1; 'Sonnets to the Atlantic' 66; *Sonnets to the Universe* 66–7; *The Triumph of Love* 66; 'The True Self' 19; 'What Think Ye of Christ?' 76–7
poetry teaching 47, 67
Prestolee School 4, 161
primary schools *see* elementary schools
private education 111; dame schools 42–3; public schools 22–4, 34n3, 111, 132–3
prize system 106, 111
progressive schools 4, 105, 132–4, 137, 151n8
Protestant Ascendency 20
Protestantism 80, 99
Prussia 138, 139, 140, 151n12
public schools 22–4, 34n3, 111, 132–3
punishment: corporal 45, 97–8, 103; *see also* discipline in schools
pupil teachers 40, 63n3, 120
Pusey, Edward 27

quantum theory 159
Quest Society 11, 18n7, 67

rational recreationists 44
reading, teaching of 47–8
recreational activities *see* leisure activities
Reddie, Cecil 4, 17, 111, 133, 136
religion: Arnold 13–14, 29–31; crisis in Victorian faith 13–14, 70–1, 85; 'high' church approach 27–8; in Holmes' early life 22, 23–4; and leftist thinking 146–7; Original Sin 11, 57, 79, 90n7, 95, 98, 102, 114, 115, 166; at Oxford University 26, 27–33
religious teaching 23–4, 25, 81–2, 84, 109–10, 147
religious voluntary schools 81

religious writings 10, 69–90, 94–5; *The Albigensian or Catharist Heresy* 138; *All is One: a Plea for Higher Pantheism* 145; anonymity of 69, 70; on Buddha 32, 86, 87, 94, 96, 157, 158; on Christ 32, 75–7, 78, 84, 148, 154; compared with Nietzsche 82–4; *A Confession of Faith* 52, 69; *The Cosmic Commonwealth* 145, 148, 149; *The Creed of Buddha* 69, 86, 94; *The Creed of Christ* 52, 69–70, 94; critiques of Western religion 27–9, 67, 69–85, 88–9; on dualism 80–2, 85, 154–5; Eastern mysticism in 11, 19, 67, 68, 84, 85–9, 94, 153–4, 158; on externalism 77–80; later writings 144–5, 146–8; Nature in 30–1, 52; poetry 76–7; science in 71–5; *The Secret of the Cross* 154
Rennie, Belle 130
Repton School 33–4
ressentiment 84
Revised Codes (1862) 39, 48
revolutionary events 145
Richards, Colin 3, 8, 162
Richards, N.J. 81
Roman Catholic Church 26, 27, 28, 71, 99
Romanticism 14, 52, 68, 74, 82, 98, 102–3, 134
Rome 10, 59
Ronge, Bertha 104, 121n5
Rosen, Michael 109
rote learning 7, 25, 48, 107–8, 140, 162
Rousseau, Jean-Jacques 1, 14, 74, 95
Rowntree, Seebohm 127, 150n3
Runciman, Walter 5, 57, 58, 59, 60, 61, 62, 63, 64n13
Runciman Papers 57, 58, 59, 61, 62
Ruskin College 164
Russell, Bertrand 11, 135, 154
Rutherford, Ernest 159

Sadler, Michael 28, 49, 62, 70, 90n4, 130
St John's College, Oxford 25–7
St Paul's School 23
Scheele, Judith 77
Schelling, Friedrich 82–3, 98
Scholar-Gypsy, The (Arnold) 31
school buildings, poor design and maintenance 40
School Manager, The 51
Schoolmaster, The 61, 62, 63, 92, 118
school playgrounds 52

science 71–5, 131–2, 158–9, 162
science teaching 72
Scott Holland, Henry 114, 122n10
Scout movement 143
secondary schools 49, 101, 104, 105–7
Secret of the Cross, The (Holmes) 154
secularism 99, 109–10
Seeley, J.R. 71, 78
self-education 57, 115, 125
self-expression 11, 56, 98, 111–13, 116
self-interest 147
self-loss 31, 67, 156
self-realization 12, 16, 17, 66, 67, 73, 75, 89, 100, 102, 111, 112, 144, 148, 149, 156, 166
Self-Realization (Holmes) 80
self-transcendence 31, 146, 148, 154, 156
Selleck, R.J.W. 4, 8, 9, 58, 92, 105, 130
sensualism 34, 46, 87, 110, 158, 161
Sharwood Smith, E. 5, 6, 18n3, 93, 117, 121n2, 130, 152
Shaw, George Bernard 117, 161
Shelley, Percy Bysshe 65, 82
Shirreff, Emily 104, 121n4
Shute, Chris 3
Silence of Love, The (Holmes) 66
Silver, Harold 12
Silver, Keith 14
Simon, Brian 12, 161
Simpson, J.H. 6, 92–3, 121n1
Simpson, Matthew 95
Sinnett, A.P. 38, 85
Skidelsky, Robert 4, 133, 136
Skinner, Quentin 3
Smiles, Samuel 102
Smith, S.F. 118
Social Development in Young Children (Isaacs) 133
socialism 12, 97, 127, 145–7
social mobility 119–20
social reform 52–3, 95
social survey movement 44
Sompting School, West Sussex 8, 52, 53, 56–7, 115–17, 126, 130
sonnet form 68, 90n1
Sonnets to the Universe (Holmes) 66–7
Sorley, Charles Hamilton 135, 151n10
soul-growth 11, 75, 104, 132, 147; *see also* out-growth; spiritual growth
Specimen Schemes of Instructions 50
Spenser, Edmund 23
Spinoza, Baruch 158

Spiritism 159
spiritual emancipation 12
spiritual growth 11, 32, 41, 79–80, 109–11, 116, 132, 133, 141, 143; *see also* out-growth; soul-growth
spiritual idealism 157
spiritual science 132
Spitalfield Weavers 16, 44
Stanford, Charles Villiers 20–1
State, theory of the 139–40
'state of the nation' question 13, 53, 58, 126–7
state schools and religion 81–2
Steedman, Carolyn 53
Steiner, Rudolf 38, 85, 131–2
Stephens, W.B. 42
Stewart, W.A.C. 4, 105
Stinton, Judith 1
Stoicism 80
Stone, Lawrence 103
Stratford-upon-Avon 129
Strauss, Richard 82
strikes 145, 146
Summerhill School 75, 134
supernaturalism 29, 99, 148, 156
Sursum Corda: A Defence of Idealism (Holmes) 31–2, 60, 150
Sweet, William 29
Syme, Florence Mary 45, 64n7, 153
Synge, John Millington 20

tabula rasa 75, 103
Taylor, Tony 81
teachers: autonomy 50; distrust of children 57, 106, 107–8, 140; Holmes' criticisms of 43–4, 59, 108; modern constraints on 7–8; pupil 40, 63n3, 120; unqualified 40, 49–50, 120
teacher training 49–50
teacher training institutions 37
'teaching to the test' 25, 105–6; *see also* examinations and testing
Telegraph, The 61
testing *see* examinations and testing
Theosophical Fraternity in Education 6, 131–2
Theosophical Society 18n7, 131
Theosophist schools 134
Theosophy 38, 70, 71, 131
Thomas, Richard Hinton 83
Thomas White Scholarship 24, 26
Thompson, Lewis 86, 91n12

Thring, Edward 111, 121n8
Times, The 152
Tiptree Hall 134
Tory Party 16, 45
To the Isis (Holmes) 31
Townley, James 22
Tractarian Movement 27
trade unions 45, 127, 145, 146, 147
Tragedy of Education, The (Holmes) 93, 113
transcendent God 28, 72, 76, 80–1, 85, 112
tri-partite school systems 131, 161
Triumph of Love, The (Holmes) 66
trust, lack of *see* distrust of children
Turnbull, W.P. 41
Turner, Barry 133
Turner, David 23

United Methodist Church 71
unity 29, 80, 84, 86, 88, 89, 101, 137, 154, 157
Universe 31, 80, 128, 154–5, 158–9; in poetry 66–7
University of Newcastle 59
unselfishness 146, 158
Upanishads 86, 87, 89, 91n13, 94, 153, 157
Uppingham School 111, 121n8
Utopia 14, 16, 53, 115–17, 130, 134

van der Eyken, Willem 133
Vanity Fair 24, 35n4
Village School, A (Holmes) 56–7
Voluntary Schools Act (1897) 81

Wandervogel youth groups 83, 90n9, 135
Wanted – A New Logic (Holmes) 155
war poets 135, 151n10
Watson, Peter 94
Webster, John 23

Weller, Harriet *see* Finlay-Johnson, Harriet
Wellington College 33
Wells, H.G. 117
Wesley, John 79, 90n8, 103
West Riding district, Yorkshire 33, 36, 42
What is and What Might Be (Holmes) 3, 6–7, 8, 69, 92–3, 96, 99, 101, 105–9, 117, 119, 124, 134
White, John 4–5, 28, 99–100, 120
White, Sir Thomas 26
Wholeness 29, 67, 128
Whyte, William 27
Wickham, Edward Charles 33
Wilkinson, M.J. 5, 59, 60, 63
Willis, Paul 102
Winchelsea, 11th Earl of 33, 34, 36
Wittgenstein, Ludwig 154
Wooldridge, Adrian 44, 72
Wordsworth, William 13, 21, 31, 66
working classes: dame schools 42–3; desire for good education system 119–20; leisure activities 16, 44, 60
World of Self or Spirit: A Scheme of Life, The (Holmes) 157
writing career 8–11, 37; anonymity 57, 67, 69, 70; autobiography 16, 20, 23, 24, 31, 37, 45, 66, 67, 159, 160; First World War 137, 138–43; later writings 144–50; *see also* educational writings; philosophy and philosophical writings; poetry; religious writings
Wynter, Philip 26

Yamasaki, Yoko 4
Yeats, W.B. 20, 144
Yorkshire 33, 36, 42
Yoxall, Sir James 60, 62